*Ideas and
Institutions*

A volume in the series

Cornell Studies in Political Economy

<small>EDITED BY PETER J. KATZENSTEIN</small>

A full list of titles in the series appears at the end of the book

Ideas and Institutions

Developmentalism in Brazil and Argentina

Kathryn Sikkink

Cornell University Press

Ithaca and London

First published 1991 by Cornell University Press.
First printing, Cornell Paperbacks, 2012
International Standard Book Number 0-8014-2488-7
Library of Congress Catalog Card Number 90-55713

Printed in the United States of America

Librarians: Library of Congress cataloging information appears on the last page of the book.

⊗ The paper in this book meets the minimum requirements of the American National Standard for Information Sciences—Permanence of Paper for Printed Library Materials, ANSI Z39.48-1984.

FOR MY PARENTS,

Arlene Angel Sikkink and Donald Sikkink

Contents

List of Tables and Figures

Preface

In a commercial district of Buenos Aires, on a narrow road recently renamed Juan D. Perón Street, stands an old residential building that holds the Frondizi presidential archives. (It is poetic justice that Frondizi's archives should be haunted by Perón's name, just as his presidency was overshadowed by Perón's legacy.) The building is dark inside; a silent old doorman unlocks the door for the few visitors who arrive. The bronze plate by the door says "Centro de Estudios Nacionales." It was once the hub of developmentalist activity before Frondizi took office, the brain center of a movement that promised Argentina a modern development program.

It was winter when I first visited. The building was cold, the ceilings stained and peeling where water had leaked through. In the library, a gas heater kept the room warm, and in the middle of the morning the librarian and the cleaning woman drank maté near it. In another room were box after box of newspaper clippings mixed with government papers, stored haphazardly and covered with dust. One day, as I sat poring over papers, Frondizi himself walked through the room in one of his infrequent visits to the center. At first I thought I had seen a ghost.

On the highest point in Brasília, the city Kubitschek built, stands a squat white marble building designed by Oscar Niemeyer, the architect of Brasília. Visitors enter the Juscelino Kubitschek Memorial through a tunnel under a reflecting pool that surrounds the building. At the door, they are met by a guide in a crisp white suit. The day I went, a group of schoolchildren were visiting. First we moved to a room filled with enlarged photographs of factories and smokestacks. This is the Room of the Targets, explained the guide, who then described the economic program, the Targets Program, implemented by the Kubitschek government. Also on the ground level is Kubitschek's personal library, moved and reconstructed at the memorial. I searched the shelves for some clues to the man behind the myth being constructed here but instead found beautifully bound sets of standard literature. Down the hall are a series of pictures of the Kubitschek presidency, including one classic of Juscelino walking on a huge felled tree as he inspects progress on the Belém-Brasília highway.

Above, in a dimly lighted room, are memorabilia from the presidency: the suit he wore to the inauguration, medals, more photographs. In a circular chamber in the center of the room, under red and purple stained glass, is a black marble casket with only the words *O Fundador* inscribed on it. The Founder—of Brasília that is. I am reminded of Napoleon's tomb at Les Invalides in Paris, but on a more modern and modest scale. A serious attempt at myth making is afoot. Nearby, in an auditorium with comfortable plush seats, a weekly seminar series is commemorating thirty years since the beginning of the Kubitschek presidency. The audience that night is sparse, perhaps because the topic, Kubitschek's transportation policy, is less than gripping.

A photograph of a meeting between Juscelino Kubitschek and Arturo Frondizi in Buenos Aires shows two intense men who shared the same dream: to usher their countries into the future as modern industrial powers. The economic program put forward by both Kubitschek and Frondizi was called developmentalism—*desarrollismo* in Spanish, *desenvolvimentismo* in Portuguese. It would become one of the most prevalent economic models in postwar Latin America and would be adopted eventually by other developing countries around the world. But in 1956, when Kubitschek was elected in Brazil, and in 1958, when Frondizi was elected in Argentina, it was quite new. It was a reaction to new opportunities and constraints in the international system, and to new ideas about development. Some of these ideas were Latin American products, like those advocated by Raúl Prebisch and his team at the Economic Commission for Latin America (ECLA in English, CEPAL in Spanish) in Santiago, Chile. Others were new adaptations of old ideas about protectionism and industrialization. The developmentalists were imbued with great optimism about the power of technical progress; under the leadership of the right man with the right ideas, and with the help of capital, technology, and know-how, development seemed within reach.

Developmentalism in Latin America was similar in its origins and functions to Keynesianism in Western Europe. Both were postwar phenomena, born of a reevaluation of economics in light of the experience of the Great Depression and the Second World War. One economist went so far as to refer to developmentalism as "Keynesianism in the tropics," but this overstates the similarities. Nevertheless, developmentalist ideas caught the imagination in Latin America in the same way that Keynesian ideas caught on in Europe and the United States. Like Keynesianism, developmentalism was a compromise ideology, mediating between increased internal demands for the state to intervene in the economy to protect its citizens, and the demands of the international system.

I have examined one slice of history in Argentina and Brazil, the seven-year period after the fall of Perón and Vargas, comparing the developmentalist governments of Juscelino Kubitschek (1956–1961) and Arturo Frondizi (1958–1962). The two young presidents represent the purest examples of developmentalist ideology in Latin America. But in spite of the similarities of their ideas, the outcomes of the Frondizi and Kubitschek governments were quite different. Kubitschek secured wide support for his ambitious Targets Program and was able to implement the bulk of his policies before completing his term. Frondizi, on the other hand, was removed from office by a military coup after having alienated many of his initial followers and truncated his development program. In Argentina this was a period of divergence, when even groups who shared basic beliefs about the way the economy should be managed were divided politically. But in Brazil it was a period of convergence, when various groups, bound to a common goal of rapid state-sponsored industrialization, temporarily overlooked differences in order to cooperate with and support the Targets Plan.

This book is concerned with two central questions: why were similar developmentalist policies adopted in Brazil and Argentina? and why did these economic policies have such different outcomes in the two countries? As Latin American countries in the 1980s and 1990s embark on a new set of economic policies of a more liberal bent, it is important to understand the origins and the tenacity of past policies based on import-substituting industrialization. The increasingly common comparisons drawn between Latin America and the East Asian "tigers" have pointed to the Latin America decision to adopt and to maintain import-substituting industrialization as one of the main factors explaining the differences in development patterns in the two regions. Yet much of this theorizing has tended to look back from the vantage of the 1980s on supposedly flawed decisions of the past, rather than grapple with why certain models are adopted and maintained. A study of decisions to adopt a development model in the 1950s can contribute to our understanding of the factors that lead countries to choose new economic policies and to the "stickiness" of these policies once adopted.

It is impossible to answer these research questions, I will argue, without understanding the impact of ideas and the manner in which ideas become embedded in institutions. Developmentalism was adopted in the mid-1950s in Brazil, Argentina, and elsewhere in the region as a response to changes in the international environment and to emerging new ideas about development. Changes in the international environment did not translate directly into policy changes; rather, policy changes depended on how relevant actors perceived the social and economic setting and structured the kinds of options available. In adopting developmentalist policies, elites were influenced by opportunities and constraints in the international arena. But they were also constrained by historical memory, by imagination, and by the economic models that structured their ideas and the ideas of their populations. We frequently focus on the material constraints but less often on the ideological constraints. What policies were imagined to be possible and impossible, which were "captivating," and why?

The second question is why these policies led to different outcomes in Brazil and Argentina. (By "different outcomes" I refer to two separate but related issues: implementation and consolidation of policies.) First, to what degree were developmentalist policies implemented? Were the policies put into effect, and did they meet the goals set for them by the policy makers? The answers to these questions are related to issues of state purpose and state capacity: that is, how particular ideas became embodied in state institutions, and how effective the state was at carrying out the policies it adopted. Differences in state capacity can be explained by differences in the networks of state institutions, the rules and procedures governing institutional life, and the prevalent attitudes about the nature and the role of the state.

The issue of consolidation concerns whether the policies generated and received broad support from the public and from key economic groups. Successful consolidation depends on the ability of leaders to mobilize domestic support for new development policies. Ideas become embodied in state institutions and are symbolized by key political leaders. Greater domestic consensus is likely to emerge around an economic model if new development ideas "fit" with preexisting political and economic ideas within a country.

When I first drafted the introductory chapter to this book, I lamented the lack of theoretical material exploring how economic policy ideas shape political action. In the past few years, however, there has been a revival of interest in the influence of ideas and ideologies in politics, foreign policy, and economic policy. Peter Hall's book on the political power of economic ideas gave me hope that cross-regional theorizing on the influence of economic ideas may be fruitful, since there are important parallels between the differential influence of Keynesian ideas in Europe and the influence of developmentalism in Latin America. Emanuel Adler's book on technological change in Brazil and Argentina convinced me that explanations focusing on ideas and institutions are useful for understanding other issues and time periods in the same countries. The concluding chapter of this book situates my conclusions in relation to recent literature on the role of ideas in politics.

It is only appropriate that a project concerned with the influence of ideas and institutions should acknowledge its own intellectual and institutional debts. As this project evolved I have increasingly realized how much I owe to the direct and indirect influence of my teachers and colleagues. John Ruggie helped define the intellectual context in which the original topic and questions were formulated. Douglas Chalmers offered consistent, critical support and assistance throughout the life of the project and first introduced me to interpretive methodologies. Thanks also go to Alfred Stepan for first directing my attention to the role of the state in Latin America, for good advice at key moments, and for a stellar final reading. My friend and colleague Margaret Keck helped most with the first drafts, offering theoretical critique, moral support, editorial assistance, and frequent tea and shortbread.

Douglas Johnson, my husband and compañero, spent twenty months with me in Argentina, Brazil, and Chile while I completed the field research for the book. And not only that, he enjoyed it. This book could not have been written without his support and encouragement. Some people say that writing a book is like giving birth, but having done both at the same time (the bulk of the first draft was written while I was pregnant), I believe that writing a book is more difficult by far, and the final product is not nearly so pleasing. I have come to think of the book as the "ugly child," but one that I love in spite of its imperfections. I cannot say that our son Daniel helped me write the book, but he certainly kept life in perspective.

Albert O. Hirschman provided both intellectual inspiration and concrete help. It has been my great privilege to benefit from his comments. While in Argentina, I was fortunate to be associated with the Centro de Estudios de Estado y Sociedad (CEDES), which offered an ideal work environment, both stimulating and friendly. Marcelo Cavarozzi and Catalina Smulovitz were particularly helpful, as was Monica

Hirst of the Facultad Latinoamericana de Ciencias Sociales (FLACSO). Judith Evans helped me to arrange some crucial interviews. The *desarrollistas* themselves were accessible and forthcoming; in particular, Oscar Camilion and Rogelio Frigerio helped facilitate my research.

Simon Schwartzman and the Instituto Universitario de Pesquisa do Rio de Janeiro (IUPERJ) provided office space while I was working in Brazil. I am grateful to Ricardo Bielschowsky, Lourdes Sola, and Maria Antonieta Leopoldi for sharing their work with me while I was in Brazil, and to the Fundação Getúlio Vargas and its Centro de Pesquisa e Documentação de História Contemporânea do Brasil (CPDPC) for access to their materials.

The research was assisted by a grant from the Joint Committee on Latin America of the Social Science Research Council and the American Council of Learned Societies (with funds provided by the Ford Foundation, the Hewlett Foundation, the National Endowment for the Humanities, and the Andrew W. Mellon Foundation), a grant from the Doherty Foundation, and a grant from the Institute for the Study of World Politics.

The Yale Center for International and Area Studies, where I was a visiting fellow, provided office space while I worked on early versions of the manuscript, and the Political Science Department at the University of Minnesota provided a conducive intellectual atmosphere and the support to see me through the later versions. My colleagues Raymond Duvall and John Freemen made timely and insightful comments on portions of the manuscript. Thomas E. Skidmore generously offered comments on the entire text. Two anonymous reviewers gave very helpful comments that structured the final revisions. At Cornell University Press, Roger Haydon played a vital and helpful role. Thanks also go to Glenn Adler, Ann Clark, Michael Coppedge, Mary Dietz, Anna DiLellio, William Drake, Edwin Fogelman, Robert Jervis, Robert Kaufman, Friedrich Kratochwil, Kurt von Mettemheim, David Sylvan, Michael Weis, Eliza Willis, Carol Wise, and Gary Wynia for their help, comments, and support at different stages of the project.

This book is dedicated to my parents, who first took me abroad, encouraged my language studies, financed my early trips to Latin America, and instilled in me a love of ideas and of politics.

KATHRYN SIKKINK

Minneapolis, Minnesota

Abbreviations

BNDE	Brazilian National Economic Development Bank (Banco Nacional do Desenvolvimento Econômico)
CEPAL	Economic Commission for Latin America (Comisión Económico para América Latina)
CGE	General Economic Confederation (Confederación General Económico)
CGT	General Labor Confederation (Confederación General de Trabajo)
CNI	National Industrial Confederation (Confederação Nacional da Industria)
CONADE	National Development Council (Consejo Nacional de Desarrollo)
CPDOC	Research and Documentation Center on Contemporary Brazilian History (Centro de Pesquisa e Documentação de História Contemporânea do Brasil)
DASP	Administrative Department of Public Service (Departamento Administrativo do Serviço Público)
ESG	Superior War College (Escola Superior de Guerra)
FIESP	São Paulo Industrialists Federation (Federação de Indústrias do Estado do São Paulo)
ISEB	Higher Institute of Brazilian Studies (Instituto Superior de Estudos Brasileiros)
ISI	Import-Substituting Industrialization
NOVACAP	Urban Authority for a New Capital [Brasília] (Companhia Urbanizadora da Nova Capital)
OAS	Organization of American States
PSD	Social Democratic Party (Partido Social Democrático)

PTB   Brazilian Labor Party (Partido Trabalhista Brasileiro)

SRA   Argentine Rural Society (Sociedad Rural Argentina)

SUDENE   Superintendency for the Development of the Northeast (Super-intendência do Desenvolvimento do Nordeste)

SUMOC   Superintendency of Money and Credit (Superintendência da Moeda e Crédito)

UCRI   Intransigent Radical Civic Union Party (Unión Cívica Radical Intransigente)

UCRP   Radical Civic Union of the People Party (Unión Cívica Radical del Pueblo)

UDN   National Democratic Union (União Democrática National)

UIA   Argentine Industrial Union (Unión Industrial Argentina)

YPF   Argentine state oil company (Yacímentos Petrolíferos Fiscales)

*Ideas and
Institutions*

CHAPTER ONE

Introduction

It is a paradox that scholars, whose entire existence is centered on the production and understanding of ideas, should grant ideas so little significance for explaining political life. In the subfields of international relations, international political economy, and Latin American politics, very little theorizing is concerned with the influence of ideas on politics, while much theoretical energy is expended demonstrating that it is not necessary to know what political actors think in order to explain how they will act.

The particular type of idea that interests me here is that concerned with economic development in the periphery, what Albert Hirschman called "ideologies of economic development," sets of "distinctive beliefs, principles and attitudes."[1] I prefer to speak of ideas about development, or models of economic policy making. Sets of ideas connected by a theory or group of theories form a model of economic development. These models help give meaning to a political economic situation and thus permit purposeful action within it.[2]

1. Albert O. Hirschman, "Ideologies of Economic Development in Latin America," in *Latin American Issues* (New York: Twentieth Century Fund, 1961), p. 3. Work by Hirschman on these topics inspired and informed my research. Celso Furtado, in a book that is both an autobiography and a history of economic ideas in Brazil, says of the 1950s there, "The role of ideas in the life of countries is frequently underestimated, and even more so in those countries that live by importing ideas. To the degree that the country's economy stopped being regulated (or disregulated) from abroad, economic ideas began to take on importance among us." Celso Furtado, *A fantasia organizada* (Rio de Janeiro: Paz e Terra, 1985), p. 141.

2. These sets of ideas often involve a critique of an existing situation and a blueprint for a desired future. Models are characterized by a specific language, terms and concepts imbued with special meaning, including the use of metaphorical and symbolic language. Clifford Geertz, "Ideology as a Cultural System," in *Ideology and Discontent*, ed. David Apter (Glencoe: Free Press, 1964), pp. 47–73.

1

This book focuses on three separate but interrelated issues: the adoption, implementation, and consolidation of an economic model in Latin America. I argue that developmentalist ideas were adopted in Brazil and Argentina in the 1950s in response to new ideas held by policy makers and to changes in the international and domestic economy. To be successfully implemented, however, the developmentalist model had to become embedded in state institutions that had the organizational capacity to carry out the policies. In order for the model to become consolidated, or to persist, an elite consensus and a broad-based societal consensus had to emerge around it. Such consensus is more likely to emerge if the developmentalist ideas articulate well with the existing ideologies of groups in a country.

Ideas matter at each of these three stages, but in different ways. The ideas of top policy makers influence the adoption of new economic models. In strong presidential systems like those in Latin America, ideas held by the president and his economic advisers are fundamentally important for an understanding of what policies were adopted. For successful implementation, however, these ideas have to become embedded in state institutions. When new development ideas arise, they are able to survive and flourish to the degree that they find an institutional home or sponsor. Rarely do new ideas thrive in the modern world outside of institutional networks. Ideas within an institution become embodied in its statement of purpose, its self-definition, and its research or training program, which in turn tends to perpetuate and extend the ideas. Once ideas become embedded in institutions, ideational change comes slowly and in an episodic manner.

For an economic model to become consolidated, however, a high level of consensus must emerge around the new model. New ideas do not enter an ideological vacuum. They are inserted into a political space already occupied by historically formed ideologies.[3] Whether or not consolidation occurs often depends on the degree to which the new model fits with existing ideologies of important economic and social groups. One way that political leaders mobilize support for economic policies is by framing their ideas in terms of existing ideologies and by using symbolic appeals to commonly held beliefs.

Only a few alternative economic models were perceived as available

---

3. Peter Hall has referred to the prevailing set of political ideas into which economic ideas are inserted as the structure of political discourse of a nation. *The Political Power of Economic Ideas: Keynesianism across Nations* (Princeton: Princeton University Press, 1989), p. 383.

to policy makers in Latin America in the postwar period: liberalism, developmentalism, national populism, and socialism.[4] A fifth model, industrialization that focused on export promotion, later adopted by a number of East Asian countries, was another logical alternative that did not become a practical one in Latin America until the 1970s and 1980s. A low-growth or ecological development model was not even considered a possibility in the 1950s. In principle, Latin American policy makers might have perceived any of these models as options in the postwar period. In practice, they did not see most as viable alternatives. Why was this so? One central constraint was ideological—the limits imposed by historical memory and the presence and absence of certain ideas in the debates over economic policy in Latin America. A profound sense of pessimism influenced the postwar reception of models that focused on exports, whether primary product exports or industrial exports. Thus, two of the most important alternative models in Latin America, national populism and developmentalism, both emphasized import-substituting industrialization (ISI) and downplayed exports.

Import-substituting industrialization was not the only viable choice in Latin America during the postwar period. Especially in retrospect it seems logical that some form of industrial export promotion might have proved more successful given the boom in world trade. Yet a state-sponsored industrial export promotion strategy was rarely discussed at the time. Powerful actors, especially rural groups, continued to advocate liberalism, but it never had strong popular support. For the majority of the population, some form of import-substituting industrialization, whether national populist or developmentalist, was the most compelling option.

Developmentalism was a model of economic development common in Latin America in the 1950s and 1960s.[5] The variants of it that ap-

4. These are "pure" models of economic development, while in the real world models are often less than clear-cut and frequently blur. Thus, whereas Perón adopted a fairly clear national populist model, Vargas adopted policies that tended to fall between national populism and developmentalism. Nevertheless, it is useful to think of the separate models as the perceived alternatives open to Latin American countries during this period.

5. Seminal discussions of developmentalism appear in Fernando Henrique Cardoso and Enzo Faletto, *Dependency and Development in Latin America* (Berkeley: University of California Press, 1979), and in Marcelo Cavarozzi's reflection on and extension of the Cardoso and Faletto analysis of developmentalism. "El 'desarrollismo' y las relaciones entre democracia y capitalismo dependiente en 'Dependencia y desarrollo en América Latina,'" *Latin American Research Review* 17 (1982), 152–65.

peared all had similar maps of the situation and blueprints for the future. These had three interrelated policy components: (1) a policy of intensive vertical import-substituting industrialization focused on priority basic industrial sectors such as steel, energy, chemicals, machinery, vehicles, and capital goods; (2) attempts to expand capital accumulation rapidly to support the industrialization effort, which emphasized reliance on foreign private and public sources of capital; (3) expanded involvement of the state in directing the development effort, generally by utilizing some form of indicative planning to channel private initiative into priority areas.

National populism, like developmentalism, focused on import-substituting industrialization. But that model favored national industrialists over foreign capitalists. As a result, national populist policies stressed horizontal industrialization and consumer goods rather than vertical industrialization with emphasis on heavy industry. In the national populist model, the domestic market is seen as the primary engine for economic growth; the expansion of the consumption capacity of wage earners creates increased demand that in turn stimulates industrialization, especially the production of consumer goods.

Both developmentalism and national populism were simultaneously counterhegemonic and hegemonic models of development. They challenged the pattern by which Third World countries were integrated into the international economic system primarily as producers of primary goods and importers of manufactured products, but did not challenge the capitalist system itself. Neither urged uncoupling the economies of developing countries from the global capitalist system. Rather, their advocates hoped to improve the terms on which their countries were incorporated into the international economic order.[6]

In its attempt to propel itself to a more privileged position in the global capitalist system, Brazil succeeded more spectacularly than did Argentina. During the postwar period Brazil moved up rapidly from the periphery to the top of the semiperiphery, while Argentina moved more slowly and, in a relative sense, declined. One of the great puzzles of Latin American economic history is how Argentina, once so wealthy and promising, fell far behind Brazil in growth and industrial devel-

6. There is some confusion about the relationship between developmentalism and dependency theory. Prebisch and the developmentalists provided a bridge to dependency theory. Dependency theorists both built upon the theorizing of developmentalists (especially their ideas of declining terms of trade, emphasis on industry, and concepts of center and periphery) and reacted against it, criticizing its reliance on foreign sources of capital and technology and its failure to promote structural reforms.

opment.[7] While explanations differ, there is general agreement that the coherence and continuity of Brazil's economic policy making over the last fifty years contributed to its surprising pattern of growth, while the discontinuity and zigzags of Argentine policy undermined development efforts. Continuity was possible in Brazil because elites were more united around the basic elements of a single model of growth: a developmentalist model.[8] These shared developmentalist ideas were part of the glue that held together Brazilian elites. In Argentina, profound political divisions of elites prevented consensus on a desirable model of growth.

ADOPTION OF DEVELOPMENTALIST POLICIES

Given the universe of possible models, why was developmentalism adopted instead of an alternative model? How important were ideas for understanding outcomes? This question relates to the classic debate over ideas versus interests. Some theorists see ideas as the veneer selected by individuals and groups to mystify and legitimize actions taken in their own self-interest: what one author terms "the battlefield image of society as a clash of interests thinly disguised as a clash of principles."[9] The other extreme is the view that ideas have a totally autonomous impact on political outcomes. Most recent theorizing on the role of ideas falls between these two extremes and is concerned with understanding the interrelationship of ideas and interests. Some discuss ideas as an "intermediate variable" mediating between interests and political outcomes. I argue that the belief in the separation of ideas and interests is fundamentally flawed. Political and ideological factors influence the very meaning and interpretation of economic ideas and recommendations. Except in its crudest form, the comprehension and formulation of facts and interests implies the existence of a conceptual apparatus. To conceive of ideas as intellectual justifications of actions that

7. For a discussion of this puzzle, see Carlos Diaz Alejandro, "No Less than One Hundred Years of Argentine Economic History, Plus Some Comparisons," Economic Growth Center, Yale University, Center Discussion Paper no. 392, January 1982; and Carlos Waisman, *Reversal of Development in Argentina: Postwar Counterrevolutionary Policies and Their Structural Consequences* (Princeton: Princeton University Press, 1987).

8. The issue of elite consensus appears frequently in literature on Brazil. See, for example, Peter Evans, *Dependent Development: The Alliance of Multinational, State, and Local Capital in Brazil* (Princeton: Princeton University Press, 1979), pp. 12, 13.

9. Geertz, "Ideology as a Cultural System," p. 53.

people wanted to take anyway is to obscure the role of ideas in helping people grasp, formulate, and communicate social realities.

Nevertheless, for analytical purposes it may be useful to attempt to separate ideas and interests initially, and discuss whether policies can be understood primarily on the basis of plausibly inferred interests of key actors, or whether it is necessary to know about the existence and content of ideas to understand policy outcomes. This permits one to explore alternative explanations for the adoption and implementation of economic policies.

The field of international political economy has been particularly deficient in coming to grips with the problem of the influence of ideas on the transformation of social reality. The dominance of the realist perspective in international relations in the postwar period has relegated the role of ideas to that of epiphenomenon along the lines of the "battlefield image" mentioned above. But a new generation of theorizing by scholars who work in the area of comparative political economy has opened the inquiry to an examination of the role of ideas and institutions in the study of economic policy making.[10] Few of these scholars have focused on the contemporary Third World, however, or specifically on Latin America. The study of economic policy making in the Third World is still dominated by alternative approaches that deemphasize the role of ideas and institutions in the adoption of economic models.[11]

ALTERNATIVE EXPLANATIONS

Do ideas matter, or is it possible to explain policy outcomes on the basis of plausibly inferred interests of the relevant actors? To explore these issues, it may be useful to consider a number of alternative explanations that have frequently been used to explain the process of economic policy making in Latin America and the Third World: economic interest group theories, relative autonomy of the state theories, theories

10. See, for example, Hall, ed., *The Political Power of Economic Ideas*; John Odell, *U.S. International Monetary Policy: Markets, Power, and Ideas as Sources of Change* (Princeton: Princeton University Press, 1982); D. Michael Shafer, *Deadly Paradigms: The Failure of U.S. Counterinsurgency Policy* (Princeton: Princeton University Press, 1988); Judith Goldstein, "Ideas, Institutions, and American Trade Policy," *International Organization* 42 (Winter 1988), and "The Impact of Ideas on Trade Policy: The Origins of U.S. Agricultural and Manufacturing Policies," *International Organization* 43 (Winter 1989), 31–71.

11. An exception to this trend is Emanuel Adler, *The Power of Ideology: The Quest for Technological Autonomy in Argentina and Brazil* (Berkeley: University of California Press, 1987).

on discourse and power, and rational choice/political survival theories, all of which define "interests" in different ways and place very little emphasis on the role of ideas.

Economic Interest Groups

This type of argument attributes the adoption of economic models and policies to the pressures of powerful economic interests, usually the industrial bourgeoisie or the rural oligarchy, or some fraction of these classes. Changing policies are the result of the changing power of different classes or class fractions, or of shifting alliances between classes. Within this framework, developmentalism is portrayed as the ideology and project of internationalized fractions of the national industrial bourgeoisie in Latin America. In this view the adoption of developmentalism is seen as the result of the increasing strength of this fraction of the bourgeoisie and its ability to impose its project on national policy making. This position is consistent with the work of dependency theorists like Fernando Henrique Cardoso and Enzo Faletto, and with the early work of Guillermo O'Donnell and Peter Evans.

In spite of Cardoso and Faletto's proviso that "intellectual evaluation of a given situation and ideas about what is to be done are crucial in politics," the thrust of their historical structural approach to dependency theory stresses different domestic and international class alliances as the primary explanation for economic policy choices in the periphery.[12] The same is true of the early work of Guillermo O'Donnell, which interprets economic policies and political developments as the result of the logic of a particular stage of capitalist development and of different class alliances.[13]

I began my research with a similar approach, interpreting developmentalism as the project of a fraction of the industrial bourgeoisie and of their technocratic allies in the state. It seemed clearly in the interests

12. Cardoso and Faletto, *Dependency and Development in Latin America*, p. xi. Cardoso and Faletto discuss a populist-developmentalist alliance of the industrial bourgeoisie, the state bureaucracy, and the worker-popular sectors against the interests of the agro-exporting group. Throughout the text, however, they fail to distinguish clearly between national populist and developmentalist versions of ISI (pp. 131, 152).

13. See Guillermo A. O'Donnell, *Modernization and Bureaucratic-Authoritarianism: Studies in South American Politics* (Berkeley: Institute of International Studies, University of California, 1973), and "Estado y alianzas en la Argentina, 1956–1976," *Desarrollo economico* 16 (January–March 1977). Peter Evans stresses the "triple alliance" between the state, multinational corporations, and the local industrial bourgeoisie in explaining the types of policies adopted by dependent capitalist countries in the semiperiphery. Evans, *Dependent Development*.

of the industrial bourgeoisie to support the active pro-industrialization policies of developmentalism. Developmentalism proposed prioritizing industrialization, through providing incentives and subsidies for industrial development and improving financial and exchange policies to facilitate industrial growth. Some of these policies benefited all industrialists, others only those basic capital-intensive industries that were prioritized by developmentalists. Likewise, since developmentalism called on the state to help plan and direct the economy, it provided a privileged economic and policy role for highly trained state technocrats, who benefited from their participation in developmentalist policy making. For this explanation to be convincing, one needs to show a pattern of industrialist support for and championing of developmentalist policies, and a pattern of alliances between state *técnicos* (professionals and technical experts) and industrialists which promoted or facilitated the adoption of developmentalist policies.

The results of my research in Argentina and Brazil increasingly called into question a simple version of the economic interest group theories. Particularly problematic for this interpretation was that most Argentine industrialists failed to promote or even to support actively the developmentalist policies of the Prebisch Plan of 1956 or the Frondizi government. In the Argentine case, the developmentalist ideas were promoted by politicians and intellectuals, often faced with an unconvinced and uncooperative industrial elite. One of the leading desarrollistas in Argentina commented regarding the lack of support of industrialists for the Frondizi economic program: "We couldn't believe that a class would act against its interests. It was clear to me that the Frondizi policies benefited all the entrepreneurs of Argentina. Frondizi adopted an intensely capitalist policy, and he couldn't understand why he didn't receive support. Many large industrialists were frigerista [supporters of Rogelio Frigerio, Frondizi's closest adviser], but the Union Industrial was permanently anti-Frondizi."[14]

The crucial difference between industrialists in Brazil and Argentina during the developmentalist period was that in Brazil industrialists conceived of themselves and acted as protagonists and leaders of the industrial program, while in Argentina they were willing to take advantage of the incentives offered by the program but never took a leadership position in forwarding the developmentalist program. In Brazil industrial association defended the government politically, while in Argentina they were either indifferent or occasionally involved in moves to undermine the government. These differences are less the

---

14. Interview with Oscar Camilion, Buenos Aires, August 5, 1985.

result of the strength or composition of the industrial bourgeoisie in the two countries than of their economic and political ideologies. Brazilian industrialists were more developmentalist than their Argentine counterparts, who continued to espouse more liberal economic ideas.

Alliances between industrialists and state technocrats were an important factor explaining the adoption and implementation of developmentalism in Brazil. But support for Kubitschek's developmentalist policies was much broader than I had anticipated, involving important parts of the working class and middle class, intellectuals as well as industrialists, and even some portions of the rural elite.

Although there is much that is convincing about economic interest group theories, these explanations often presuppose that one can know the interests of a social or economic group without understanding their historically specific ideologies, assuming, for example, that we can infer the interests of industrialists without knowing how they themselves define their interests. These approaches also assume that interests are universal—they will be approximately the same in different countries experiencing similar development paths. Yet it is not clear that the "objective" interests of Brazilian and Argentine industrial groups were so different as to explain their very different positions on developmentalism without reference to the ideological predispositions that shaped their perceptions of their interests, and thus their position toward developmentalist governments.

Economic and political interests are not directly perceived by political actors. Rather, these interests are perceived through the lens of the existing ideologies in various historical settings. Thus, for example, in order to understand the positions of Argentine industrialists toward the Frondizi administration, we need to know that large industrialists perceived their interests through the lens of their anti-Peronism. The government was judged more by its policies toward Peronism than by the essence of its industrial policy. And Brazilian industrialists' perceptions of Kubitschek's policies were shaped by the strong developmentalist orientation of Brazilian industrial associations, dating to the ideological and institutional leadership of Roberto Simonsen in the 1940s. Thus any explanation for the adoption and implementation of these policies must take into account the ideologies of powerful economic groups which led them to interpret their interests in different ways.

In addition, the ability of powerful economic groups in Argentina and Brazil to veto policies that they perceived as directly threatening their interests was much stronger than their ability to advocate precise alternatives. Powerful rural producers, for example, were able to veto agrarian reform proposals but could not impose their own development model. The economic interests of powerful groups helped set the limits of what was possible but did not determine choice within those limits.

State Autonomy Arguments

Neo-Marxist theories of the state can provide an alternative to economic interest group explanations of the adoption of developmentalist policies. These theories focus on the degree to which the state can formulate and pursue goals that are not simply reflective of the demands or interests of social groups, classes, or society. Poulantzas reconceptualizes the state as the "material condensation of a relationship of forces among classes and class fragments." He thus rejects both the understanding of the state as a tool of the dominant class with no autonomy whatsoever and of the state as a subject external to social classes. Because of the materiality of the state and the contradictions among various components within it, the state possesses a certain degree of "relative autonomy" from any given class fraction which permits it to represent and organize the long-term interests of the dominant class as a whole. Policies are the result of class conflict mediated through a relatively autonomous state.[15]

Lindblom presents a somewhat similar argument from a non-Marxist position. Since in a market-oriented system major decisions affecting the well-being of society and government rest in the hands of businesspersons, officials cannot be indifferent to how business performs. The government cannot perform most of these tasks itself, and it cannot command business to produce; it can only induce business to perform through financial and political benefits. As a result, government officials grant business a privileged role. By the nature of the market system, the government is dependent on the performance of a sector that it can only induce to perform.[16] Like Poulantzas, Lindblom essentially argues that the state will act in the long-term interest of capital, regardless of direct pressures from business interests.

A number of authors have applied the insights of theories of state autonomy to study policy making in Latin America.[17] But these theories

15. Nicos Poulantzas, *State, Power, Socialism* (London: New Left Books, Verso, 1978), pp. 128–29.

16. See Charles E. Lindblom, *Politics and Markets* (New York: Basic Books, 1977), p. 175.

17. See, for example, Nora Hamilton, *The Limits of State Autonomy: Post-Revolutionary Mexico* (Princeton: Princeton University Press, 1982).

suffer from some of the same problems as economic interest group theories. They help us understand why, in the context of the capitalist state, certain alternatives that are directly threatening to capitalists are excluded (a socialist alternative, for example); but they do not help us understand the content of the policies that are actually adopted. How do state policy makers know what kinds of policies will benefit the capitalist system, even when individual capitalists themselves do not know? What gives policy makers a kind of vision that is lacking in industrial groups? A number of different kinds of policies could plausibly be construed as providing for the long-term interests of capital. Why do policy makers adopt one type of policy over another?

In the 1980s it would appear that Latin American policy makers would have been acting in the long-term interests of capitalism if they had sponsored state-led industrial export promotion rather than ISI. Then why was state-led industrial export promotion rarely considered an option? One of the problems with the state-autonomy approach is that many state actions can be justified post hoc in terms of the long-term interests of the capitalist state. Less clear is whether these theories can help us specify what kinds of policies will be adopted. It is necessary to know the economic ideas held by policy makers in order to understand why certain alternatives are chosen above others.

The state-centric approaches that are more useful for understanding the adoption and implementation of developmentalist policies are those that focus more on issues of state capacity and purpose rather than on state autonomy. Since the concept of state autonomy does not focus on concrete aspects of state structure and institutions, it fails to capture important differences in the nature of the states in Brazil and Argentina. These differences are more related to state capacity than to state strength or state autonomy. State capacity involves the administrative and coercive abilities of the state apparatus to implement official goals. State capacity is a relational concept: the state is strong or capable in relation to the tasks it sets for itself or that are set for it.[18] Thus state capacity cannot be measured in an absolute sense but only in terms of the fit or disjunction of state capacity with the functions of the state.

A second state characteristic not captured well by notions of either strength or autonomy has to do with the centrality of the state to political life. In Brazil all politics revolves around the state. The state is the major arena, the major power broker, the center of political debate and action. The dilemma of the Argentine state is both its lack of capacity

18. I am indebted to Margaret Keck for helping me clarify this argument.

and its lack of centrality to the political process. Argentine politics takes place outside the bureaucratic apparatus of the state. "The Argentine bureaucracy failed so completely to act as a power broker that most accounts of Argentine politics ignore it entirely."[19]

A third aspect of the state that influenced the developmentalist period was that of state purpose: the ideas or orientations embedded in its institutions which do not change dramatically from one government to another.[20] In the case of Brazil, developmentalist ideas, with their emphasis on technical solutions and state direction of the economy, found special resonance with the ethos of the insulated bureaucracy in Brazil and became part of the embedded orientation of the Brazilian state. No single economic model has emerged as the orientation of the Argentine state.

Power and Discourse Arguments

Others argue that developmentalism is not indigenous to Latin America. This view presents developmentalism as a discourse on underdevelopment constructed in the developed countries and imposed on unwilling Latin Americans as a precondition for receiving military and economic aid. Developmentalism is seen as part of the discourse of development associated with the whole apparatus of development, such as the World Bank and the International Monetary Fund, by which "western countries have been able to manage and control and, in many ways, even create the Third World politically, economically, sociologically, and culturally."[21] In this view developmentalism is not a reflection of the perceived needs for the economic development of these countries but rather is a direct or indirect reflection of the interests and needs of foreign governments and foreign capitalists. This assertion needs to be considered both as regards the theoretical origins of devel-

19. William Ascher, "Planners, Politics, and Technocracy in Argentina and Chile" (Ph.D. diss., Yale University, 1975), p. 163.

20. In their study of the Mexican state and the transnational auto industry, Douglas Bennett and Kenneth Sharpe distinguish between the power and the interests of the state, concepts similar to the capacity and purpose of the state. They perceive the interests of the state as "embedded orientations . . . institutionalized in the ministries and agencies of the state—in their habitual ways of diagnosing and remedying problems and in their organization of staff responsibilities and resources." *Transnational Corporations versus the State: The Political Economy of the Mexican Auto Industry* (Princeton: Princeton University Press, 1985), p. 43.

21. Arturo Escobar, "Discourse and Power in Development: Michel Foucault and the Relevance of His Work to the Third World," *Alternatives* 10 (1984), 383–84.

opmentalism and the institutional linkages between developmentalist governments and foreign governments, international firms and international financial institutions.

It is often assumed that developmentalism in Latin America was directly linked to the emergence of certain strands of modernization theory in the U.S. academic community in the 1950s and 1960s, and as such was an ideology reflecting U.S. political and economic interests. Some authors have argued that developmentalism is essentially a synonym for modernization theory and in general for all U.S. theorizing about Latin America in the 1960s, a paradigm surrogate for U.S. scholars who study Latin America.[22]

There is no doubt that developmentalists were heavily influenced by the examples of the developed world. They saw in the developed countries many of the characteristics they aspired to for their countries: industry, autonomy, technical progress, and modernity. To say that developmentalists were thus influenced, however, is quite different from suggesting that developmentalism was imposed on the Third World, or that Western countries managed or controlled their development. Intellectuals and political leaders consciously chose policies that both attempted to imitate some of the development patterns of the West and at the same time challenged many of the orthodoxies of international financial institutions.

Although there are similarities between some aspects of modernization theory and developmentalism, the linkages have been overemphasized. Most modernization theory did not share the intense emphasis on heavy industry and indicative planning that was central to developmentalism. In most cases, both the practice and the theorizing of developmentalists in Latin America predated the most important publications of modernization theorists.[23] A number of Brazilian developmentalist policy makers attended U.S. universities in the 1940s, where they were exposed to the early work of development economics. But Argentine developmentalists had less such exposure than their Brazilian colleagues. Much of the important work in development economics was

22. Susanne Bodenheimer, *The Ideology of Developmentalism: The American Paradigm-Surrogate for Latin American Studies* (Berkeley: Sage Publications, 1969).

23. See, for example, Seymour Martin Lipset and Aldo Solari, *Elites in Latin America* (New York: Oxford University Press, 1967); Gabriel Almond and James Coleman, *The Politics of Developing Areas* (Princeton: Princeton University Press, 1960); or Kalman Silvert, "The Politics of Social and Economic Change in Latin America," *Sociological Review Monographs*, no. 11, Latin American Sociological Studies, University of Keele, ed. Paul Halmos (London: Routledge and Kegan Paul, 1967), pp. 47–58.

published during or after the developmentalist experiences in Brazil and Argentina.[24]

The Eisenhower administration in the United States viewed the presidencies of Kubitschek and Frondizi favorably.[25] They appeared to be the kind of leaders the United States wanted to encourage: young, "modern," and favorable to U.S. investment in the region. But Frondizi and Kubitschek wanted more than verbal support from Eisenhower; their programs depended on substantial foreign financial resources. In 1960 Eisenhower proposed a new aid program for Latin America, later named the Social Progress Trust Fund, which aimed at combating communism in Latin America by supporting health, education, housing, and land reform projects. Both Frondizi and Kubitschek, however, were skeptical of the program. It was too little, too late, and it focused on the wrong kind of assistance. The developmentalist presidents argued that Latin America needed massive infusions of capital for the large infrastructural and industrial projects that formed the centerpiece of the developmentalist program.[26]

In other words, the United States supported the Frondizi and Kubitschek presidencies but was not particularly supportive of the developmentalist component of their programs. The U.S. government was encouraged by their open policies toward foreign investment, but did not endorse the protectionist, pro-industrialization priorities of these governments. Developmentalist policies often were adopted or

24. For example, Walter Rostow's most influential work, *The Stages of Economic Growth: A Non-Communist Manifesto*, was not published until 1960. Albert Hirschman's early work on industrialization and linkages was published in 1958, after the Frondizi and Kubitschek programs were already under way. Hirschman's ideas in *Strategy of Economic Development* are sometimes attributed as sources for developmentalist policies in Argentina. But Hirschman himself points out that his book was not translated into Spanish until 1961. Albert O. Hirschman, "Argentina's Economic Development and Policies during the Frondizi Period (1958–1962): Comments on the Paper by Alberto Petrecolla," unpublished manuscript to be published in a volume edited by Guido DiTella.

25. Vice-President Richard Nixon attended both the Frondizi and Kubitschek inaugurations. During his trip to the Frondizi inauguration, Nixon also toured Peru, Uruguay, and Venezuela, where he was confronted with angry demonstrators protesting U.S. policy toward Latin America. In particular, the United States was blamed for its support of dictatorships that blocked social change in the region and for its failure to provide economic assistance for Latin American development. While publicly blaming Communists for the attacks on Nixon, the Eisenhower administration nevertheless undertook a reevaluation of U.S. policy toward Latin America. As a result of this reevaluation, Eisenhower approved a National Security memorandum that called for "special encouragement" to representative governments, like those of Frondizi and Kubitschek. Stephen G. Rabe, *Eisenhower and Latin America: The Foreign Policy of Anticommunism* (Chapel Hill: University of North Carolina Press, 1988), p. 104.

26. Ibid., pp. 141–44.

maintained in the face of opposition from international financial institutions. For example, the International Monetary Fund (IMF) tried to get both Frondizi and Kubitschek to abandon some of the basic elements of the developmentalist industrial policy. As a result, Kubitschek eventually broke off negotiations with the IMF in order to complete the implementation of the developmentalist programs. Frondizi implemented a harsh IMF-style stabilization program, but not without conflict between the advocates of orthodox stabilization and the developmentalists within his ruling coalition.

One of the problems with viewing developmentalism as an ideology imposed by external forces is that this approach presents a political world in which Third World countries are treated as objects rather than subjects, and in which the ideas held by both policy makers and the public are either false consciousness or thinly veiled justifications. To frame the ideas of Latin American intellectuals like Raúl Prebisch and other developmentalist thinkers mainly as means to effect Western domination over Third World countries is to debase the validity of many Latin American contributions to the global development debate. But even more serious, this view misrepresents the chronology and genealogy of intellectual currents and the nature of linkages and conflicts between external and internal factors.

Rational Choice/Political Survival Arguments

Rational choice theories focus on individual policy makers, arguing that policy makers are rational and will choose policies that maximize their goals. Given a set of preferences and a set of alternatives from which to choose, policy makers choose the alternatives that maximize their chances of achieving their goals. Rational choice theorists do not attempt to explain preferences but rather suggest that "it is the synthesis of a creative and plausible attribution of preferences to actors with the rational choice assumptions themselves which results in the most compelling instances of this approach."[27] Barry Ames, one of the few to apply rational choice theory to policy making in Latin America, argues that preferences are of two kinds: survival and substantive. Survival preferences include what must be done to stay in office. Substantive preferences—those the executive can implement if he or she gains and maintains office—include everything else. Since "true" substantive

27. Barbara Geddes, "Toward a Rational Actor Account of Political Development," memorandum for the workshop "Understanding the Political Economy of NICs: Current Conceptual Debates," San Diego, January 5–6, 1990, p. 1.

preferences are "unknowable," Ames assumes that the predominant interest of leaders is holding on to their jobs.[28] Survival preferences involve calculating the costs of attracting new supporters and maintaining old ones. Ames argues that his theory of political survival explains variation in public spending patterns among administrations. Politicians will use the budget to reward and recruit followers. In particular, Ames discusses an "electoral-expenditure cycle" in Latin America: spending in response to elections designed to provide jobs and projects for supporters and allies.

In the sense that rational choice theorists do not attempt to explain substantive preferences, the model may be inappropriate to explain the adoption of economic policies. Most of them claim that rational choice theory will tell us what will promote our aims, but not how preferences themselves are determined. Still, it seems important to consider the possibility that developmentalist policies can primarily be understood as survival strategies, or whether it is possible to synthesize a creative and plausible attribution of preferences with the rational choice assumptions to explain the adoption and implementation of developmentalism.

Political survival arguments can help us understand how policy was carried out, but not how major policy choices were made. Ames discusses both the Kubitschek and the Frondizi periods specifically, but his discussions fail to identify the central dynamic in development policy or in development spending during these administrations.[29] Kubitschek used a wide variety of techniques, including pork barrel spending and expansion of public sector employment, to gain the support of politicians for his program. But the central economic policy of the period, the Targets Program, cannot be explained in terms of pork barrel politics, and the institutions that implemented it were those least affected by clientelism. Ames can explain how Kubitschek gained support for

28. Barry Ames, *Political Survival: Politicians and Public Policy in Latin America* (Berkeley: University of California Press, 1987), p. 4.

29. Ames characterizes the Kubitschek administration as one in which the Congress was consistently more conservative than the president, producing a legislative deadlock. Yet research on congressional roll call votes shows that Congress gave the president wide multiparty support on the major issues essential for the implementation of his program. Wanderley Guilherme dos Santos, "The Calculus of Conflict: Impasse in Brazilian Politics and the Crisis of 1964" (Ph.D. diss., Stanford University, 1979), p. 143; and Maria Isabel Valladão de Carvalho, "A colaboração do legislativo para o desempenho do executivo durante of governo JK" (masters thesis, Instituto Universitario de Pesquisa do Rio de Janeiro, 1977), p. 51.

his program in Congress but not how and why the program was adopted in the first place. For example, to win congressional support for the construction of Brasília, Kubitschek created a bipartisan commission to oversee the construction, which became a source of patronage for both parties. A political survival argument can explain how Kubitschek tried to win support for Brasília but not why he decided to build a new capital in the first place. Likewise, Ames explains how Frondizi tried to win support for his developmentalist program by offering major wage increases at the beginning of his presidency. But once again, the survival argument cannot tell us why developmentalist policies were adopted, or why Frondizi decided to reward certain sectors but not others.

Indeed, Frondizi's understanding of survival politics only makes sense within the intricate logic of his developmentalist thought. Most observers of the Frondizi period are struck by his ability to alienate so many of his initial followers early in his administration. Yet Frondizi was clearly a rational political leader. When it became apparent during the election campaign that he might lose, Frondizi secured an electoral alliance with the banned Peronist leadership to attract Peronist votes. When he understood that one of the key problems with the balance of payments was payment for imported petroleum, he took measures to increase Argentine domestic oil production by bringing in foreign investment to explore and exploit Argentine oil. But Frondizi's rational moves were interpreted very differently by political leaders and the public in Argentina. Frondizi's rational actions were simultaneously irrational in that they undermined his long-term political survival. In order to act rationally in a way that would insure his survival, he had to be aware of the political and symbolic impact of his actions on the Argentine public.

The political survival perspective is useful in that it helps us understand that much of politics involves creating coalitions to gain or maintain political power. But what is the process through which coalitions are built? Political survival is ensured not only by "buying off" different groups, but also through mobilizing support. One of the most important means for mobilizing support is an appeal to commonly held ideas, a "project" that captivates and inspires people. In turn, ideas may often serve as the glue that holds together otherwise disparate coalitions. Focusing solely on the economics of survival politics while ignoring the ideational dimension impoverishes our concept of politics and weakens our ability to explain the adoption of policies and the formation of coalitions.

Horizontal ISI policies can be understood as an attempt to court the support of urban dwellers and the middle class by providing previously unavailable consumer goods. But vertical ISI cannot be explained this way, since it often involves short-term sacrifices for the public for the sake of long-term development. The tools used to gain support for the program are ideological and symbolic as well as economic. In order to accept some of the delayed gratification and sacrifices of the developmentalist program, the people were wooed with images of industrialization, "technification," and the future greatness of their country.

The political survival approach cannot provide a satisfactory explanation of the decision to adopt developmentalist policies, because it is unable to deal with the question of politicians' substantive preferences. It proposes, indeed, that the substantive preferences of political leaders are "unknowable." I argue, to the contrary, that the substantive preferences of political leaders are knowable, and that the survival strategies of most political leaders are inseparable from their substantive preferences and their beliefs about the polity. That is, any survival strategy presupposes a knowledge of how the public, or how specific political and economic groups, will respond to policies. So many different types of activities can plausibly be construed as a preference structured by the desire to stay in office. But how do we explain why one survival strategy is adopted instead of another? In the case of Frondizi, how do we explain why he chose policies that appeared to be irrational survival strategies? Both Frondizi and Kubitschek were political entrepreneurs whose programs were much more ambitious and varied than those required for survival. Why do some politicians simply survive and some lead? And why do some appear to have an instinct for self-destruction?

My goal has not been to dismiss each of these alternative theories, but rather to point to some of their weaknesses in trying to answer the specific questions addressed in this volume: why were developmentalist policies adopted in Brazil and Argentina during this period? and why were they implemented and consolidated more successfully in Brazil than in Argentina? These alternative explanations offer powerful understandings of why not just any model was available to policy makers during this period. But the most they can tell us is that there are certain types of policies that are ruled out, such as those that directly contradict the interests of capitalists or those that threaten the immediate political survival of a politician. These theories also offer insights into the types of strategies used to win support for the program once adopted. But they do little to determine within a set of equally plausible survival strategies, or strategies for furthering the interests of capitalism, why policies are actually chosen.[30] In particular, they have difficulty explaining why policies like those chosen in East Asia, policies of state-led export promotion, were not considered viable alternatives in Latin America during this period. To understand the power of export pessimism and the appeal of import-substituting industrialization in its different variants, it is necessary to grapple with the influence of ideas on the policy-making process, not only the ideas of individual policy makers, but also those on development shared by large groups in society.

The Role of Ideas

As the discussion above makes clear, ideas did not operate unfettered by material constraints. In their choices of economic models the countries of the periphery and semiperiphery were constrained by their subordinate position in the international economic order, by the limited size of their domestic markets, and by powerful domestic groups who vetoed certain alternatives. The debate over development models operates within a "material matrix of affirmations and sanctions," in the language of Goran Therborn.[31] Developmentalism was a compromise program constructed within a matrix of international and domestic constraints and opportunities.

International and domestic constraints and opportunities, however, do not exist outside of individual cognition; rather, they are perceived by policy makers based on their conceptual frameworks. For example, the expanded availability of international investment could be perceived of as an opportunity or as a danger, depending on the ideas held by policy makers. The choice of a "plausible" or "rational" alterna-

30. I am indebted to a memorandum by John Ferejohn and to Robert Keohane's comments on that memo for helping me reconceptualize some of the arguments presented in this section. Ferejohn argues that in many game situations, multiple equilibria are possible, and thus auxiliary assumptions are needed to select between plausible alternatives. Ferejohn suggests that at this point there is room for cooperation between rational and interpretive accounts. Interpretive approaches may need rational accounts to help us narrow the range of possible interpretations, while rational choice theorists can "select among equilibria by appeals to culturally shared understandings and meanings." John Ferejohn, "Rationality and Interpretation: Parliamentary Elections in Early Stuart England," memorandum presented at the SSRC Workshop on Politics and Ideas," Stanford University, January 18–20, 1990, pp. 9–10.

31. Goran Therborn, *The Ideology of Power and the Power of Ideology* (London: New Left Books, Verso, 1980), pp. 33–34.

tive depends on the way ideas structure the understanding of policy makers and the public about what is desirable and possible.

John Ruggie provides one theoretical framework to examine these issues: the "economic regimes" that arise during a historical period are the result of a convergence between an international power structure (primarily the existence or nonexistence of a hegemonic power able and willing to enforce certain rules of the game) and the structure of legitimate social purpose characteristic of the hegemon and the core states. Legitimate social purpose is defined by the nature of state-society relations emerging from a fusion of a particular class configuration and a specific ideology.

Thus Europe's move to a free trade system was related to the political and cultural ascendance of the middle class, which in turn provided fertile soil for the ideology of the free market as "an increasingly captivating social metaphor."[32] Likewise, the change to a regime of "embedded liberalism" in the postwar era was the result in part of the increasing political strength of the working class in the core and the general acceptance of the doctrine that the state should take more responsibility for domestic social security and economic stability. In this explanation, it is the convergence of new ideas with a particular international power structure and class relations that determines the emergence of new economic models. But Ruggie overemphasizes the degree to which the emergence and strength of new ideas is connected to the ascendance of a class or class fraction that is particularly receptive to a new ideology.

In the postwar period a new social purpose was also emerging in the periphery, not totally unlike that in the center. New state-society relations had begun to redefine the legitimate social purpose in pursuit of which state power was expected to be employed; the new goal in the periphery was the pursuit by the state of economic growth through rapid import-substituting industrialization. Developmentalism provided "captivating social metaphors": the concept of state-supported heavy industry as the route to autonomy and wealth, the mystique of planning and technification as tools that would allow the leap into the future. The debates over economic policy in Brazil and Argentina in the 1950s and 1960s show the degree to which people were caught up by the mystique of industrial development and planning, and the grip of developmentalist ideas on the collective consciousness of a generation.

32. John G. Ruggie, "International Regimes, Transactions, and Change: Embedded Liberalism in the Postwar Economic Order," *International Organization* 36 (Spring 1982), 386.

These ideas captured the imagination of a broad segment of the population, not only of the industrialists or the new technocratic elite. The degree to which the metaphors of developmentalism found fertile ground, however, varied from country to country, depending on the existing ideological conditions, the manner in which the new ideas were introduced, and the institutional supports for the new ideas.

THE IMPLEMENTATION AND CONSOLIDATION OF DEVELOPMENTALISM

Developmentalism was adopted in Brazil and Argentina during this period because of new constraints and opportunities in the international system, and because of the existence of new ideas about development. But once adopted, these ideas were more successfully implemented and consolidated in Brazil than in Argentina. In Brazil, a stronger consensus emerged around developmentalism both within the institutions of the state and among the powerful groups in society. In Argentina, no such consensus ever emerged on developmentalist policies. This is in part the result of the stronger institutional capacity of the Brazilian state and the way developmentalist ideas became embodied by institutions in Brazil. The greater leadership skills of the Kubitschek administration in mobilizing financial, technical, and political support for the program, and the fact that developmentalist ideas "fit" better with existing ideas and ideologies of important groups in Brazil, also contributed to implementing and consolidating developmentalist ideas in Brazil.

More consensus emerged in Brazil because developmentalism came to take on a different meaning in Brazil than it did in Argentina. Even though the policies of Kubitschek and Frondizi were very similar, they had different meanings in the two different political contexts. The meanings of new ideas derive not only from their content but also from the nature of the political and ideological context into which they are introduced.[33] Any economic model is open to a number of different interpretations, depending on which aspects are emphasized.[34] Frondizi interpreted developmentalism as nationalist; Peronists interpreted it as *entreguista*—selling out to foreign interests. Some interpretations come

33. Kathryn Sikkink, "The Influence of Raúl Prebisch on Economic Policy Making in Argentina, 1950–1962," *Latin American Research Review* 23 (1988), 91–114.
34. Peter Hall makes this point eloquently as regards the adoption of Keynesian ideas in Europe. *The Political Power of Economic Ideas*, p. 370.

to dominate others, and those dominant interpretations infuse meaning into models in particular contexts. Frondizi lost the interpretive struggle. In Argentina, desarrollismo came to be associated with antinationalism. In Brazil, developmentalism was able more closely to maintain its association with nationalism, which contributed to the consolidation of the model.

The Importance of Institutions

Brazil has been characterized by a strong centralized state and a relatively weak civil society. Argentina is just the opposite: the state is comparatively weak, whereas elements in civil society, especially the labor unions and the political parties, are strong.[35] But for state-centric approaches to be useful, we need to be more precise about the specific state characteristics that contribute to policy outcomes in the economic policy arena.[36] The existence of an "insulated" bureaucracy in Brazil provided the technical pockets to embody and implement the developmentalist program, while the Argentine state had no such insulated sector.

This emphasis on the comparative institutional capacity of the Brazilian and Argentine states is similar to the institutional approach, which highlights the role of executive officials or organizational structures of the state in determining political outcomes.[37] This work differs from the theories of state autonomy discussed above in that it is more concerned with the ability of the state to carry out its goals than with the degree of autonomy of the state from dominant classes. Once set up, state institutions tend to endure, and thus take on influence beyond that of the particular coalitions and conditions that led to their emer-

35. For an engaging discussion of the differences between the state and society in Brazil and Argentina, see Guillermo O'Donnell, "Y a mi, que me importa? Notas sobre sociabilidad y política en Argentina y Brasil," Estudios CEDES 10 (November 1984), 33–35.

36. Theda Skocpol's introduction, "Bringing the State Back In: Strategies of Analysis in Current Research," in *Bringing the State Back In*, ed. Peter Evans, Dietrich Rueschemeyer, and Theda Skocpol (New York: Cambridge University Press, 1985), highlights a number of studies on the possibilities for autonomous state action. Among other factors, she suggests that state capacity relates to insulated state bureaucracies and to the state's ability to attract and retain elite university graduates with sophisticated technical training (p. 16).

37. Some examples of this approach include Stephen Skowronek, *Building a New American State* (Cambridge: Cambridge University Press, 1982); Peter Hall, *Governing the Economy* (New York: Oxford University Press, 1986); and the authors of "The State and American Foreign Economic Policy," a recent special issue of *International Organization* 42 (Winter 1988).

gence.[38] Although the institutional approach is more open to the role of ideas in economic policy making, it does not offer a systematic attempt to explain how ideas, institutions, and individuals interact to produce policy outcomes.[39]

Our most durable economic models become embodied or codified in institutions (including such institutional arrangements as rules and regulations), but primarily in concrete institutions—organizations. These institutions may be within the state or outside of the state—domestic, regional, or international.[40] Some institutions may have a class base, such as national business associations or labor unions, but others are more autonomous of class influences, such as universities, research institutions, or international organizations. But not all institutions become equally imbued with ideas. A minimum level of institutional and personnel continuity is a necessary precondition for ideas to become embodied in institutions.

By institutions I mean established organizations and the rules and practices that govern how these organizations function internally and relate to one another and to society. The rules and practices governing these institutions can be formal (that is, embodied in laws and regulations) or informal and implicit.[41] I am concerned with those institutions that relate to economic policy making. Most of these institutions are organizations within the state, such as national development banks and planning agencies, but international institutions such as CEPAL and domestic institutions such as organizations of industrialists are also explored.

The institutional approach has been divided between those who focus primarily on domestic politics and state structures and others who study international institutions. Those who study international institutions have not paid sufficient attention to domestic politics, and

38. G. John Ikenberry, "Conclusion: An Institutional Approach to American Foreign Economic Policy," *International Organization* 42 (Winter 1988), 224–25.

39. A recent contribution to the institutional literature which directly addresses the role of ideas and institutions is Goldstein, "The Impact of Ideas on Trade Policy," pp. 224–25.

40. Other authors have made similar points regarding the role of institutions as carriers or disseminators of ideologies. Peter Hall, in *Governing the Economy*, argues that ideas acquire force when they find organizational means of expression, especially when they are taken up by a powerful political organization (p. 280). Emanuel Adler stresses how institutions are carriers of certain ideologies, or "constellations of collective understanding." *The Power of Ideology*, pp. 11–13.

41. This is similar to Keohane's definition of "specific institutions" as "discrete entities, identifiable in space and time" with "unique life histories." Robert O. Keohane, "International Institutions: Two Approaches," *International Studies Quarterly* 32 (1988), 383–84.

those who study domestic institutions have not always made clear the linkages between domestic and international institutions. Throughout this book, I situate domestic policy making and economic institutions within the international political and economic context, and I explore the linkages between domestic and international institutions.

In the case of developmentalism, the institutional links and lack thereof are clear and interesting. At the international level, developmentalism found its expression in some pockets of the United Nations, and regionally in the Economic Commission for Latin America. At the domestic level in Argentina, the penetration of developmentalist ideas in institutions was incomplete; its only true institutional home was the political party apparatus associated with Frondizi, and even there it contested institutional terrain with national populist ideas still embraced by many members of the Radical party. Developmentalist ideas were not embedded in the institutional memories or apparatus of the organizations of the national industrial bourgeoisie until much later. In contrast, in Brazil developmentalist ideas found a number of institutional homes. They were embraced by the industrial associations at the national level and in the state of São Paulo, and they became part of the institutional identity of the National Development Bank, the Development Council, and parts of the Banco do Brasil and the Foreign Ministry. As part of the institutional identity of these organizations, developmentalist ideas were transmitted in training programs and embodied in laws, procedures, and publications.

Institutional and personnel continuity is necessary for ideas to become embodied in institutions and for policies to be successfully implemented. Although economic institutions existed in both countries, in Brazil the web of institutions was more complex and had more continuity than in the case of Argentina. Kubitschek was also able to build on the institutional infrastructure and expertise accumulated during previous governments.[42] Kubitschek's skill was less that of an innovator than of a borrower who took existing people, institutions, and instruments and rearranged them to carry out his economic program. In Argentina, many of the economic institutions created by the Peronist government were later dismantled. Frondizi attempted to form a "parallel administration," but it was not comparable to the complex institutional framework erected in Brazil.

In states where institutions are fairly new, such as Argentina and

42. Luciano Martins has pointed out that such continuity allowed the bureaucracy to fill the important function as the memory of the system. Luciano Martins, "Politique et developpement economique: Structures de pouvoir et systeme de decisions au Bresil, 1930–1964" (Ph.D. diss., University of Paris, René Descartes, 1973), p. 558.

Brazil, continuity of individuals is the primary mechanism for continuity and coherence of policy. Individuals experience "political learning" and serve as the memory of the system.[43] Personnel continuity did not necessarily mean that the same people stayed in the same job for long periods of time. But in Brazil during this ten-year period most of the top policy makers were drawn from the same pool and rotated among positions within the bureaucracy, acquiring experience and forming networks. In Argentina, there was virtually *no* continuity of personnel between different administrations, limiting the possibility for policy continuity via political learning and accumulated administrative experience.

As a result of the much stronger institutional base, developmentalist ideas had a stronger and more lasting influence on policy making in Brazil and received greater domestic support. In Argentina, the influence of developmentalist ideas was much more contested, and many policies were undermined and reversed as soon as Frondizi left office.

An Institutional-Interpretive Approach

Unfortunately, much of the attention to the state capacity or to state administrative structures has been applied in a mechanistic way, more reminiscent of a study of public administration than of politics. These state institutions, and their rules and procedures, do not exist outside of political life. Essential in the study of state capacity is the dynamic interaction between the institutions, rules, and procedures of the state and society, and the people, groups, and ideas in political life. These state structures represent potential resources, but for development to proceed potential resources must be mobilized. Mobilization of resources is the game of politics at its richest and involves ideas, inspiration, leadership, and the unquantifiable qualities that motivate people to believe and to act.

Because of this concern with institutions and with ideas and meanings, I think of this as an interpretive-institutional approach—institutional because of the focus on institutions of the state and outside the state, interpretive because of the concern with the process of how certain meanings emerge around certain policies, ideas, and institutions.[44]

43. For a discussion of political learning, see Hugh Heclo, *Modern Social Politics in Britain and Sweden* (New Haven: Yale University Press, 1974), pp. 304–22.

44. The notion of an interpretive approach is not unlike what Keohane calls a "reflective approach . . . which stresses the impact of human subjectivity and the embeddedness of contemporary international institutions in pre-existing practices." Keohane, "International Institutions," p. 379.

In trying to understand how the protagonists saw their world, I have taken seriously the intentions of the participants in these debates as they were expressed in interviews and publications. I have been concerned not only with what they say but how they say it: the words, images, metaphors, and symbols of political life.[45]

Interpretive institutionalism, however, is only an approach or framework. It directs our attention to areas of concern without yielding many specific theoretical arguments about the types of relationships we will find. If we are to take it further, we need to begin to specify when and how an interpretive institutional approach is more useful than other approaches. When do ideas and institutions take on greatest importance?

The adoption of new models is the result of the ideas of top policy makers, who respond to what they perceive as the constraints and opportunities in the international and domestic economic situation. Ideas held by powerful individuals are the key to understanding the adoption of policies.[46] Ideas in institutions are less important at the adoption stage. The Frondizi administration was able to adopt a full-fledged developmentalist program in spite of the fragile institutional support for developmentalist ideas in Argentina. If powerful individuals in key positions "change their minds," as Frondizi and his top advisers did in 1957–1958, they can oversee the adoption of a new economic model.

Successful implementation and consolidation of new models, however, requires that these ideas become embodied in capable institutions and that they receive broad support from societal groups. New ideas are more likely to be influential if they "fit" well with existing ideas and ideologies in a particular historical setting. Peter Hall has made this point about the adoption of Keynesianism in Europe. New ideas enter a terrain already defined by a prevailing set of political ideas, which Hall refers to as the political discourse of a nation.[47] This was also the case in Latin America. Developmentalism took on a different meaning in Brazil and Argentina because it articulated differently with existing ideologies and with the prevailing terms of political discourse. In Brazil, developmentalism resonated better with existing ideas than in Ar-

45. Research in Latin America convinced me that the symbolic and discursive dimensions of development policy in Latin America had been neglected. As I developed this theme, one source of inspiration was Murray Edelman, *The Symbolic Uses of Politics* (Urbana: University of Illinois Press, 1985).

46. This conclusion coincides with Judith Goldstein's argument that "ideas influence policy only when they are carried by individuals or groups with political clout." "The Impact of Ideas on Trade Policy," p. 71.

47. Peter Hall, "Conclusion: The Politics of Keynesian Ideas," in *The Political Power of Economic Ideas*, pp. 383–84.

gentina. The better fit between new ideas and the political discourse helps explain the more successful consolidation of developmentalism in Brazil.

At the level of the implementation and consolidation of developmentalist policies, state institutions and the manner in which ideas are embodied in state institutions are more central to the explanation. How do certain state institutions become imbued with a particular "purpose"—that is, how do certain ideas become embodied in state institutions? I suggest that the organizational infrastructure, the operating procedures, and the accumulation of intellectual talent in an insulated portion of the bureaucracy are the principal differences between the institutional structure in Brazil and Argentina, and that they help explain differences in the implementation of developmentalist policy. In Argentina, a historical failure to undertake necessary administrative reforms and a chronic distrust of the state has led to the emergence of weak and ineffectual institutions for the ongoing formulation and implementation of economic policy. Such institutions are unlikely to acquire a strong institutional "purpose" or become identified with a set of ideas.

We all too often speak of state structures as if political leadership had no role at all. Ideas become embodied in institutions but are often symbolized by the leader, who is the most important spokesperson and representative of the idea. Kubitschek and Frondizi are clear examples of leaders who symbolized a school of thought: developmentalism. Their personal histories thus become entwined with the histories of the ideas they championed. This study of economic policy making examines the complex interaction between ideas, institutions, and individuals which undergirds the policy process.

Chapter 2 discusses developmentalist ideas more closely and provides an overview of the changing international conditions in the postwar period and their influence on the region and Brazil and Argentina, which contributed to the emergence of developmentalist policies. Chapters 3 and 4 then tell the stories of the developmentalist experiments in Argentina and Brazil. Beginning with the end of the populist government in each country, with the downfall of Perón and the suicide of Vargas, these chapters trace the adoption, implementation, and consolidation of developmentalism in the two countries. To explore consolidation, I examine the domestic responses of different groups to developmentalist policies. Although the chapters end respectively with the fall of Frondizi and the end of the Kubitschek term, they briefly trace the political paths that developmentalists chose as both countries moved toward authoritarianism in 1964 and 1966. The nature of the state in both countries played an important role in the formulation and implementation of developmentalist policies. Chapter 5 focuses on how the differences in state autonomy, state capacity, and state purpose influenced the implementation of developmentalist policies. Chapter 6 then compares and contrasts the two developmentalist experiments, drawing attention to the different economic and political outcomes. While the convergence of a set of international preconditions and the emergence of new ideas led to the adoption of developmentalist policies, the internal success and consolidation of the developmentalist model depended primarily on domestic political factors. In the second part of Chapter 5, I discuss how the differences in the mobilization of financial, technical, political, and symbolic resources in Brazil and Argentina influenced the implementation of developmentalist programs. Although Brazil mobilized financial and technical resources more successfully than did Argentina, it was Kubitschek's mobilization of political and symbolic resources that sets the Brazilian developmentalist period apart from that of Argentina. Chapter 7 situates the conclusions of the book in relation to some of the recent literature on ideas and institutions.

CHAPTER TWO

The International Setting and
the Origins of Developmentalism

The study of economic models in Latin America has tended to divide the options into only nationalist and internationalist models. Sometimes this distinction is referred to as structuralism versus monetarism, other times as national populism versus liberalism.[1] But in the focus on only two models, developmentalism falls in between. It is both internationalist and protectionist. This view blurs the distinction both between liberal economic and developmentalist economic models, and between national populist models and developmentalism. I argue above that a number of different models were open to Latin America in the postwar period, but that the debate focused primarily on three models: developmentalism and national populism, both of which focused on import-substituting industrialization (ISI) and liberalism.

Latin America's negative experience with the loss of traditional export markets during the Depression and the Second World War made it wary of export promotion models, even those that focused on manufactured or nontraditional exports. During the war both Brazil and Argentina were forced to produce many products that had previously been imported, and the experience of this industrialization by necessity, together with the sense of vulnerability caused by the loss of mar-

---

1. See, for example, Roberto Campos, "Two Views on Inflation in Latin America," in *Latin American Issues*, ed. Albert O. Hirschman (New York: Twentieth Century Fund, 1961); Richard Mallon and Juan Sourrille, *Èconomic Policy Making in a Conflict Society: The Argentine Case* (Cambridge, Mass.: Harvard University Press, 1975). Robert Kaufman, "Liberalization and Democratization in South America: Perspectives from the 1970s," in *Transitions from Authoritarian Rule*, ed. Guillermo O'Donnell, Philippe Schmitter, and Laurence Whitehead (Baltimore: Johns Hopkins University Press, 1986), pp. 86–87, refers to "internationalist economic models."

kets and supplies during the war, led to the continuation of ISI policies after the war. Given the magnitude of the external shocks they experienced, it is not surprising that after the war many Latin American governments adopted economic models designed to give their countries greater self-sufficiency in the production of industrial goods.

During this period both national populist and developmentalist models tended to have an antiexport bias. In the case of national populism, this antiexport bias may have been inherent to the model. In the case of developmentalism, it may have been a temporary stage of developmentalism rather than a permanent characteristic. Some developmentalists believed that after basic industries had been established, efforts could be made to promote export of these industries' products. This was the case, for example, with the policy makers who oversaw the establishment of the automobile industry in Brazil and Argentina, and who hoped that these factories would eventually export vehicles to the rest of the region.

The Socialist model was not seriously considered as a practical alternative in Latin America. Although mentioned here as a possible alternative, it was not one of the important alternative models contemplated by most political and economic actors in Latin America in the 1950s. Even the Communist parties in Brazil and Argentina did not seriously advocate a Socialist economic model for these countries in the 1950s, because they believed that the countries had not yet reached an adequate level of economic development to create the right conditions for socialism. It was also believed that a Socialist model would be unacceptable to the United States and thus was not politically viable. These assumptions were questioned after the Cuban revolution in 1959, but this questioning came too late to have much of an impact during the period under study.

Because both national populist and developmentalist models are proindustrialization models emphasizing import-substituting industrialization, there is sometimes a tendency to confuse them. They are lumped together as ISI models, or even as inward-looking growth models (*desarrollo hacia adentro*). But this obscures important differences between them. Whereas in national populism the internal market and domestic consumption are seen as the engine of growth, in developmentalism growth is promoted by directed investment in priority areas, which in turn creates possibilities for forward and backward linkages to other industrial areas. National populism is a demand-driven economic model, and developmentalism is an investment-driven model. Thus national populism is more of an inward-looking growth model than is developmentalism, which looks outward for sources of finance. We need to examine the similarities and differences between the national populist and the developmentalist models.

NATIONAL POPULIST ECONOMIC MODEL

Two central features distinguish the national populist from the developmentalist model. The national populist model favors domestic industry over foreign industry, which in turn leads to a built-in bias in favor of small and medium-sized industry over heavy or basic industry. Since national capitalists in most Latin American countries have neither the financial nor technical resources to set up large industrial concerns for the production of heavy basic industry, the preference for national capital reinforces the emphasis on smaller-scale industry. But medium-sized industry also produces the types of consumer goods that the populist coalition demands. This has been referred to as national populism's emphasis on horizontal industrialization as compared to developmentalism's emphasis on vertical industrialization.

National populists also advocate greater state involvement in production than do developmentalists, seeing state industry as far preferable to foreign involvement either through foreign borrowing or foreign investment. Foreign borrowing, one of the central pillars of developmentalism, is viewed unfavorably in the national populist model.

The economic policies of the first Peronist government serve as the prototype of national populist economic policies. The Peronist administration looked so unfavorably on foreign borrowing that it refused to become a member of either the World Bank or the IMF. Peronists believed that increased wages in popular sectors led to increased demand for domestic consumer goods, stimulating the expansion of domestic industry.[2] Horizontal industrialization focused on the internal market and aimed at protecting the country from vulnerability to external shocks. "If, then, a country does not try to enlarge its internal market and to progress along the path of being the first transformer of its own raw materials, it will remain dangerously exposed to the shocks of these

---

2. According to one author, the theoretical inspiration for these policies was a version of Keynesian economics modified to suit the needs of an underdeveloped economy. Gary Wynia, *Argentina in the Postwar Era: Politics and Economic Policy Making in a Divided Society* (Alburquerque: University of New Mexico Press, 1990), p. 46. I have found, however, no clear indication that Peronists were well informed in Keynesian economics, and it seems unlikely that Keynesianism served as a specific inspiration for Peronist policies.

unpredictable variations and in a position of permanent instability."[3] The national populists viewed the international market as unreliable, more as a result of diverse and antagonistic economic policies of other countries than as a result of the structure of the international economy.[4]

DEVELOPMENTALIST ECONOMIC MODEL

Developmentalism can be understood as an economic model that was based on certain theories, embraced a series of values, and advocated a set of policies. In one form or another, all developmentalism was based on the belief that industrialization was necessary for development, a belief common to both national populism and developmentalism. In most cases this belief was implicitly reinforced by the theory of declining terms of trade for agricultural products, first elaborated by Raúl Prebisch in documents prepared for CEPAL in 1948, although rarely was this influence directly attributed. A second belief that distinguished developmentalism and national populism was that not all forms of industrialization were equal, or contributed equally to development. Specifically, vertical industrialization, the establishment of basic or heavy industry and the basic infrastructure that would facilitate the emergence of an integrated industrial structure, was central to the developmentalist model. The theoretical origins of this belief are less clear. Albert Hirschman captured this idea with his theories of unbalanced growth and forward and backward linkages. At the time in Brazil references were made to concepts of "bottlenecks" and "growing points" as key areas where state-sponsored industrial and infrastructure projects should concentrate to have the most effect. The necessity of vertical

3. Banco de Credito Industrial Argentino, *Memoria y balance 1944* (Buenos Aires, 1945), p. 16.
4. The Peronists were aware of the emerging developmentalist thought at CEPAL. Peron's minister of economics, Alfredo Gomez Morales, in his lectures in 1951, used terminology and concepts indicating that he was familiar with Prebisch's work, although he did not specifically mention Prebisch or CEPAL. Alfredo Gomez Morales, *Politica Economica Peronista* (Buenos Aires: Escuela Superior Peronista, 1951). No Peronist ever credited Prebisch as an influence on Peronist economic policy; some even suggested that CEPAL derived its ideas from Peronism and not the other way around. For example, in 1953 Perón said, "ECLA has established that the only solution for those semi-developed countries lies in industrialization. . . . We said the same ten years ago, and for the past ten years we have been carrying it out in the Argentine Republic." Cited in Carlos H. Waisman, *Reversal of Development in Argentina* (Princeton: Princeton University Press, 1987), pp. 172–73. Prebisch disputed this claim at the same time as he recognized similarities between CEPAL's ideas and Perón's position on industrialization. Interview with Raúl Prebisch, Buenos Aires, October 23, 1985.

industrialization for development was supplemented by a third belief: domestic savings were inadequate to fund the heavy industrialization project. The fourth basic belief was that although private initiative should be primarily responsible for development, it could not carry out industrialization without direction and assistance from the state.

From these four basic beliefs flowed the three interrelated policy components that characterize developmentalism: (1) intensive vertical import-substituting industrialization focused on high-priority basic industrial sectors; (2) rapid capital accumulation that emphasized foreign private and public sources of capital; (3) state involvement to channel private initiative into priority areas.

The economic ideas of both Frondizi and Kubitschek were classic examples of developmentalist thought, embracing explicitly all of the points outlined above. Both called for an intense process of industrialization concentrating in key industrial sectors—for example, steel, energy, automobiles, transport. Both believed that national savings were insufficient to generate the necessary funds for their industrialization projects, and thus saw extensive investment and technical assistance from foreign capital as essential to the success of their development program.[5] Although these policies were based on the beliefs described above, they were not always based on elaborate economic theories. Often the policies were adopted first and the theorizing came later.

Like national populism, developmentalism emphasizes import substitution but favors granting protectionism and incentives to those industries specializing in the priority areas. Unlike national populism, developmentalism is indifferent to the origin of investment and investors, providing incentives to both national and foreign capital. Since it favors heavy industry and capital goods industry with capital and technical demands often beyond the capacity of domestic entrepreneurs, it tends to have a built-in bias toward foreign capital. Developmentalism places primary emphasis on the role of private initiative, but the state has an

5. Using a simplified cognitive mapping technique, I prepared maps of the causal logic of Kubitschek and Frondizi's ideas about development, as they presented them in their initial speeches to Congress and in speeches made after five and six months in government, summing up initial progress on their programs. The resulting maps are strikingly similar. Cognitive mapping helped to check the validity of more general statements on the ideas of Kubitschek and Frondizi based on a much broader survey of speeches and documents and on secondary source materials on Kubitschek's and Frondizi's ideas—especially Mirium Limoeiro Cardoso, *Ideologia do desenvolvimento, Brasil: JK-JQ* (Rio de Janeiro: Paz e Terra, 1978); and Mario Barrera, *Information and Ideology: A Case Study of Arturo Frondizi* (Beverly Hills: Sage Publications, 1973)—than the cognitive mapping technique alone permits. For a discussion of the cognitive mapping technique, see Robert Axelrod, ed., *The Structure of Decision: The Cognitive Maps of Political Elites* (Princeton: Princeton University Press, 1976).

essential role to play in guiding and planning economic activity. The state establishes priority areas for investment, offers incentives to investors, evaluates investment projects, finances development projects, and constructs the basic infrastructure necessary for industrialization. In some cases the state may become involved in wholly owned or public-private mixed enterprises for those priority areas where private initiative is unable or unwilling to invest. Implicit in the policies outlined above are a series of political and economic values that accompanied and underpinned the developmentalist program.

Developmentalism and Democracy

Developmentalists tended to see economic development as a necessary precondition for many other cherished political values. It was common for developmentalists to see economic development as the means not only for the greater well-being of the population but also for democracy, freedom, security, national autonomy, and national greatness. Thus, Kubitschek argued that economic development would "consolidate a free and powerful nation, a nation capable of reciprocating in prosperity, justice, security, and well-being all the prolonged efforts of its sons."[6] His faith in development was so intense that Kubitschek would claim that "the struggle in defense of the style of life we have adopted, our Christian character, our love of liberty and democracy, requires that Brazil utilize and transform its mineral reserves and its raw materials."[7] Frondizi echoed the same thought. "The path of stagnation leads to hate, to dictatorship, and to national disintegration. We have chosen the path of development, which leads to conciliation and liberty."[8]

In this sense, democracy played a secondary role in the political world view of developmentalists, in that it was subordinated to the demands of economic policy. The belief that political rights could only be insured through promoting economic development had potentially negative implications for democratic political practice. But this subordination of democracy to economic goals was not unique to developmentalists; it was shared by many other political actors in Brazil and Argentina.

6. Juscelino Kubitschek de Oliveira, *Mensagem ão Congresso Nacional, 1956* (Rio de Janeiro: Departamento de Imprensa Nacional, 1956), p. 62.
7. Juscelino Kubitschek de Oliveira, *Discursos, 1956* (Rio de Janeiro: Serviço de Documentação da Presidência da República, 1958), p. 21.
8. Arturo Frondizi, *Mensajes presidenciales, 1958–1962*, Vol. 1: 1958 (Buenos Aires: Ediciones Centro de Estudios Nacionales, 1978), p. 167.

Development and Security

Frondizi and Kubitschek also emphasized a connection between development and security issues. While at times this discourse was part of a strategy to gain broader international financial support for their development efforts, it seems clear that developmentalists in both countries perceived their policies as a peaceful alternative to more radical change. Frondizi declared, "The only dilemma that exists in our continent is: development by democratic means, or development by violent means. People will no longer accept living in stagnant misery or ignorance."[9] In the same vein, Kubitschek stated, "The economic situation of Latin America must improve if democracy is going to survive. . . . Today, economic development is inseparable from the concept of collective security and it constitutes the necessary condition to protect our liberty."[10]

In spite of the similarities of discourse, the foreign policies of the two administrations reveal that Kubitschek's was more clearly aligned with the U.S. cold war position, while Frondizi pursued a more nonaligned stance, although he understood that emphasizing the security problem would lead to increased development assistance. After the Cuban revolution in 1959, this argument became all the more effective and was frequently used by developmentalists.[11]

Redistribution

Developmentalism was not a redistributive model. Developmentalists argued that in the underdeveloped economy the primary problem was production and growth rather than redistribution of income. For developmentalists, distribution of income in underdeveloped economies implied the distribution of poverty. Instead developmentalism called for intense emphasis on capital accumulation and vertical industrialization, which they argued would eventually expand the pie for the entire population. For example, Frondizi argued that "the fundamental problem of Latin American countries is not distribution; it is production. It is not justice; it is the need for technical-economic transformation."[12]

9. Felix Luna, *Diálogos con Frondizi* (Buenos Aires: Editorial Desarrollo, 1963), p. 103.

10. Juscelino Kubitschek de Oliveira, *Discursos, 1958* (Rio de Janiero: Serviço de Documentação da Presidência de República, 1960), pp. 386–87.

11. For example, on a trip to Washington in 1961, Frondizi's closest adviser, Rogelio Frigerio, made a presentation titled "Cuba or Argentina: Two Alternatives to a Common Problem: Underdevelopment." He argued that Argentina was pursuing "the other way," the opposite of what was being done in Cuba.

12. Luna, *Diálogos con Frondizi*, p. 158.

Positive Investment Climate

Because investment in general, and foreign investment in particular, was so essential to the success of the developmentalist program, both Kubitschek and Frondizi stressed the importance of creating positive conditions for investment, reestablishing credit abroad and confidence in the government. This was to be achieved by reducing internal political tensions, adopting responsible financial policies—including the reduction of inflation and government deficits through establishing clear legal guidelines for foreign investment—and resolving past investment disputes that undermined investor confidence. Thus issues of financial stability, inflation, and balance of payments were central to the thinking of developmentalist policy makers. They were always subordinated, however, to the priorities of investment and industrialization, seen as a necessary means to reach more central goals of development.

Speed

Both presidents emphasized the need for speed in the development process, essential in breaking down the old economic system and installing the new. Both expressed a sense of urgency; if the country did not move quickly to promote development, history might pass it by. The addiction to speed was one of Kubitschek's most noticeable character traits; it was reflected in all his activities. His political slogan was "Fifty years in five," and he considered the great achievements of his administrations the large public works built in record time, of which Brasília is the most notable example.[13]

Frondizi and his colleagues had other reasons for speed. Not only did they feel they had to make up for lost time, as they noticed their neighbor to the north, Brazil, undertaking its massive industrialization project, but they were also worried that the Argentine military would not allow the government to complete its term in office. They worked under the assumption that they would have perhaps one or two years in power to undertake all of the changes they hoped to implement.

13. It was not surprising that Kubitschek was killed in 1977 in an auto accident in which his car was apparently going well over the speed limit, as was his custom. He was a man in a hurry. On the walls of his home library hung four of his most treasured awards: the Legion of Honor of France; Doctor Honoris Causa from the University of Coimbra in Portugal; the Knight of the Grand Cross of the Order of Saint Michael and St. George, signed by Queen Elizabeth II of England; and a small award stating that he was a member in good standing of the "Mach Busters Club," awarded by North American Aviation, Inc. to all those people who had broken the sound barrier in their airplanes.

The Limits of State Action

While Kubitschek and Frondizi galvanized the state to plan and channel the development process, they both thought that the state should primarily provide incentives for private initiative rather than substitute for it. In his campaign documents Kubitschek presented a phrase that would become a kind of slogan for the government's attitude toward the role of the state: "The state will be predominantly a manipulator of incentives and not a controller of decisions; a pioneer and supplemental investor instead of an absorbing Leviathan."[14] In his inaugural speech to Congress, Frondizi expressed a very similar position: "The function of the state should not be to replace private activity except in those areas where it cannot develop efficiently. The government has the necessary means to channel private action in the manner most compatible with general welfare, without needing to replace it directly."[15]

In spite of their general agreement on the limits of state action, the discourse of the two presidents stresses different aspects of the role of the state. Kubitschek promoted the need for "harmonious government support for private initiative."[16] In his vision, a "government that plans, deliberates, and executes, works and produces, animated by vitality and creative enthusiasm," was an essential partner with private initiative in the promotion of development.[17] He was thus also more likely to refer to planning and its positive contribution.

Frondizi, on the other hand, presented a more negative view of state action, the "evils of the bureaucracy," and the financial burden of public administration.[18] Thus his emphasis was more on the need for administrative rationalization than on the harmonious interaction of government and the private sector. It is noteworthy that in these early speeches he does not refer to planning.

Technical Orientation

Developmentalism placed a high premium on technical improvements and skills in the development process. Technical improvements

---

14. Juscelino Kubitschek de Oliveira, *Directrizes gerais do plano nacional de desenvolvimento* (Belo Horizonte: Livraria Oscar Nicolai, 1955), p. 27.

15. Frondizi, "Mensaje Inaugural," in *Mensajes presidenciales*, Vol. 1, pp. 38–39.

16. Kubitschek, *Mensagem ão Congresso Nacional, 1956*, p. 49.

17. Kubitschek, *Discursos, 1956*, p. 113.

18. Frondizi, "Mensaje Inaugural," p. 27.

in agriculture and industry would improve productivity and expand growth. Issues of agriculture and agricultural production tended to be marginalized in developmentalist thought, except for emphasis on the need for increasing "technification and mechanization" of agriculture to expand production and improve rural life. New rational planning and evaluation methods used by the state would permit more sophisticated forms of state direction of the economy. This technical orientation sometimes led developmentalists to see the very exercise of politics as an obstacle to realization of the program. It set in motion a tension between developmentalist methods and democratic accountability, as policy makers tried to insulate economic policy from the pressures arising from civil society, while at the same time the government faced increasing demands to make economic policy responsive to public demands.

Models from the Developed World

International developmentalism is associated with a collective awakening of the Third World and a recognition of the shared dilemma of underdevelopment. The discourse of neither Kubitschek nor Frondizi, however, demonstrates a strong sense of affinity with the Third World. In the early 1950s, CEPAL theorists such as Furtado began to realize that the state of underdevelopment was quite unlike the previous situation of the industrialized countries. It was not a phase but rather something qualitatively different.[19] Still, the writings and speeches of Kubitschek and Frondizi reveal that they turned to the industrialized countries of the north as models for the future progress of their own countries. Frondizi portrayed the United States as the logical model of what Argentina could achieve with correct policies and correct consciousness. He was more likely to quote Franklin Roosevelt, Ulysses S. Grant, or Alexander Hamilton than to cite an example of Third World development.[20]

Kubitschek also saw models for the future of Brazil in the development patterns of Europe and the United States. His travels to Europe and the United States convinced him further of the possibility of Brazil following their lead. In his autobiography, he recalled his impressions after a 1948 visit to the United States and Canada: "I saw and I felt the path that we would have to follow. The effort that would have to be made. And, even more important, the orientation, the direction, the

19. Celso Furtado, *A fantasia organizada* (Rio de Janeiro: Paz e Terra, 1985), p. 88.
20. For citations of Grant and Hamilton on the issue of protectionism, see Frondizi, *Industria Argentina y desarrollo nacional* (Buenos Aires: Ediciones Qué, 1957), pp. 70, 81.

route, that the governments of our country would have to imprint on our progress."[21]

In spite of the similarities in the developmentalist thought and discourse of Kubitschek and Frondizi, there were also important differences. In addition to their differences on the nature of state intervention, mentioned above, the positions they took on specific issues also varied. The most important differences were on the issues of petroleum and stabilization policy and planning (which will be discussed in greater detail in Chapters 4 and 5.)

COSMOPOLITANS AND NATIONALISTS: ACCUMULATORS AND REFORMERS

Developmentalists can be divided into two groups: the so-called cosmopolitan developmentalists and the nationalist developmentalists. This typology has been used to discuss Brazilian developmentalists, but it is useful in categorizing developmentalists in general.[22] Cosmopolitan and nationalist developmentalists agreed on the basic core of the developmentalist program—vertical industrialization programs promoted by vigorous state action—but they disagreed over the role of foreign investment and the degree of state involvement in the economy. Cosmopolitans favored more reliance on private initiative and encouraged extensive foreign investment. Nationalist developmentalists called for less foreign investment and greater state participation in both production and welfare issues.

In his essay "The Turn to Authoritarianism in Latin America and the Search for Its Economic Determinants," Albert Hirschman identifies two principal tasks or functions that must be accomplished in the course of the growth process: the entrepreneurial or accumulation function and the distributive or reform function. The accumulation function involves the capital accumulation process necessary for growth; the reform function refers to the social reforms needed to improve the welfare of neglected groups and to redistribute wealth in general. Hirschman argues that "how well these two functions are performed and coordinated is crucial for both economic and political outcomes of

21. Juscelino Kubitschek, *Meu caminho para Brasília: A escalada política* (Rio de Janeiro: Bloch Editores, 1976), p. 153.

22. This terminology was first used by Helio Jaguaribe in *Desenvolvimento econômico e desenvolvimento político* (Rio de Janeiro: Fondo de Cultura, 1962), pp. 195–210, and later adapted by Lourdes Sola to distinguish between técnicos within the developmentalist camp.

the growth process."[23] But rather than focus on the functions themselves, he draws our attention to the role of ideology in support of accumulation and reform as one explanation for the strength of each function.

Developmentalism stressed primarily the accumulation function. Its main aim was to accelerate accumulation in order to permit rapid vertical industrialization of key industrial sectors. But various developmentalists advocated striking a different balance between the accumulation and reform functions. This is one useful way to envision the split between cosmopolitan and nationalist developmentalists. The cosmopolitan developmentalists put more emphasis on the accumulation function, while the nationalists argued for a better balance between accumulation and reform.

In Brazil a tactical alliance between the cosmopolitans and the nationalists gave Kubitschek the support he needed to carry out his program. Kubitschek was more successful in temporarily achieving an alliance between developmentalists and national populists under the leadership of developmentalists. In Brazil developmentalist ideas merged well with existing ideologies and political traditions, including some of the embedded orientations of the state inherited from the Estado Nôvo (of the 1937–1945 period) and the second Vargas administration, and the pro-industrialization ideas of a good part of the Brazilian industrial class and the military. Kubitschek's political bargaining skills, using the role of the president as arbiter as well as his receptivity to the symbolic importance of key issues, helped him hold together the developmentalist coalition during most of his term.

In Argentina the alliance between cosmopolitans and nationalists broke down within the first year of the Frondizi government. Here liberal economic ideas held a tighter grip on the political imagination. In the late 1800s and the early 1900s Argentina had grown wealthy in its role as a supplier of wheat and beef to the world economy. Important segments of the elite, especially the powerful agricultural interests, saw no reason to alter the formula that once had worked so well. They advocated a liberal model of only minimal state intervention in the economy to guarantee the functioning of the market.

But more harmful to the consolidation of developmentalism in Argentina than competition from the liberal model was the lack of unity

---

23. Albert O. Hirschman, "The Turn to Authoritarianism in Latin America and the Search for Its Economic Determinants," in *The New Authoritarianism in Latin America*, ed. David Collier (Princeton: Princeton University Press, 1979) p. 88.

of all the fractions of what I have called the potential developmentalist alliance. In spite of the similarities in their positions on economic issues, this potential developmentalist coalition was politically fractured. Although Frondizi attempted to woo the Peronists, he was not able to establish an alliance with nationalist populists. Second, industrialists and the military gave Frondizi less support than anticipated. Third, members of other fractions of the Radical party who shared similar ideas on economic policy were bitter enemies of the Frondizi government.

The essential unity of Brazilian elites around a basic economic model was only a temporary "tactical alliance" between groups who shared some ideas and differed on others. Shared ideas about state-sponsored vertical industrialization served as the common ground to bring together nationalist and cosmopolitan developmentalists as well as national populists in support of the economic program of the Kubitschek government. This alliance gave Kubitschek the political support he needed to carry out his rapid development program. Argentina was more profoundly divided over economic models, since powerful groups in society still embraced liberal economic ideas. More debilitating, however, to the developmentalist government of Frondizi were the divisions within the potential developmentalist coalition and between the developmentalists and the national populists. This failure to gain consensus on a single economic model was not unique in Argentina. It was only one in a string of failed attempts to gain support for a particular economic model.

BRIEF HISTORICAL OVERVIEW

The Great Depression and the Second World War created the preconditions for adoption of the type of industrialization policies later associated with national populism and developmentalism. These events did not determine the nature or content of policies; they only created certain predispositions and attitudes. In particular, the Depression and World War II cracked the ideological hegemony of the liberal economic model and encouraged a range of experimental policies that stressed nationalism, growth, and domestic import-substituting industrialization. A decade of trying to revive traditional export markets, and almost fifteen years of shortages of foreign industrial imports, undermined faith in free trade and comparative advantage. The success of the heterogeneous policies adopted by Latin American states in the

1930s and 1940s created confidence in alternative paths to development.[24]

Both Brazil and Argentina faced substantial external shocks during the Second World War, including the loss of export markets and severe supply shortages. The almost absolute natural protection provided by the war led to an upsurge in import-substituting industrialization, but at the same time supply shortages exacerbated the deterioration of the physical capital base. The different policies adopted by each country during the war, however, influenced the degree to which they were affected by the external shocks.

Argentina's decision to pursue a policy of intransigent neutrality limited the country's access to export markets, credits, and all types of imports and supplies during the war and in the postwar era. Following Argentina's refusal to break off relations with the Axis, the United States initiated an economic boycott of Argentina which severely limited essential exports to that country.[25] The war and the boycott led to shortages of fuels, essential materials, and capital goods, creating production difficulties.[26]

After an initial period of neutrality, Brazil decided to collaborate with the Allies during the war and garnered economic rewards as a result, such as U.S. funding of construction of the Volta Redonda steel complex. Brazil's participation in the war was not merely symbolic but involved extensive mutual planning with the United States, significant arms transfers, and eventually the participation of a Brazilian Expedi-

24. Carlos Diaz Alejandro, "The 1940s in Latin America," Economic Growth Center, Center Discussion Paper no. 394, February 1982, p. 36.

25. For example, the United States prohibited exports to Argentina of electrical equipment, chemical products, equipment or parts for petroleum companies, and other essential goods. Only materials essential to operate the meat packing plants and the beryllium and tungsten mines, the output of which were sold to the United States, were exempt from control. The United States also used diplomatic pressure and supply agreements with other Allied nations to limit exports to Argentina. By the terms of the Lend-Lease agreement, Britain was debarred from supplying Argentina with tin plate, steel sheets, and galvanized wire. Through its relations with other Latin American countries, the United States worked to limit exports to Argentina of Bolivian rubber, tin, sulfates, and quinine; Chilean copper and copper nitrate; and Brazilian coal and rubber. For a discussion of the boycott, see Carlos Escude, *La declinación Argentina, 1942–1949* (Buenos Aires: Editorial Belgrano, 1983).

26. During this period, Argentine industry and railroads were obliged to burn corn, wheat, peanut shells, and rice husks as energy sources. In 1944, the worst year of the fuel shortage, such sources provided 31.4 percent of Argentina's total energy consumption. Carl E. Solberg, *Oil and Nationalism in Argentina: A History* (Stanford: Stanford University Press, 1979), p. 162. Argentine imports of iron products fell from 696,000 tons in 1939 to 76,000 tons in 1943, in large part as a result of the U.S. boycott. Escude, *La declinación Argentina*, p. 259.

tionary Force in the Mediterranean theater during the last years of the war.[27] Brazil's participation in the war resulted in supply difficulties that were not as dramatic as Argentina's. In both countries, however, the impact of external shocks on export and import levels was severe. Argentine exports suffered more during World War II than they had during the Depression. In Brazil export quantum during this period also fell in comparison with the 1930s, although not as severely as in Argentina. The fall in import quantum was much more drastic in both countries than was the decline in exports.[28]

Brazil's cooperation with the Allies during the war linked it more closely to the United States and Europe, creating a positive precedent for international economic collaboration that would shape the ideas of policy makers and public alike. Argentina's neutrality, and the far greater international hostility and ostracism that it faced, also helps explain its greater insulation from international developments in the postwar period. Argentina stayed neutral in the Second World War until the United States insisted that it would not be allowed to join the United Nations if it did not declare war. Because of its neutrality it was unable to claim international assistance in compensation for contributing to the war effort. Argentine hostility to international economic institutions made it less permeable to some international ideas about development. Its version of developmentalism was more home-grown than the Brazilian variant.

The postwar industrialization drive was financed primarily by national savings rather than by foreign capital. Both Argentina and Brazil had accumulated large foreign exchange surpluses during the war, and they used these surpluses to finance postwar industrialization. Even if they had wished to rely primarily on international sources of finance, however, the international situation was not amenable. Europe's resources were directed toward its own urgent reconstruction effort, while the United States mounted a massive aid drive to support Euro-

27. A detailed discussion of U.S.-Brazilian relations during the war and joint military planning is found in Frank McCann, *The Brazilian American Alliance, 1937–1945* (Princeton: Princeton University Press, 1973).

28. In Argentina the average annual import quantum in 1940–1945 was 48 percent below the annual level in 1935–1939 and per capita quantum fell by a full 50 percent. The fall of imports in Brazil, although serious, was significantly less than in Argentina; depending on the source, the average annual import quantum in 1940–1945 was 12–20 percent below the level for 1935–1939. Annibal Villela and Wilson Suzigan, *Política do governo e crescimento do economia brasileira, 1889–1945* (Rio de Janeiro: IPEA/INPES Monografia 10, 1973), p. 441; and United Nations, Economic Commission for Latin America, *Economic Survey of Latin America, 1949* (New York: United Nations, 1951), pp. 111, 211.

pean reconstruction. Latin Americans argued for a "Marshall Plan for Latin America," but their pleas went unanswered as Washington devoted its funds and energies to the perceived priority of reconstruction. U.S. foreign investors focused on the rehabilitation and restocking of previously established enterprises in Europe.

Although the Depression and the Second World War increased pro-industrialization sentiment in Latin America, it was not until the mid-1950s that additional conditions created an impetus for specifically developmentalist policies. The international system is often perceived as only imposing constraints on domestic economic policy making. But developmentalist policy makers were conscious of both the constraints and the opportunities presented by the international environment to developing countries during the postwar period. Often, the same phenomena offered simultaneously an opportunity and a constraint for policy makers. The most important international factors influencing developmentalism were: the recovery of Europe, and to a lesser degree of Japan, from the war; the expansion of private foreign investment to less developed countries, and the changing nature of private investment targets; the increased availability of multilateral and bilateral public and private finance for development and of technical assistance programs motivated in part by the fear of the spread of communism to less developed regions; and the diffusion of international developmentalist ideas via the network of postwar international organizations.

None of these factors led to a change of the investment "regime," since the flow of capital continued to be guided by the same basic principles and norms that had existed prior to the Second World War: an open door for investment and the protection of property rights of foreign investors.[29] What changed was the scope and direction of investments as sources, targets, and vehicles of investment diversified and total investment expanded. The diversification of sources of investment, in turn, created competition among investing countries and gave somewhat greater bargaining leverage to investment recipients. This leverage was used not to try to modify the rules of the investment regime but to exercise greater control over types of investment, and to capture a slightly higher margin of profits.

By the mid-fifties the international situation had changed. European reconstruction had succeeded so dramatically that European countries were beginning to export capital once again, both direct foreign invest-

29. Raymond Duvall and Alexander Wendt, "The International Capital Regime and the Internationalization of the State," paper prepared for the German-American Conference on International Relations Theory, Bad Homburg, Federal Republic of Germany, May 31–June 4, 1987.

ment and medium-term suppliers' credits.[30] In 1959, the height of the developmentalist experiment in Brazil, total European foreign investment accounted for 35.8 percent of foreign investment in Brazil, almost as much as total foreign investment from the United States (37.5 percent). European investment tended to concentrate in the basic industrial areas prioritized by the developmentalist program.[31] In Argentina European investment totaled more than 40 percent of foreign investment during the period 1958–1965.[32]

International companies looked abroad for markets. Facing the high tariff barriers erected as part of the national populist policies of the 1940s, these companies began to see tariff-jumping direct foreign investment as the best means of holding on to markets in the newly industrializing countries.[33] Aside from Canada, Latin America was one of the areas where U.S. foreign investment expanded most rapidly.

The United States fostered a political and economic order at the end of World War II which facilitated the overseas expansion of U.S. corporations.[34] The United States encouraged private investors to increase their holdings abroad and foreign countries to promote a positive climate for international investment. In many cases financial assistance was effectively conditioned on the adoption of measures for the protection of investment. International financial institutions also helped insure that countries observe the rules of the game regarding foreign investment. IMF conditionality and World Bank loan agreements often were used to encourage positive policies toward investment. In spite of isolated cases of expropriations, throughout the 1950s an international regime for the protection of foreign investment was in place, a regime

30. Pedro Malan has stressed the importance of European recovery for Brazilian economic policy making in the 1950s. A changing international situation created by European imports, European direct foreign investment, European trade credits, and European currencies' limited convertibility after 1955 allowed Brazil to pursue its policies in the face of the refusal of the International Bank for Reconstruction and Development to lend and of the IMF to uphold Brazilian practices. He also emphasizes the importance of suppliers' credits as development finance during this period. Cited by Lourdes Sola, "Political and Ideological Constraints to Economic Management in Brazil, 1945–1963" (Ph.D. diss., Oxford University, 1982), p. 145.

31. Gertrude E. Heare, U.S. Department of Commerce, Bureau of International Programs, *Brazil: Information for United States Businessmen* (Washington D.C.: U.S. Government Printing Office, 1961), pp. 12–13.

32. Oficina de Estudios para la Colaboración Económica (OECEI), Buenos Aires, 1966.

33. U.S. Department of Commerce, Office of Business Economics, *U.S. Business Investments in Foreign Countries* (Washington D.C.: U.S. Government Printing Office, 1960), p. 1.

34. Robert Gilpin, *U.S. Power and the Multinational Corporation* (New York: Basic Books, 1975), p. 5.

based in part on the implicit threat of U.S. sanctions.[35] Foreign businesspersons and their governments assumed that foreign investments were generally safe. It was not until after the Cuban confiscations of U.S. businesses that these assumptions began to be questioned.[36]

Total U.S. foreign investment increased dramatically in the 1950s, expanding from $11.8 billion in 1950 to $29.7 billion in 1959. U.S. foreign investment in Latin American rose from $4.6 billion in 1950 to $9.0 billion in 1959.[37] Most of this increase is accounted for by the expansion of transnational corporations (TNCs). From 1950 to 1966 the number of affiliates of U.S. TNCs alone rose from seven thousand to more than twenty-three thousand. The growth was especially rapid between 1957 and 1966.[38] By the mid- to late 1950s Latin American countries had foreign capital available to them on a new scale. And contrary to previous capital flows, much of the new investment was attracted to the areas of petroleum and manufacturing, which also interested the developmentalists.

In addition to direct foreign investment, a second phenomenon of the mid-1950s was the rapid expansion of suppliers' credits to developing countries. As early as September 1954 the president of the World Bank recognized that a transition was in progress from a sellers' to a buyers' market in the international availability of capital equipment. He observed that "a competitive race is developing among suppliers all over the world," taking the form "not only of competition in terms of price, quality, and delivery date, but also competition in the offer of medium-term suppliers' credits." He suggested that suppliers' credits could be misused and overused, and that "there is some disturbing evidence that this is happening—too much credit given under the pres-

35. In 1958, a representative of the International Chamber of Commerce could report that "international law on the subject of expropriation and prompt and adequate compensation is fairly well established and rules for non-discrimination against foreign investment have received recognition by most countries of the free world. . . . Expropriations always receive the greatest amount of publicity. While these are serious . . . fortunately they occur infrequently." American Society of International Law, *Proceedings of the Second International Investment Law Conference* (Washington, D.C.: 1958), pp. 3, 7.

36. Charles Lipson, *Standing Guard: Protecting Foreign Capital in the Nineteenth and Twentieth Centuries* (Berkeley: University of California Press, 1985), pp. 103, 204. During the 1950s foreign assistance was in part conditioned on the adoption of measures to protect foreign investment, but it was not until the adoption of the Hickenlooper amendment in 1962 that an explicit statutory link was made between repayment for expropriation and disbursement of foreign assistance (p. 202).

37. U.S. Department of Commerce, *U.S. Business Investments in Foreign Countries*, p. 1.

38. Joan Edelman Spero, *The Politics of International Economic Relations* (New York: St. Martin's Press, 1977), p. 91.

sure of competition, sometimes on inappropriate terms and for the wrong purposes."[39]

Although suppliers' credits are basically private transactions between a company and its client, by the mid-1950s the governments in the creditor and the debtor nations had begun to play an increasingly important role in promoting suppliers' credits by offering insurance and guarantees. A system that blended public and private lending for export transactions emerged. Thus while export credits themselves were not new, the public insurance and guarantees and the competition between creditor countries led to the expansion of these credits and the lengthening of terms from two to three years to five or ten years and even longer. An estimated 90 percent of the flow of guaranteed export credits to developing countries in this period came from Western Europe and Japan, and only 10 percent from the United States. After the recovery from World War II, European countries began to increase short-term private export credits, which had always existed as a form of financing trade, to medium-term forms guaranteed by their governments.[40] The interests of industrialized countries' exporters and governments in augmenting the flow of exports coincided with the demands of developing countries' companies and governments to expand imports of capital goods.

Suppliers' credits became a common form of development finance, though they were not intended for this purpose, because of the absence of acceptable alternative sources of finance. In most Latin American countries domestic financial markets were not well enough developed to supply funds for import requirements of local firms. In other cases, public and semipublic agencies also relied on suppliers' credits as sources of finance. One alternative means of increasing government funding—increasing the taxing capabilities of the central government—was often perceived as politically untenable. Other bilateral and multilateral sources of capital were meager in comparison to the capital needs of the newly industrializing countries, and they often carried onerous conditions that were not in tune with the development programs being adopted.

The developmentalist governments relied heavily on these medium-

---

39. Cited in IBRD, *Suppliers' Credits from Industrialized to Developing Countries*, a study by the staff of the World Bank requested by the United Nations Conference on Trade and Development, rev. ed., April 3, 1967, pp. 1–2.

40. The Berne Union, consisting of twenty-six public and private export credit insurance institutions, tried to develop guidelines for the terms for granting suppliers' credits, but by the mid-1950s these terms were progressively relaxed. Ibid., pp. 6, 13.

term credits to finance the bulk of capital goods and industrial imports essential to their economic program. In Brazil and Argentina during the developmentalist governments, suppliers' and trade credits in some years accounted for 60–70 percent of all external finance excluding foreign investment. For a number of years the inflow of suppliers' credits exceeded the inflow of direct foreign investment. Given the great financial demands of the developmentalist economic programs, the absence of extensive alternative sources of assistance, and the ready availability of suppliers' credits, the reliance on suppliers' credits was a path of least resistance for developmentalist governments. Suppliers' credits were a relatively ready form of finance in ample supply that involved little outside scrutiny of policies and projects and few immediate sacrifices for domestic populations.

By the mid-1950s many Latin American countries began to experience chronic balance-of-payments crises and shortages of foreign exchange. (See figure 1.) These shortages, in combination with the new availability of foreign capital from private and public sources, made a developmentalist program of rapid industrialization with support from foreign capital a rational policy option. But the international conjuncture of the mid-1950s provided both opportunities for and limitations on the activities of Latin American governments. The increased availability of foreign capital made the development program possible, but it also imposed limitations on the types of policies these governments could adopt. Policies had to be designed to attract and maintain foreign capital. Meanwhile, international financial institutions such as the World Bank and the IMF had increased leverage over domestic economic policies, since their seal of approval was often a precondition for other sources of finance. During this period both the World Bank and the IMF endorsed orthodox prescriptions of domestic economic health, which were difficult for governments to reconcile with domestic political demands. The intransigence of these institutions forced the developmentalists to rely more heavily on private foreign investment, and on suppliers' credits, or on Export-Import Bank loans.[41]

The developmentalist governments were well aware of the trends in international investment patterns, of which they hoped to take advantage. Policy makers in Brazil and Argentina saw the recuperation of

41. The IMF began to impose stricter conditions on the receipt of credit and to write precise economic policy objectives into the standby agreements for the first time around 1957 and 1958. David Pion-Berlin, "The Role of Ideas: The International Monetary Fund and Third World Policy Choices," paper presented at the American Political Science Association Meeting, New Orleans, August 29–September 1, 1985, p. 1.

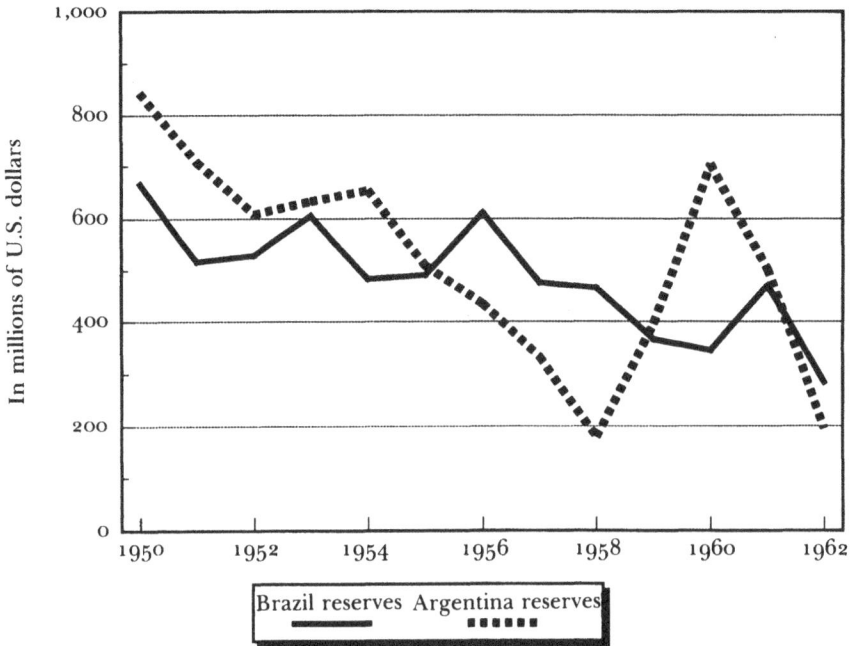

Figure 1. International reserves, Brazil and Argentina, 1950–1962

Europe and Japan, and the resulting competition among industrialized countries for exports, as an opportunity that could be exploited for the benefit of their countries.[42] Both governments succeeded in attracting large amounts of foreign investment and in gaining political and economic support from the United States. But while the absolute levels of direct foreign investment in the two countries were roughly equal, Brazil received larger amounts of other forms of international assistance, such as technical assistance grants from the United States and loans from the IBRD and the U.S. Export-Import Bank.

42. An Argentine government document analyzing tendencies in international capital flows observed that 1955–1958 had been a period of expanding international investment, and that somewhat less than half of this capital was flowing to underdeveloped countries. The memo emphasized that the major change in the last years was that "Western Europe is acquiring an increasingly large capacity for the export of private capital." It also notes the increasing importance of short- and medium-term capital, especially suppliers' credits. Presidencia de la Nación Argentina, Secretaria de Relaciones Económico-Sociales, "Tendencia de las corrientes de capital en los ultimos años" (no date, probably 1958), pp. 1–3.

U.S. POLICY AND DEVELOPMENTALISM

A second opportunity and restraint of the international system was created by the postwar cold war climate and exacerbated by the Cuban revolution in 1959 and the fear of "another Cuba." During the 1950s a cold war security approach to political development was favored in U.S. policy circles. This led to the United States's willingness to consider the issues of poverty and underdevelopment, which U.S. and Latin American experts identified as causes of radicalism.[43] Truman's Point Four Program attempted to transfer the principles of the Truman Doctrine and the Marshall Plan to the Third World, establishing for the first time economic development of underdeveloped areas as a goal of U.S. policy.[44]

The Cuban revolution and the Alliance for Progress increased the salience of Latin American development issues in U.S. policy circles. Both Kubitschek and Frondizi were in office when the Cuban revolution rocked the continent in January 1959, but Kubitschek served most of his term before the Cuban revolution, whereas Frondizi served most of his after it. The Right in Brazil and Argentina accused Kubitschek and Frondizi of benefiting from Communist support or of having Communist sympathies, but these accusations had greater impact in Argentina, where anticommunism was heightened in the wake of the Cuban revolution. At the same time, Frondizi was able to benefit from greater regional polarization; he framed his appeal for economic support from the newly elected Kennedy administration by arguing that Argentine developmentalism offered a viable alternative to revolution.

During an early visit to the United States, Frondizi's top adviser, Rogelio Frigerio, argued that Argentine developmentalism offered one of the only valid alternatives to revolution, and thus the United States should support developmentalism for its own self-interest. "In Argentina . . . we are doing the opposite of what is being done in Cuba. If the great western powers do not act with speed and determination, the underdeveloped world will accept the assistance of the other side. No ideological consideration can be allowed to stand in the way."[45]

---

43. Robert A. Packenham points out that in the 1950s and early 1960s U.S. officials continued to believe that "poverty has a positive and linear relationship to Communism." He cites a 1959 Legislative Reference Service Report that says, "The simple assumption that communism flows from poverty is so widely accepted in America that it is almost an article of faith." *Liberal America and the Third World* (Princeton: Princeton University Press, 1973), p. 52.

44. Ibid., p. 105.

45. Frigerio, "Cuba or Argentina," pp. 1–3, 15–16.

Kubitschek left office before the fear of "another Cuba" translated into increased development assistance, but he used similar rhetoric with his vision of "Operation Pan America" to appeal to U.S. self-interest in order to generate more development financing. Under Operation Pan America, Kubitschek requested concrete measures of assistance: increased investments, expanded technical assistance programs, measures to combat fluctuations in prices of commodities, and increase of resources and liberalization of the rules of international financial agencies.[46]

Like other international opportunities, the new fear of communism operated simultaneously as a restraint. The other side of the new concern with revolution was increased anticommunism among the Latin American military and other elites, which limited the developmentalist governments' freedom in formulating their foreign policy and choice of advisers.

Developmentalism emerged during this conjuncture. The experience of the Depression and World War II had broken down the ideological hegemony of free market ideas and given birth to new heterodox ideas about the economy and development. The vulnerability the countries had experienced and the success of their forced import substitution gave impetus to industrialization policies. At the same time, new sources of international finance, both public and private, became available, and the United States and international financial institutions encouraged policies of openness to foreign capital.

Yet in many ways the international situation would have been more permissive toward the adoption of liberal free trade policies or to industrial export promotion than developmentalist policies in the Third World. The attitude of international financial institutions, of the U.S. government, and of international capital was much more favorable toward liberal policies in Latin America, with low tariffs and an open door for all kinds of investment and trade. But liberalism was no longer acceptable to the majority of the population in Brazil and Argentina. Nationalist pro-industrialization policies had taken firm root in domestic consciousness. Liberalism ran counter to the new social purpose in these countries, but national populist policies were increasingly difficult to sustain financially and technologically. By the mid-fifties the reserves accumulated during the war were gone, and domestic sources seemed unable to provide the resources and know-how for the industrialization drive. In this context, developmentalism emerged as a com-

46. Juscelino Kubitschek, speech on Operation Pan America, delivered in Rio de Janeiro, June 20, 1958.

promise between the domestic demands for industrialization and state intervention on the one hand, and international demands for openness on the other. In these circumstances, the move toward developmentalist policies was a rational one, but it was not the only rational set of policies.

One additional element encouraged the adoption of developmentalist policies. In the postwar period economics as a profession came into its own. For the first time, individual economists in Latin American countries began to have the skills and confidence to help direct development policy from positions within the state. We see the emergence in this generation of "new economic professionals" who will take responsibility for economic policy making. Initially many of these new economic professionals received their training in economics abroad. But during the 1950s the region's schools of economics were reorganized and curricula updated so that these countries could begin to train the técnicos needed for economic policy posts.[47]

By the mid-1950s the motivation, opportunities and constraints, new ideas, and intellectual talent were in place to create the preconditions for adoption of developmentalist policies in Latin America. The striking simultaneous emergence of similar developmentalist projects in a number of different countries throughout the region indicates that these preconditions created a strong impetus for policy makers to choose developmentalist policies. Not only were such policies adopted in Brazil in 1956 and Argentina in 1958 but similar models were used in Venezuela beginning in 1958, in Peru in 1962, and in Chile in 1964.

THE ORIGINS OF DEVELOPMENTALISM

The emergence of developmentalism in the south was linked indirectly to the emergence of Keynesian ideas in the north. Albert Hirschman, in his essay "The Rise and Decline of Development Economics," argues that Keynesianism succeeded in breaking the monopoly of the claim of "monoeconomics," the notion that a single system of economic thought could explain all economic situations. By suggesting that there were two kinds of economics, one that applied to the fully employed economy and another where there was substantial unemployment of human and material resources, Keynes opened the door for the possi-

47. Pan American Union, *The Teaching of Economics in Latin America* (Washington, D.C.: General Secretariat, Organization of American States, 1961).

bility of a special kind of economics for underdeveloped areas as well.[48] But for the developmentalists, Keynes was more important in breaking down old ways of thinking about economics than as a source of ideas for developmentalism.[49]

Important differences separate Keynesianism from developmentalism. Developmentalism was primarily concerned with economic growth, whereas Keynesianism did not have an explicit growth perspective. Employment, so central to Keynesian analysis, was surprisingly absent from developmentalist discourse. Developmentalists assumed, of course, that industrialization strategies would increase employment opportunities, but employment was not a major element in developmentalist arguments. Keynesian ideas opened up an intellectual space and set the tone for the vibrant postwar economic debate that helped nourish the debate about development. Few developmentalists, however, describe themselves as Keynesians, or credit Keynes as a major influence on the formation of their ideas.

Because of the strong protectionist bent of developmentalism and its emphasis on protecting nascent domestic industry from foreign competition, one also looks to List and Manoilescu as possible influences. Yet few references to these theorists are found in the writings, speeches, or interviews with key developmentalists. Although List's ideas were influential in Chile in the late 1800s and early 1900s, they seem to have had little influence elsewhere in Latin America.[50] Rumanian economist Mihail Manoilescu, who denounced the international division of labor and advocated protection of domestic industries, had somewhat more influence on developmentalists, especially among Brazilian industrialists.[51]

48. Albert O. Hirschman, *Essays in Trespassing: Economics to Politics and Beyond* (New York: Cambridge University Press, 1981), p. 6.

49. Some of the leading developmentalist economists were well versed in Keynesian thought. Raúl Prebisch wrote one of the first introductory texts to Keynesian thought in Spanish. Prebisch later argued that he was never a Keynesian, but he believed that Keynes's most important contribution was his recommendation of expansionist policies of state spending and investment to combat the Great Depression. Raúl Prebisch, *La crisis del desarrollo argentino* (Buenos Aires: El Ateneo, 1986), p. 164. Roberto Campos had studied Keynesian ideas while a graduate student at Columbia University and described himself as "more Keynesian" than his other Brazilian colleagues at the Bretton Woods Conference. Interview with Roberto Campos, Rio de Janeiro, June 20, 1986.

50. Joseph Love, "Economic Ideas and Ideologies in Latin America, 1930–1970," draft chapter for *Cambridge History of Latin America*, p. 5.

51. The leader of Brazilian private sector developmentalism, Roberto Simonsen backed up his positions with references to works by List and Manoilescu. He arranged for Manoilescu's book to be translated and published by the Brazilian industrialists' confederation as early as 1931. Mihail Manoilescu, *Teoria do protecionismo e da permuta internacional* (Sao Paulo: CIESP, 1931).

But by the Second World War Manoilescsu's ideas "were slowly abandoned for more practical and circumstantial arguments," perhaps because of the frontal attacks by Jacob Viner and other neoclassical theorists of Manoilescu's work.[52] Industrialists in the 1950s, accused of being followers of Manoilescu, explained their ideology: "The São Paulo industrialist doesn't need Manoilescu's book to embark on the crusade for our country's economic independence. . . . The businessman has even less use for Adam Smith's liberalism, since today his principles are inapplicable because they are anachronistic."[53]

Raúl Prebisch makes no reference to Manoilescu in his early writings,[54] nor does Argentine developmentalist Rogelio Frigerio. In his surveys of national and foreign economic theories and theorists, Frigerio discusses the classical economists, especially Ricardo and Marx, and devotes attention to the ideas of Keynes and Prebisch, but does not refer at all to either List or Manoilescu.[55]

Indeed, on the whole, many of the developmentalists were surprisingly atheoretical. Juscelino Kubitschek, in one of his autobiographies, mentions only one economic theorist—Gunnar Myrdal—and only in passing.[56] The developmentalists drew their inspiration from a multiplicity of sources, and they were very practically oriented. The main common ground seems to have been similar interpretations of the shared experiences of the past decades. They were more influenced by the examples of particular countries, such as the early U.S. protection of its infant industries, than by specific theorists.

The United Nations as a Source of Ideas

The emergence of developmentalism was connected to ideas advocated in the United Nations in the immediate postwar period. Al-

52. Love, "Economic Ideas and Ideologies in Latin America," p. 7.

53. FIESP, *Boletim informativo* 450 (May 21, 1958), cited in Maria Jose Trevisan, *50 anos em 5: A FIESP e o desenvolvimentismo* (Petropolis: Vozes, 1986), p. 141.

54. Prebisch himself confirmed the absence of such an influence even though articles discussing Manoilescu's theories were published in the late 1930s in the journal of the Economics Department at the University of Buenos Aires, where Prebisch taught. Joseph Love, "Raúl Prebisch and the Origins of the Doctrine of Unequal Exchange," *Latin American Research Review* 15 (1980), 62.

55. See, for example, Rogelio Frigerio, *Economia política y política económica nacional* (Buenos Aires: Hachette, 1981), and *Estatuto del subdesarrollo: Las corrientes del pensamiento económico argentino* (Buenos Aires: Libreria del Jurista, 1983).

56. "I repeat now, so that there is no doubt as to our position, that only by finding our way to that 'shortcut' that Myrdal mentions, will Latin America speed up the growth of the per capita income of its inhabitants. It is clear, and all the true students of the problem will agree with me, that the bulk of investments, if not almost the totality, should be

though developmentalism is usually associated with the ideas of the U.N. Economic Commission for Latin America (CEPAL), these ideas had already been voiced in U.N. debates before the creation of CEPAL. One Brazilian developmentalist who had worked at the United Nations said, "Really, the ideology of development was born at the U.N. . . . The U.N. was the oven where those ideas were cooked."[57] International developmentalism emerged from a debate that began in both the north and the south during the period after the depression and during and after the Second World War. The United Nations' contribution was to bring together the various strands and currents of the debate previously carried on in isolation and provide international institutional support for the new ideas. Although developmentalist ideas were present in U.N. debates from its inception, developmentalism was not the hegemonic ideology of the United Nations during this period.

Three strands of ideas reinforced in the U.N. had particular importance for the emergence of developmentalism. The first is the belief that, increasingly, issues of economic and social development were linked to security concerns. The second is the notion of "economic rights and duties of states." And the third is the belief, reinforced by Keynesianism, in the "scientific" correctness of greater state control over domestic economic policies.[58]

The connection of economic and social development to security concerns emerged from an analysis of the causes of the Second World War. It came to be accepted that a repetition of the violence of the Second World War could be avoided in part through attention to improving economic and social conditions throughout the world. This added a component of self-interest to the practice of international aid and assistance and moved it out of the category of charity.[59] The linkage

---

directed to the basic and infrastructural sectors of the Latin America economies." Juscelino Kubitschek, *A marcha do amanhecer* (São Paulo: Importadora de Livros, 1962), p. 150.

57. Interview with Cleantho de Paiva Leite, Rio de Janeiro, May 21, 1986.

58. The second and third strands of thought are identified and discussed by Craig Murphy in "What the Third World Wants: An Interpretation of the Development and Meaning of the New International Economic Order Ideology," *International Studies Quarterly* 27 (March 1983), 62.

59. This linkage between security and economic and social development is presented clearly in the U.N. Charter's section on international economic and social cooperation, article 55: "With a view to the creation of conditions of stability and well-being which are necessary for peaceful and friendly relations between nations . . . the United Nations shall promote: a) higher standards of living, full employment, and conditions of economic and social progress and development; b) solution of international economic, social, health and related problems and international cultural and educational cooperation."

between security and economic well-being served as the theoretical underpinning of the Marshall Plan and of Truman's Point Four Program. But it was also in the discourse of the Latin American states in early U.N. meetings, where they advocated greater attention to problems of development in the underdeveloped countries in the name of future security and peace.[60] As explained above, a similar connection between poverty and communism served as an important justification for economic assistance programs in the postwar period and as leverage for developing countries requesting aid.

The doctrine of the "economic rights and duties of states" which emerged from the early work of the United Nations both legitimized the idea that states had the sovereign right to formulate their own economic policies and promoted the idea that other states had the duty to help them achieve adequate levels of development.[61] In practice, however, the idea of economic rights and duties of states had much less influence on the developmentalist debate than the more self-interested idea that economic development and international security were intimately linked. The appeals made by developmentalist governments for economic assistance were usually framed in terms of the Western world's self-interest in promoting development and thus democracy.

During the early U.N. debates on economic issues Latin American countries argued that the organization should give more attention to development issues. At this point, the United Nations was immersed in the tasks of reconstruction, and many of the more developed countries argued that no other task should be allowed to distract attention from this essential task. Early U.N. debates show the representatives of underdeveloped countries making sophisticated arguments for the equal importance of reconstruction and development in the tasks of the new organization.[62] Brazilian delegate Roberto Campos, who would later be a key economic policy maker in the Kubitschek government, concluded

60. See, for example, comments by the Argentine delegate, Summary Records of Meetings, General Assembly, Second Committee, 1947, p. 31.

61. Murphy, "What the Third World Wants," p. 62. Murphy does not refer to these new ideas as developmentalism but rather sees them as the seeds of the new international economic order (NIEO) ideology. I argue that developmentalism is a forerunner of NIEO ideas.

62. Brazil, among the countries making sophisticated arguments along these lines, stressed the "principle of economic interdependence" to counter the "regional or continental view of the problem," which gave priority to European reconstruction. This "internationalist" view emphasized that reconstruction cannot be separated from the general issues of world economic recovery and reviving international trade. Thus reconstruction and development were two essential and complementary parts of the same task. See comments by the Brazilian delegate, Summary Records of Meetings, General Assembly, Second Committee, 1946, p. 89, and 1947, p. 30.

that the United Nations should concentrate its efforts on technical assistance and research and studies of problems of economic development,[63] a position common among less developed countries in the United Nations and supported by the U.N. Department of Economic Affairs.[64] The vindication of development as a central and shared concern was an important product of these debates.

Although the view of the less developed countries lost out in the definition of the postwar economic order to the U.S. view, their position was not then lost or absent from the U.N. system or from international consciousness. Rather, pockets in the U.N. continued to reflect and support this point of view, especially those agencies that dealt with issues of economic and social development. International developmentalism was not the dominant view of the United Nations, nor was it reflected in the mandate of the IMF or even the World Bank. Still, it was a minority view that continued to flourish in the Secretariat, and which captured certain parts of the bureaucracy.

The Economic Commission for Latin America

One important source of developmentalist ideas within the U.N. system was the Economic Commission for Latin America, created against the will of both the United States and the USSR in 1948. The creation of CEPAL reflected the realization of Latin American and other Third World delegations that the U.N. needed to address the issues of development and industrialization. As Hirschman has pointed out, CEPAL mirrored the new feelings, gave expression and direction to diffuse currents, and turned them to constructive tasks.[65]

The Chilean delegate made the original proposal for the formation of an economic commission for Latin America, arguing that it was necessary to develop the industry of Latin American countries to improve the standard of living of its inhabitants. All twenty Latin American countries and a number of other underdeveloped countries supported the proposal for an economic commission for Latin America and in general favored greater U.N. cooperation in support of economic and social development of underdeveloped countries.[66] This was the occa-

63. Ibid., 1948, pp. 168–73.
64. Interview with Cleantho de Paiva Leite, Rio de Janeiro, May 21, 1986; and Hernan Santa Cruz, *La CEPAL: Encarnación de una esperanza de América Latina* (Santiago, Chile: United Nations, Cuadernos de La CEPAL 50, 1985).
65. Albert O. Hirschman, "Ideologies of Economic Development in Latin America," in *Latin American Issues* (New York: Twentieth Century Fund, 1961).
66. See the debate in Summary Records of Meetings, General Assembly, Second Committee, 1947.

sion when the General Assembly first initiated its great debate over economic development, which later would become one of its main themes of discussion.[67]

The Brazilian delegate gave a rousing speech in favor of the creation of CEPAL, in which he advocated the greater use of planning as a means of promoting development of less developed countries, a position then considered daring and original. Although the proposal to establish an economic commission for Latin America was passed by a strong majority,[68] its existence during the first few years was precarious, since it was given only a temporary mandate.

Once established, CEPAL set up shop in Santiago, Chile, and began to work on the preparation of a document summarizing the economic conditions of the Latin American republics. In 1949 CEPAL had Argentine economist Raúl Prebisch prepare a study on the economic situation of Latin America, which he would present at the 1949 CEPAL conference in Havana. This text, a ringing critique of the international division of labor and declining terms of trade for the producers of primary products, called for industrialization as the only path to development in the underdeveloped countries of Latin America.[69] The tone of the document, and the fact that soon afterward Prebisch would accept an invitation to become the executive secretary of CEPAL, indicated that the new economic commission would chart a more vocal and independent path than had been anticipated.

CEPAL's existence was far from secure. The United States had opposed its formation, and the activist stance of CEPAL's early work did nothing to endear the new organization to the country. The United States believed that CEPAL duplicated and competed with work that was being carried out under the Organization for American States (OAS), an entity more open to U.S. influence. At a conference in 1951 the United States and its allies argued that the work of CEPAL should be transferred to the OAS. The situation looked bleak. What finally swung the tide of the debate was a telegram from the Brazilian presidential palace, expressing President Vargas's personal wish that the autonomy of CEPAL be defended.[70] The United States, unwilling to provoke an open confrontation, backed down, and CEPAL's continued existence was assured.

67. Santa Cruz, *La CEPAL*, p. 19.
68. Thirteen votes in favor, no votes against, and four abstentions—the United States, Canada, the USSR, and Byelorussia.
69. Raúl Prebisch, *The Economic Development of Latin America and Its Principal Problems* (New York: United Nations, Economic Commission for Latin America, 1950).
70. Furtado, *A fantasia organizada*, pp. 104, 111–16. Also, interview with Cleantho de Paiva Leite, Rio de Janeiro, May 21, 1986.

The creation of CEPAL was a product of incipient developmentalism and pro-industrialization sentiment among the Latin American delegation, the staff of the Economic Department of the United Nations, and key allies of other Third World states, as well as some developed countries like France. The continued intellectual production, and continued existence and vitality of CEPAL, was a mutual outcome of a fruitful and occasionally precarious balance and exchange between CEPAL and its allies in the rest of the continent. Noted Latin American economists like Prebisch infused CEPAL's work with originality and dynamism, while Latin American statesmen and diplomats contributed to the creation and continued existence of the organization. At the same time, CEPAL reports, theory, technical assistance teams, and training workshops gave information, evidence, and support to governments throughout the region. Economists who worked at CEPAL found their work enriched by the broader regional perspective that informed CEPAL analysis.

But developmentalist ideas are not simply synonymous with the ideas of CEPAL or a result of its influence. CEPAL was only one of the multiple influences and roots of developmentalist thought in Brazil and Argentina, and CEPAL ideas had little direct influence on the thought of Frondizi, Kubitschek, and their top advisers. In Argentina CEPAL thought was marginal to policy making during the Frondizi government, primarily because of the previous political involvement of Prebisch with conservative governments and his identification with anti-Peronist politics in Argentina.[71] In Brazil CEPAL was more influential than in Argentina, although even in Brazil CEPAL thought was more important in legitimizing and providing strong analytical arguments for policies already being adopted than as the generator of new policy ideas.[72]

DOMESTIC ORIGINS OF DEVELOPMENTALISM

Developmentalism, as it emerged in both Argentina and Brazil, was rooted in an analysis of the impact of the Great Depression and the Second World War on the domestic economies, and the countries' responses to these crises. In Argentina this implied that developmentalism was founded on a critique of the conservative governments of the

71. See Kathryn Sikkink, "The Influence of Raúl Prebisch on Economic Policy Making in Argentina, 1950–1962," *Latin American Research Review* 23 (1988), 91–114.

72. See, for example, Ricardo Bielschowsky, "Brazilian Economic Thought (1945–1964): The Ideological Cycle of Developmentalism" (Ph.D. diss., University of Leicester, 1985).

1930s and the Peronist experiment. In Brazil developmentalism was a response to and continuation of the Vargas policies.

Argentine desarrollistas frequently trace the origins of their ideas to early Argentine advocates of industrialization and protectionism rather than to international influence. This emphasis on Argentine sources of developmentalism is part of a belief that foreign models are not appropriate to the Argentine context. "Models are not exported," argued Frigerio. "They are the result of a rigorous study of the reality in each country and its historical formation."[73] It also reflects a preference of some desarrollistas for practical thinkers as opposed to theorists. Thus Frigerio argued that it was more beneficial to read the speeches of Argentine industrialist Carlos Pellegrini than many books on economic development.[74]

Nevertheless, when Argentine developmentalists looked outside their country for inspiration, they were likely to cite examples from the U.S. development experience. Early Argentine advocates of industrialization in the late 1800s and early 1900s frequently referred to the U.S. example of protection of infant industries.[75] The developmentalists who followed them also cited U.S. examples. One Argentine developmentalist quoted Alexander Hamilton and Thomas Jefferson as sources of his ideas,[76] and President Frondizi was fond of referring to Franklin Roosevelt. In his history of the Argentine economy, Rogelio Frigerio cites an early Argentine advocate of industrialization telling the story of Benjamin Franklin's pride in wearing suits of homespun American cloth in European courts.[77]

Developmentalism in Argentina was profoundly rooted in an analysis of the 1930s and of the Peronist experience. The Great Depression was seen as having caused an irreversible breakdown in the agro-import structure of the country. Developmentalists believed that the conservative governments' insistence on maintaining a free trade policy and attempting to preserve Argentina's position as an exporter of primary products during the crisis of the Great Depression led to progressive impoverishment of the country and loss of its international position.[78]

73. Rogelio Frigerio, written response to interview questions, received July 15, 1985.

74. Rogelio Frigerio, *Estatuto del subdesarrollo*, p. 54.

75. Mario Rapoport, *De Pellegrini a Martinez de Hoz: El modelo liberal* (Buenos Aires: Centro Editor de America Latina, 1984), p. 24.

76. Interview with Alberto Virgilio Tedin, Buenos Aires, August 10, 1985.

77. Rogelio Frigerio, *Sintesis de la historia crítica de la economia Argentina desde la conquista hasta nuestros dias* (Buenos Aires: Hachette, 1983), p. 67.

78. Ibid., p. 83. But the desarrollistas ignored some of the innovative pro-industrialization policies advocated by Raúl Prebisch as director of the Central Bank in the early 1940s.

The positive and negative aspects of the Peronist experience was perhaps the most important influence on desarrollismo in Argentina. Peronist economic policy was national populist rather than developmentalist. As opposed to the other critics of Peronism, who seemed to view it as a bad dream or a historical accident, the fruit of demagoguery and false consciousness, developmentalists analyzed what they considered the positive and negative contributions of Peronism. They supported Perón's industrialist vision but criticized his government's emphasis on production of light and intermediate consumer goods rather than on basic heavy industry.[79] Likewise, they argued that the Peronists had been excessively concerned with distributive issues at the expense of the creation of an integrated industrial sector.

At the same time, the desarrollistas recognized advances in the economic and political situation made under Perón.[80] In particular, the developmentalists favored the kind of coalition that Perón had engineered as the backbone of his government: national entrepreneurs and workers. Developmentalists hoped to recreate the old Peronist coalition of entrepreneurs and workers, add to it their own blend of intellectuals, técnicos, and the "modern" middle class, and place it under the developmentalist leadership and ideology. Since this implied "capturing" the Peronist movement without Perón, desarrollista discourse always combined a blend of praise and criticism of the Peronist experience. In spite of these affinities between developmentalism and Peronism, there were few personnel or institutional linkages between the Peronist and the developmentalist administration, as was the case in Brazil between the Vargas and Kubitschek administrations.

One interesting question is whether there was any cross-fertilization between the developmentalists in Brazil and Argentina. There is little evidence that the Brazilians were influenced by the Argentines. Kubitschek took office two full years before Frondizi. Shortly before taking office, Frondizi undertook a tour of three Latin American republics: Brazil, Peru, and Chile. Kubitschek recalled Frondizi's pre-inaugural visit in his memoirs:

---

79. Fanor Diaz, *Conversaciones con Rogelio Frigerio* (Buenos Aires: Hachette, 1977), p. 34.

80. They argued that during the Peronist government, the country had recovered control of its money and credit, repatriated the foreign debt, nationalized the railroads and gas and telephone companies, expanded the merchant marine, and created many new sources of work. With the support of state credits, light industry had expanded dramatically, and the foundations were laid for the development of the basic sectors of the economy. See, for example, Mariano Montemayor, *Claves para entender a un gobierno* (Buenos Aires: Impresiones El Sol, 1960), p. 81.

What Frondizi preached was the same as I had been doing in Brazil since the election. The one difference in our attitudes was that he was at the theoretical level. He had not yet taken the reins of government, and I already had long experience with these problems. This similarity of viewpoints facilitated the conversations we had outside of the official program. Frondizi lived, like I did, the drama of attempting to reconcile Democracy with Development. In my case, a good piece of the road had already been traveled.[81]

This statement underscores that Kubitschek knew the two presidents shared a common vision of the world, of the future they desired for their countries, and of the policies they believed would help them achieve that future. It was a unique moment of optimism, even naivete, in the continent. A full year before the Cuban revolution, still enjoying the high commodity prices that followed the Korean War, many things seemed possible, and the new leaders believed they could change the course of their countries.

While in Brazil, Frondizi had the opportunity to witness some of the initial progress of the Targets Program firsthand. But the desarrollistas were well aware before 1958 of what the Brazilian developmentalists were doing. A survey of *Qué* magazine during the 1956–1958 period shows that Argentine desarrollistas kept close track of Brazilian industrial policy and progress with a certain degree of envy. Articles with headlines such as "Brazil Sets an Industrialization Rhythm for All of Latin America," "Brazil Grows in Its Industry and on the Map While We Get Smaller," "While Brazil Builds Smokestacks, Here They Are Pulled Down," "São Paulo Advances Feverishly: The Most Rapidly Growing City in the World," "Brazil Projects Itself into the Sphere of Great World Powers," and "Industries We Reject Here Spur the Growth of São Paulo" detailed the Kubitschek economic and foreign policy and compared it favorably to the policies of the Liberating Revolution (the military government in power from 1955 to 1958) in Argentina.[82]

Brazil apparently served as a point of reference for the Argentine developmentalists. The Brazilian influence was not felt in the formulation of specific programs, with the exception of the automobile program, where the Argentines self-consciously modeled their plans after

81. Kubitschek, *Meu caminho para Brasília*, p. 197.
82. The dates of the *Qué* magazine articles listed above are respectively: no. 107, October 30, 1956, pp. 32–33; no. 156, November 12, 1957, pp. 26–27; no. 100, September 11, 1956, p. 13; no. 122, March 19, 1957; no. 164, January 7, 1958, p. 19; and no. 155, November 5, 1957, p. 18.

the Brazilian experience. Although one occasionally finds examples of Brazilian developmentalists offering specific inspiration to the Argentines, in general the Brazilian developmentalist program offered a point of comparison that spurred the Argentines but was not perceived as directly "applicable" to their context.

While developmentalism in Argentina was a critical response to and a break with the policies of the Peronist period, in Brazil there was greater continuity between developmentalism and the earlier policies adopted by the Vargas governments, both during the authoritarian Estado Nôvo period and, more significant, during the second Vargas government, from 1951 to 1954.

During the authoritarian Estado Nôvo period (1937–1945) many of the intellectual and physical bases for the developmentalist policies were laid down. Vargas and the founders of the Estado Nôvo were primarily concerned with centralizing, strengthening, and rationalizing the Brazilian state. As part of this process, Vargas expanded the federal bureaucracy and reorganized it to place more emphasis on merit and efficiency. This reorganized bureaucracy later played an important role in the formulation and implementation of developmentalist policies. In this sense, the Brazilian experience was quite different from that of Argentina. In both countries the state was expanding its role in the economy, but only in Brazil did a reform of the state bureaucracy itself take place.

Under the Estado Nôvo, the state increased its intervention in the economy, expanding federal ownership of industries and creating mixed public-private corporations. Among the more important state investment projects were the National Steel Company, which constructed a large steel complex at Volta Redonda with support from the Export-Import Bank and a state-funded iron ore mining operation. This state intervention in the economy increased when Brazil entered World War II in 1942. It was after the Brazilian entry into the war that Vargas adopted an openly pro-industrialization policy.

Later, when Vargas was elected president under a democratic regime in 1951, he carried his pro-industrialization policies a step further, establishing the national petroleum company, Petrobras, and setting up the Banco Nacional de Desenvolvimento Econômico, or the National Economic Development Bank (BNDE), to support infrastructure and basic industrial projects. Vargas also established an Industrial Development Council to make recommendations for new industrial policy. Among the subcommissions of the council was one on jeeps, tractors, trucks, and automobiles, which lay out the first blueprints for the Brazilian automobile industry later established during the Kubitschek government.

Kubitschek was a Vargas man, and thus it is not surprising that there is significant continuity between the Vargas development policies and the Kubitschek Targets Program. The developmentalists in Brazil did not need to "capture" populism the way the Frondizi forces hoped to capture Peronism in Argentina. They were its natural heirs. Vargas's suicide left the movement without its leader to compete with Kubitschek for definition of its goals. The main heir to the populist strand of the Vargas legacy, João Goulart, who might have competed with Kubitschek for the right to carry the Vargas banner, was carefully incorporated into the Kubitschek coalition as his vice-president.

Later, when Kubitschek was president, he called on some of the same men who had worked closely with Vargas. One of these advisers argued that "the germ of the Targets Program of Kubitschek was in the Economic Advisory Team of Vargas."[83] But the theoretical origins of the Targets Program were more closely linked to another group, the Joint Brazil–United States Economic Development Commission, than they were to the Vargas Advisory Team. The Joint Brazil–United States Economic Development Commission began work in 1951, the first year of the second Vargas administration. U.S. participation in the commission was based on the provisions of the Point Four Program. The commission's ultimate aim was "to create conditions for, and eliminate obstacles to, an increase in the flow of investment, public and private, foreign and domestic, needed to promote economic development." Its immediate goal called for it to prepare specific development projects, with special emphasis on transportation and electric power. By the time it issued its final report in December 1953, the commission had formulated forty-one detailed projects, issued an overall report on long-term trends in the Brazilian economy, trained Brazilian technicians in U.S. universities, and provided technical assistance.[84] In the eyes of Brazilians, however, the commission failed to meet its goals, since neither the United States nor the IBRD provided funding for the bulk of the projects formulated by the commission. Nor did the commission meet the goals of the U.S. government. In an office memorandum, a State Department official complained that "we also permitted

83. Interview with Cleantho de Paiva Leite, Rio de Janiero, May 21, 1986.
84. *Report of the of the Joint Brazil–United States Economic Development Commission* (Washington, D.C.: Institute of Inter-American Affairs, Foreign Operations Administration, U.S. Government Printing Office, 1955), pp. iii–vi.

the Brazilians to subvert the program to their own internal political ends."[85]

But if the commission failed to meet either Brazilian or U.S. goals, it did succeed in establishing the theoretical framework that would later be used in selection of targets for the Targets Program. A section of the report said to be written by Brazilian Roberto Campos stated:

> Brazil . . . offered striking evidence of the interrelationships of an economy and of how accelerated growth in one sector is often the precondition for faster growth in other sectors. Thus, the spurt in the chemical and plastics industries, while temporarily leading to an increase in import requirements, provided, for the first time, a sizable and relatively stable domestic market for certain raw materials and semi-manufactures; these markets, in turn, prompted the development of related mining and agricultural raw material and processing ventures.[86]

This paragraph foreshadows later arguments about the importance of forward and backward linkages in industrial development. Following this line of reasoning, the commission decided that to be most effective, development finance should contribute to this process by focusing on specific "bottlenecks" and "growing points" in the economy. The report argued that the basic criterion for the determination of priorities for funding should be "concentrating on investments with the highest social productivity, in terms of their importance in the elimination of structural bottlenecks to economic growth or in serving as growing points leading to economic progress."[87] Using these criteria, the commission focused almost entirely on transportation and energy, recommending only two industrial projects: an alkali industry and the expansion of cast iron pipe production. But the same criteria would be applied to determine the priority infrastructural and industrial areas to be targeted in the Targets Program.

In addition to the personal and political link between Kubitschek and Vargas, an institutional link also contributed to the influence of the Vargas policy on the developmentalists. Vargas helped set up the BNDE and appointed the top staff of the bank. Many of the staff from the Joint Brazil–United States Economic Development Commission

85. U.S. Government, office memorandum, May 6, 1953, ref. no. DE 500720. The kinds of goals sought by the United States are apparent in another confidential memorandum, which argued for using the development loans to finance the projects "as a powerful lever to encourage steps by Brasil to adopt constructive measures, most important of which might by a solution of its petroleum problem with foreign participation."
86. *Report of the Joint Brazil–United States Economic Development Commission*, p. 14.
87. Ibid., p. 73.

moved to key positions in the National Development Bank. Later Kubitschek relied heavily on the BNDE, and on some of the same staff appointed by Vargas, to formulate and implement the Targets Program.

THE DEBATE OVER DEVELOPMENT POLICY

In the period from 1945 to 1956 Brazilian and foreign economists engaged in a debate over development policy and planning, which was played out in newspapers and the public arena. The first shot of this public debate was fired by industrialist Roberto Simonsen when he presented his document in favor of economic planning to the National Council for Industrial Policy in 1945. Simonsen's position was attacked by leading liberal economist Eugenio Gudin, who declared that "the mystique of planning is . . . a genetic derivation from the failed and abandoned experiences of the American New Deal, from the Italian and German dictatorships that brought the world to catastrophe, from the five-year plans of Russia that don't have any application in other countries." CEPAL entered the fray. Brazilian economist Celso Furtado translated and arranged for the Brazilian publication of Prebisch's classic article in 1948 and later divulged CEPAL's documents on the new programming techniques. Gudin counterattacked CEPAL with a series of newspaper articles titled "The Mystique of Planning." Prebisch responded with newspaper articles attacking liberal thought titled "The Mystique of Spontaneous Equilibrium." The third major skirmish in the battle occurred in 1956, shortly after Kubitschek took power, when Gudin published another series of newspaper articles attacking recent economic policy and Kubitschek economic proposals.[88]

But the debate over development in Brazil had a very different quality than the debate in Argentina. Even at its most intense, there was an amiability unimaginable in Argentina. In Brazil this was a debate among elites who agreed to disagree, abided by certain rules of the game, and moved in the same circles. Even after his attack on planning, it was Gudin who agreed to publish Furtado's translation of Prebisch's manifesto in 1948 in his prestigious economic journal *Revista Brasileira de economia*. Within the same institution, the Fundação Getúlio Vargas

88. This debate has been documented and analyzed in João Paulo de Almeida Magalhães, *Controvérsia brasileira sôbre o desenvolvimento econômico: Uma reformulação* (Rio de Janeiro: Gráfica Record Editora, 1967), pp. 11–33; and Heitor Ferreira Lima, *História do pensamento econômico no Brasil* (São Paulo: Editora Nacional, 1978), pp. 170–83. Bielschowshy, "Brazilian Economic Thought," discusses the debate in detail.

operated two economic journals arguing different viewpoints, *Revista Brasileira de economia*, headed by Gudin, and *Conjuntura econômica*, published by the foundation's developmentalist wing from 1947 to 1952.

The other point that the much publicized "debate over development" in Brazil obscures is that in many ways by the time the debate took place the battle for developmentalism had already been won. Gudin was almost in a camp by himself, respected by fellow economists for his elegant, eloquent, and persistent defense of a liberal model. But the practical implications of his theories were largely ignored by most policy makers and intellectuals. Liberalism never took root in Brazil the way it did in Argentina.[89] The real debate in Brazil was not between the liberal model and the planning model but within the developmentalist camp between cosmopolitan and nationalist developmentalists. The much publicized debates with Gudin distract attention from the real nature of the debate on development, which was between those within the developmentalist camp who advocated more or less inflationary policies.

DEVELOPMENTALISM AND DISILLUSIONMENT

By the late 1960s and early 1970s the failure of developmentalist policies to deliver on all that they had promised and the turn to authoritarianism in the region led many to blame the developmentalist model for the ills the continent was experiencing. Developmentalism was reinterpreted in the light of its supposed failures, the victim of the high hopes it had generated and the subsequent disillusionment. But such disillusionment should not serve to cloud our vision of the importance of developmentalism in Latin America, and its successes and failures.

Many Brazilians look back to the Kubitschek period as the most democratic and hopeful period in recent Brazilian political life, whereas for the majority of Argentines the Frondizi legacy is associated with failure and frustration.[90] But this contrast is too dramatic. In one sense both

89. On why liberalism never took root in Brazil, see Wanderley Guilherme dos Santos, "Liberalism in Brazil: Ideology and Praxis," in *Terms of Conflict: Ideology in Latin American Politics*, ed. Morris J. Blachman and Ronald Hellman (Philadelphia: ISHI, 1977).

90. During the Alfonsín presidency there was considerable speculation about similarities between Frondizi and Alfonsín; both were civilian presidents from different branches of the Radical party whose authority was frequently challenged by a restive military. Because of Frondizi's negative image, Alfonsín's supporters tried to counter the comparison, once publishing on the cover of one of their magazines a picture of Alfonsín under the large headline, "Alfonsín no es Frondizi" (Alfonsín is not Frondizi). *Generación '83* 2 (March 1985).

Kubitschek and Frondizi succeeded, and in a final sense they both failed. Policy makers who followed the developmentalist governments embraced their policy goals, even when they maligned and attacked the policy makers themselves. The military government that took power in Brazil in 1964 removed Kubitschek's political rights and eventually forced him into exile, but it embraced his economic program, motivated by the dream of Brazil as a modern industrial power. Some of the most negative aspects of developmentalism came through with a vengeance: indifference to issues of equality and distribution, the naive belief that growth in and of itself would resolve all problems, disregard for the environmental impact of industrial growth, and increased internationalization of the economy.

The "success" of the developmentalist governments in implementing many of their policies had dual consequences. This was a period of rapid industrialization and capitalization in both countries. New factories sprang up, encouraged by generous incentives to industry. The automobile industry in both countries traces its birth to the developmentalist period, as does much of the petrochemical industry, the expansion of the steel industry, and many others. Huge infrastructural projects were undertaken; the construction of new roads and railroad networks, large electrical generating plants, gas pipelines, new docks and shipbuilding facilities were all initiated during the developmentalist governments. In the backlands of Brazil, a modern new capital arose out of nothing, capturing world attention with its futuristic buildings.

But at the same time the developmentalist programs exacerbated other problems in the region. Developmentalists argued that the problem in Latin America was production not distribution. But their indifference to issues of distribution and equality meant that developmentalist policies failed to mitigate the concentration of wealth in a region known for great inequality. Meanwhile, in the developmentalist euphoria of the 1950s, the great factories and infrastructural projects were set up without a thought to their impact on the environment. The roads that cut a swath across the Amazon jungle, for the first time linking it with the rest of Brazil, also opened the area to unprecedented desecration.

This is what we see of the developmentalist period looking back from the 1990s. Should someone have suggested a low-growth strategy as a means for protecting the environment in the 1950s, they would have been taken for crazy if not subversive. The goal of high growth was unquestioned. The desire for rapid industrialization was an article of faith for most of the population. Kubitschek and his advisers were totally convinced that building roads into the Amazon was the way to bring progress to a region previously cut off from the advantages of modernization.

The built-in bias of developmentalism toward basic industry and modern technology led to a large increase in the level of foreign ownership and external indebtedness of the economy. For the developmentalists, it was more important to establish the right kinds of industry than to worry about who owned the factories. But as a result of developmentalist policies, both governments increased their external dependence on foreign investors and creditors. Foreign debt, negligible up until that point, began to increase. These were among the side effects of the developmentalist program which led to increasing questioning and disillusionment.

More damaging, however, was the association that emerged between developmentalism and authoritarianism. If one defines democracy in terms of the existence of formal institutions such as elections, and the concomitant individual freedoms of speech and association which make the electoral process meaningful,[91] the Kubitschek and Frondizi governments were as democratic or more democratic than was the norm in their countries in the postwar period. The political practice of the Kubitschek government showed the greatest respect for civil and political rights of any Brazilian government in this period. Free elections were held in which all except the Communist party were allowed to participate. The franchise was still limited by literacy requirements, under the 1946 constitution, which excluded a large part of the Brazilian population from political participation. No political prisoners or reports of torture or mistreatment tarnished the government's image. But in Argentina Frondizi's hasty and extended imposition of a state of emergency and the application of search and arrest procedures led to the suspension of some vital civil and political rights. The most grievous abridgment of democratic rights during the Frondizi period was a prohibition on the participation of Peronist candidates, a proscription common to all the Argentine governments during the 1955–1973 period. At the same time, in Argentina this was a time of comparatively open debate and political participation. It is frequently recalled as the era when the university flourished and functioned with least interference from the government.

But in neither country was a democratic political regime institutionalized. Frondizi's failure was dramatic, as his tenuous and contested authority throughout his presidency and his eventual overthrow by the

91. This is similar to the definition used by Juan Linz, *The Breakdown of Democratic Regimes: Crisis, Breakdown, and Reequilibration* (Baltimore: Johns Hopkins University Press, 1978), p. 5.

military attested. His political slogan outlined the political project and the economic model: integration and development. By integration Frondizi meant the reincorporation of the Peronist voters and the Peronist working class into Argentine political life. But the Peronists were not prepared to be reintegrated into Frondizi's scheme of Peronism without Perón, and the anti-Peronist forces in Argentine society were not prepared to accept integration in any shape or form.

Kubitschek's failure was more subtle. He succeeded in completing his term and completing much of his program. But the political project of development and democracy which he promoted was almost as tenuous as it was in Argentina. It depended on the masterful fine tuning and balancing that Kubitschek himself was able to maintain, but not his predecessors. Holding together the developmentalist coalition also had a price: inflation and the limiting of consumption demands of most of the population, neither of which could be sustained indefinitely.

In both Argentina and Brazil the democratic system broke down and bureaucratic authoritarian regimes emerged four years after the end of the developmentalist experiments. O'Donnell and others have treated the emergence of bureaucratic authoritarianism as the almost inevitable result of a failure of the populist-developmentalist experiment. They argue that once the "easy stage" of import substitution was over, the economic requirements necessary for "deepening" industrial development were almost impossible to achieve under a democratic regime.[92] This argument has been questioned by many experts, since the developmentalist governments were actively undertaking the deepening of their industrial structure, and the "easy stage" of import substitution was already well past by the time of the breakdown of democracy.[93]

The early developmentalist governments of Frondizi and Kubitschek were attempts to wed the developmentalist economic model to a democratic or semidemocratic political project. As policy makers in the current civilian regimes in the southern cone look back on their histories for guidance, in many cases the developmentalist periods are the last episodes of relatively rapid economic growth during a democratic or semidemocratic regime.

This overview of developmentalist ideas in the international and the domestic setting attempts to clarify developmentalism's legacy as one of

92. Guillermo O'Donnell, *Modernization and Bureaucratic-Authoritarianism: Studies in South American Politics* (Berkeley: Institute of International Studies, University of California, 1973).

93. See essays by Robert Kaufman and Albert Hirschman in *The New Authoritarianism in Latin America*, ed. David Collier.

the most prominent economic models used in postwar Latin America. I have stressed the interconnections between the emergence of developmentalist ideas in the international arena and the new ideas and policies adopted by national governments. The United Nations was an important early arena for debates on development and for an interchange and spread of shared ideas. The creation of the Economic Commission for Latin America was one of the earliest institutional outcomes of debates on development in the United Nations. Its precarious early existence was testimony to the enduring difficulties developmentalist ideas faced. The fortuitous combination of the prestigious and innovative intellectual leadership of Prebisch, which caught the imagination of the continent's elites, and committed allies in diplomatic and policy circles helped to secure CEPAL's continued existence.

But while international developmentalism had its points of connection with domestic ideas, the concerns of domestic developmentalism were of a different nature. Developmentalist politicians like Kubitschek and Frondizi faced a political dilemma. Their ideas about development led them to focus on the need for intense capital accumulation to support the industrialization process that lies at the heart of developmentalism. They were convinced that this process of capital accumulation had to rely on foreign capital as well as on domestic savings. Thus one of the principal political and economic tasks of the developmentalist governments was the creation of an atmosphere of security and investor confidence. At the same time, groups within and outside of their political coalitions often made demands that conflicted with the basic outlines of the developmentalist model, demands for more equitable distribution of income, higher wages, more nationalist policies, higher benefits for domestic as opposed to foreign entrepreneurs, and more attention to the agricultural sector. How these politicians faced the conflicts between the demands of their developmentalist ideas and domestic political pressures is the subject of Chapters 3 and 4, which relate to the adoption, implementation, and consolidation of developmentalism in Brazil and Argentina.

CHAPTER THREE

Developmentalism in Argentina, 1955–1962

The first tentative steps toward developmentalism were taken during the last years of the government of Juan Perón. In April 1955 the Peronist government, breaking its traditional nationalist stance, signed a contract with Standard Oil of California for the exploration and exploitation of Argentine oil fields in Patagonia. The Peronists hoped the contract would help expand domestic petroleum production. "Realism recommends collaboration with private foreign firms" since "the state cannot make a similar effort," the party argued.[1] Nationalists, both inside and outside the Peronist party, firmly opposed the contract. Arturo Frondizi, then president of the National Committee of the Radical party, attacked the Peronist concessions to a foreign company. This speech brought Frondizi to national attention as a new political leader whose appeal went beyond traditional anti-Peronist groups.[2]

Arturo Frondizi, the eleventh child of middle-class Italian immigrant parents, was born in 1908 in the Province of Corrientes, Argentina. The children received a good education; many would later distinguish themselves as intellectuals.[3] When he was eighteen, Frondizi entered the law school at the University of Buenos Aires.

1. "Informe sobre la reunión del Consejo Superior del Peronismo," *La nación*, September 10, 1955. Cited in Alain Rouquié, *Poder militar y sociedad política en la Argentina II: 1943–1973* (Buenos Aires: Emecé Editores, 1982), p. 104.
2. Alain Rouquié, *Radicales y desarrollistas en la Argentina* (Buenos Aires: Schapire Editor, 1975), p. 42.
3. When Arturo Frondizi was president, his younger brother, Risieri Frondizi, was rector of the national university, and his older brother, Silvio Frondizi, was a prominent Marxist sociologist. From the time they were children, family discussions focused on scientific and philosophical themes. Rodolfo Pandolfi, *Frondizi por el mismo* (Buenos Aires: Editorial Galerna, 1968), p. 18.

While at the university, Frondizi became active in opposition to the military government that had overthrown President Yrigoyen, participating in antigovernment demonstrations and suffering his first political arrest. He enrolled in the Radical party, initiating his career in the opposition, which would continue for the next twenty-eight years, until he was elected president. Frondizi worked in opposition to the conservative governments of the period 1930–1943, later in opposition to Perón, and eventually in opposition to the military government that overthrew Perón. This constant opposition role shaped the early development of Frondizi's thought, giving it an abstract and purist quality.

During this early period Frondizi continued to work as a lawyer, specializing in commercial law. He also defended political prisoners, worked as a lawyer for the International Red Cross, and participated in the Argentine League for the Rights of Man. Through these activities he established good relations with the Argentine Left, also in opposition to the conservative government.[4] Like many Latin American intellectuals, he was influenced by Marxism, which reinforced his tendency to think in broad historical terms. During the thirties and early 1940s Frondizi's ideology focused on social reform and economic nationalism.[5] In the mid-forties he helped organize a reformist wing within the Radical party, which attempted to incorporate some aspects of populist nationalism into the Radical doctrine. In 1946 he was elected to the Congress, where he soon became a party spokesman on economic and foreign policy issues. Even his opponents respected his intellect and his carefully documented and argued presentations. Frondizi was his party's vice-presidential candidate in 1951, on a ticket with Ricardo Balbin, leader of the Radical party. By 1954, his wing of the party now in the majority, Frondizi became president of the National Committee of the Radical party. At the same time he published a book that won him fame and haunted him during his presidency. *Petroleum and Politics* was a spirited and well-documented defense of the state oil monopoly and of economic nationalism in general.

Frondizi was considered one of the most brilliant politicians of his generation. "He was dazzlingly intelligent for the environment in which he worked. He was an intellectual involved in politics, a man of ideas, one of the few Radical politicians who had a large library. He studied Argentine problems seriously."[6] His adversaries called him "the professor" or "the sphinx." His followers often deferred to him, even when

4. Ibid., p. 36.

5. Mario Barrera, *Information and Ideology: A Case Study of Arturo Frondizi* (Beverly Hills: Sage Publications, 1973), pp. 12–14.

6. Interview with Nicolas Babini, Buenos Aires, July 7, 1985.

unsure of his motives, with the phrase "Frondizi knows what he's doing."

By the late forties and early fifties Frondizi began to have some differences with the main positions of his party. He believed that the party failed to direct sufficient attention to the urgent task of creating a powerful heavy industry in the country.[7] He increasingly directed his attention to issues of production, industrialization, protectionism, planning, and the mechanization of agriculture. He found little support for his concerns within the Radical party. At this point he first met Rogelio Frigerio, businessman, editor of a popular weekly news magazine, and a driving force behind a group of intellectuals associated with the magazine. Some commentators claim that Frigerio "intellectually captured" Frondizi,[8] but it appears more likely that in Frigerio Frondizi found an expression of his own recent doubts and ideas, for which he had found no echo in his own party. The meeting seemed providential: Frigerio had new ideas and a magazine, Frondizi shared similar ideas, and he had a party and votes.[9] This meeting marked the birth of the desarrollista movement in Argentina.

Thus Frondizi experienced an ideological transformation in the mid-1950s from a traditional Radical politician, reformist and nationalist in perspective, to a full-fledged developmentalist. This involved a reversal of his position on the state oil monopoly, the role of foreign investment in the economy, agrarian reform, and income distribution, and a change in emphasis in many other areas. His changed ideas were not the result of travel abroad or of any practical administrative experience. His was a more solitary intellectual process of change from one set of ideas to another, almost a "rebirth." His contact with Frigerio was one catalyst of the change, but Frondizi was already moving in a similar direction before he met Frigerio.

Changes in Frondizi's ideas were motivated by the impact of new information, provided by surrounding events.[10] Frondizi confirmed that the Argentine experience during World War II contributed to his change in ideas regarding the new focus on development and industrialization. The war revealed Argentine dependence on imports from the industrial world, while at the same time the growth of Argentine

7. Felix Luna, *Diálogos con Frondizi* (Buenos Aires: Editorial Desarrollo, 1963), p. 65.

8. See quote by Nicolas Babini, cited in Ricardo Gallo, *1956–1958 Balbin, Frondizi y la división del radicalismo* (Buenos Aires: Editorial Belgrano, 1983), p. 96.

9. Frigerio apparently once said that Frondizi had a million votes, and he, Frigerio, had the ideas. Nicolas Babini, *Frondizi: De la oposición al gobierno* (Buenos Aires: Editorial Celtia, 1984), p. 14.

10. Barrera, *Information and Ideology*, p. 6.

import-substituting industry "demonstrated the possibilities" for an alternate path. Frondizi's reading of U.S. economic history convinced him that the protection of infant industries had been a key factor in the development of the United States. And the Japanese example showed that a large resource base was not required for a policy of heavy industrialization.[11]

Raúl Prebisch and the Liberating Revolution

The actions of the military government that overthrew Perón, called the *Revolución Libertadora*, or the Liberating Revolution, helped set the stage for the debate over developmentalism in the postpopulist period. General Lonardi, first head of the new military government, took over under the slogan "Neither victors nor vanquished." His initially conciliatory positions toward Peronist labor leaders were an attempt to reintegrate Peronists into Argentine political life. One keystone of Lonardi's program was the reestablishment of economic confidence and development.

In early October 1955 General Lonardi asked Raúl Prebisch to return to Argentina as a special economic adviser to the president and to prepare the economic plan for the new military government. Prebisch's impeccable intellectual credentials and historical ties to the Argentine establishment made him an ideal candidate in the eyes of the influential Argentine elite. Prebisch requested a three-month leave of absence from CEPAL to undertake the task.

In his youth Prebisch had been a supporter of the Socialist party and a believer in free trade, the gold standard, and the international division of labor, positions that the Socialist party supported as well. On a number of occasions in the 1920s he was employed as a consultant by the Sociedad Rural, or Rural Society, the bastion of the landholding elite of Argentina. Later, as an economic policy maker in the conservative Argentine government of General Jose Uriburu, Prebisch proposed the creation of a Central Bank and eventually served for eight years (1935–1943) as its director-general. During this period Prebisch was actively involved in the negotiations with Britain which resulted in the controversial Roca-Runciman Pact, commonly perceived as disadvantageous to Argentine interests. These activities created a strong perception in Argentine political and economic circles that Prebisch was an individual tied to traditional conservative landholding interests. From

11. Ibid., pp. 38–39.

1926 to 1948 he served as professor of economics at the University of Buenos Aires. In his research, teaching, and work at the Central Bank, Prebisch was grappling in a nontraditional manner with some of the economic dilemmas of the era. By 1934 he began to publish articles and include in his lectures concerns that he later incorporated into his theory of declining terms of trade. By 1942 the Central Bank, under Prebisch's influence, began to advocate pro-industrialization policies.[12]

Still, in many ways Prebisch was essentially a conservative man, drawn by events and his analytical mind to propose sometimes unorthodox theories and policies. "During the Great Depression, although I had been a neoclassical economist, I realized that in light of the crisis, it was necessary to industrialize. I did this with misgivings, since all my ideas ran against it. But faced with the facts, faced with the intensity of the crisis, I said that there was no other alternative. Later I began to theorize."[13] Joseph Love, who studied extensively the origins of Prebisch's ideas, argues that relatively little of Prebisch's theories of center-periphery "was derived or borrowed from other writings, and that it owed more to empirical observation and experimentation than to Prebisch's reading of other theorists—Marxist, corporatist, Keynesian, or neoclassical." Of the Third World economists who made important contributions to development theory in the early postwar years, Prebisch was probably the only one exclusively trained in the Third World.[14]

Under the Peronist government Prebisch was excluded from official posts, "perhaps because of his long and close association with the nation's traditional economic elite."[15] Thus he was free to go to Santiago to become the executive secretary of CEPAL. Still, he remained bitter toward the Peronist government for his abrupt dismissal from his positions, the dismantling of the economic team he had assembled at the Central Bank, and the reversal of some of the policies he had championed.

Once Perón was overthrown, the Liberating Revolution once again gave Prebisch the chance to shape Argentine economic policy. Aware that no serious economic plan could be written on such short notice, Prebisch adopted a dual strategy. He convinced Lonardi to invite a

12. Joseph Love, "Raúl Prebisch and the Origin of the Doctrine of Unequal Exchange," *Latin American Research Review* 15 (1980), 45–72. I also relied on information from David Pollack, based on his extensive interviews with Prebisch, and on material provided by Adalbert Krieger Vasena, in his commentary to my article "The Influence of Raúl Prebisch on Economic Policy Making in Argentina, 1950–1962," *Latin American Research Review* 23 (1988), 115–19.

13. Interview with Raúl Prebisch, Buenos Aires, October 23, 1985.

14. Love, "Raúl Prebisch," p. 65.

15. Ibid., p. 57.

CEPAL mission to Argentina to carry out an in-depth study of the Argentine economy. Simultaneously, Prebisch wrote and took personal responsibility for a diagnosis and short-term economic program, the so-called Prebisch Plan.[16]

A few weeks later, military sectors that were unhappy with the government's orientation requested that Lonardi resign. General Pedro Eugenio Aramburu assumed the presidency and immediately adopted a more punitive position toward the Peronists. He took control of the central trade union organization, the General Labor Confederation (CGT), dissolved the Peronist party, and repressed party and union members. Under the Aramburu government Prebisch prepared and presented the rest of his economic program. Thus Prebisch, and CEPAL by association, became identified with the three reports and the ideology of the Liberating Revolution and its virulent anti-Peronism.

Although Prebisch emphasized his efforts to maintain the strictest impartiality,[17] his anti-Peronist and pro–Liberating Revolution sentiments were evident in the reports and in other Prebisch statements at the time.[18] Because Prebisch failed to present his plan in clear contrast

16. The Prebisch Plan was actually a collection of three separate documents prepared by Prebisch for the provisional government during a three-month period in late 1955 and early 1956: "Informe preliminar acerca de la situación económica" (October 26, 1955); "Moneda sana o inflación incontenible"; and the "Plan de restablecimiento económico" (Buenos Aires, January 7, 1956). According to Prebisch, only the third document was the "genuine and definitive Prebisch Plan." In the minds of his supporters and critics, however, all three documents formed the Prebisch Plan. The second report became the best known, possibly because of its dramatic title, "Healthy Money or Uncontrollable Inflation." The Prebisch Plan was not actually a plan, but only a set of recommended policies. Although Prebisch drew on the expertise of the CEPAL mission, which had already begun work on the country study in Buenos Aires, the Prebisch Plan was fully a work of Prebisch and not a CEPAL document.

17. Prebisch, "Informe preliminar," p. 8.

18. Prebisch referred to "the economic disaster the country has lived through . . . in the last ten years," and to "that incredible Mr. Miranda [Perón's first minister of economics], who did so much harm to the country." He ended one presentation with an emotional evocation of General Lonardi: "that noble and austere figure who together with other officers unsheathed his sword to topple one dictator and not to set up another in this suffering land of Latin America." La Agrupación Reformista de Graduados en Ciencias Económicas, "Mesa Redonda," November 28, 1955, published December 19, 1955, pp. 5, 8. The Prebisch Plan claimed that Argentina faced the worst economic development crisis of its history. Prebisch diagnosed the Argentine economic crisis as one of production, stressing that per capita income had only increased by 3.5 percent in the previous decade. According to Prebisch, the primary obstacle to growth was the serious foreign exchange shortage, provoked by several factors: first, disincentives for technical progress and production in agriculture had led to declining production and exports, which hampered Argentine capacity to import necessary capital goods; second, a short-sighted policy of import substitution had failed to develop necessary basic industries such as steel and chemicals; and third, a failure to stimulate the national production of petro-

to the policies of both the Peronist government *and* the pre-Peronist period, his opponents accused him of simply wanting to turn back the hands of the clock and return to the golden age of the "the fat cows" in the early 1900s.[19]

A careful reading of the report makes it clear that Prebisch *did not* recommend a return to the economic policies of the 1930s. His proposal was a cosmopolitan developmentalist approach with some classical overtones, in particular its focus on sound money and inflation. The Prebisch Plan proposed the development of a more complete and viable industrial structure, and only the provincialism of Argentine political culture caused by ten years of isolation could explain interpreting the plan as an attempt to return to a pre-industrial era.[20] Prebisch recommended that relative prices be reversed to favor agricultural producers in order to expand exports and thus generate the foreign exchange necessary for the capital goods imports needed for continued industrialization. But in a country as ideologically divided between two dominant economic doctrines (national populism and liberalism), little intermediate space existed for Prebisch's cosmopolitan developmentalism. Because most allies of the Aramburu government embraced the liberal model, and the plan advocated a reversal of prices favoring the rural sector, it was rapidly identified as a liberal document.

The Prebisch Plan contained two sections: a series of emergency measures to deal with the short-term economic situation, and a set of longer-term recommendations to guide the ongoing economic program of the government. The short-term recommendations were the most traditional: a large devaluation of the peso to provide price incentives for agricultural exports, liberalization of the foreign exchange market, a freeze on salaries and wages, and an expansion of foreign loans (to be facilitated by joining the IMF and the World Bank). The longer-term recommendations called for setting up a program to "technify" the agricultural sector; establishing steel, mechanical engineering, paper and pulp, petrochemical, and basic chemical industries; increasing the efficiency and management of the railroads; expanding the state production of petroleum; and increasing electric capacity. Prebisch rec-

leum had resulted in excessive foreign oil imports. In addition, Prebisch singled out inflation and excessive state intervention as obstacles to Argentine development.

19. See, for example, Arturo Jauretche, *El plan Prebisch: Returno al coloniaje*, 5th ed. (Buenos Aires: Pena Lillo, 1984). The revolutionary socialist newspaper *Lucha obrera* referred to Prebisch "not as the agent of imperialism but as imperialism personified" (November 10, 1955).

20. Tulio Halperin Donghi, *Historia Argentina: La democracia de masas* (Buenos Aires: Editorial Paidos, 1983), pp. 90–91.

ommended eventually adopting a development program based on the in-depth CEPAL study and programming techniques, to plan long-range capital investments.

The plan was as notable for what it omitted as for what it recommended. A rapid reading of these three reports reveals little to connect their content with the Prebisch of CEPAL fame. At no point in the reports did the author make reference to his renowned categories of center and periphery, to regional integration, or to the need for agrarian reform or rearrangement of land tenure patterns. Nor did he discuss declining terms of trade, the specific problems of peripheral economies, or any problems associated with reliance on foreign capital.

On the controversial issue of foreign investment, the Prebisch Plan tried to walk a middle line by ruling out foreign investment in the petroleum sector and railroads, but advocating foreign loans in other selected areas. Prebisch argued for increased agricultural exports rather than foreign investment as the primary means to expand capital goods imports. Only at the end of the final report did he make a passing reference to the need for planning and programming economic development, which would be based on the CEPAL country study being prepared. Although a concern for industrialization pervaded the reports, it was often relegated to the background, while problems of inflation, agricultural production, and exports took precedence.

These differences led Prebisch's critics to point to inconsistencies between his work as a CEPAL theorist and his recommendations for policy in Argentina.[21] Prebisch did not have two theoretical personalities, one at CEPAL and the other in Buenos Aires; rather, his positions on Argentina always reflected the most traditional options within the bounds of his beliefs. He believed that CEPAL's ideas were applicable in Argentina, but he attempted to adapt these ideas in order to counterbalance what he considered the mistakes of the Peronist government.

Reactions to the Plan

The most favorable response to the Prebisch Plan came from the rural sector. The Sociedad Rural editorialized in favor of the plan, and a journal generally representing agro-export sectors referred to "Dr. Raúl Prebisch's masterly diagnosis."[22] In addition to devaluing the peso,

21. The most renowned criticism was a polemic book, Jauretche, *El plan Prebisch*, pp. 137–66.
22. *Review of the River Plate*, October 31, 1955.

the provisional government responded to some of the dearest demands of the Sociedad Rural, including the dismantling of the Argentine Trade Promotion Institute (IAPI), which producers opposed because it purchased commodities at low official prices and resold them at higher international prices. But the rural sector was critical of other government policies, such as a 25 percent tax on foreign exchange recommended by Prebisch to soften the inflationary impact of the rural sector's exchange windfall.[23]

Industrialists' reaction to the new economic plan was more mixed. Aramburu had dissolved the small and medium-sized business association created by the Peronist government, Confederación General Económico, or the General Economic Confederation (CGE), and resurrected in its place the old Unión Industrial Argentina (UIA), traditionally the stronghold of large industrial concerns, as the sole representative of industrial interests. The old members of the CGE were unhappy over losing their organization and believed their interests were not adequately considered by the new economic policy. The UIA endorsed many of the policies of the Prebisch Plan,[24] but its support may have been more a result of the anti-Peronism of the Aramburu government than the developmentalist policies advocated by Prebisch.

Frondizi's Radical party, which represented much of middle-class opinion, was divided over what position to take on the Prebisch Plan. Aldo Ferrer, a Radical party economist, while signaling differences between the Prebisch Plan and the Radical economic program, admitted that "the report is generally good, and there is little doubt that in the short term it would reactivate national economic development." But Raúl Scalabrini Ortiz, a renowned nationalist intellectual whom Frondizi consulted about the plan, argued that "the objective of the Prebisch plan, which is to say the objective of Great Britain, is to dismantle our industry and leave the country in the state it was in 1935."[25]

These comments point to a schism that was beginning to widen in the Radical party, generated by personality and policy differences between Frondizi and the traditional leader of the party, Ricardo Balbín. Balbín

23. Gary Wynia, *Argentina in the Postwar Era: Politics and Economic Policy Making in a Divided Society* (Albuquerque: University of New Mexico Press, 1978).

24. The UIA applauded the plan's emphasis on expanding energy production, extending import substitution of basic industrial inputs, opening the economy to more international capital, monetary stabilization, and the reorganization of the banking sector. Unión Industrial Argentina, *Memoria y balance, 1956–1957*, pp. 22–24.

25. Aldo Ferrer, "El informe Prebisch y el problema económico argentino," Frondizi archives, Centro de Estudios Nacionales, Buenos Aires, no date. Frondizi circulated this document to Scalabrini Ortiz, whose handwritten margin comments are signed and dated December 13, 1955.

argued that the party should support the Liberating Revolution and took a more conciliatory position toward the economic policies of the government. Meanwhile Frondizi was trying to profile his wing of the party as the primary opposition to the military government. Contrary to the Balbín line, he argued that the Peronists had to be reincorporated into the political system. These differences eventually led to a formal split in the party during the 1957 election campaign between Frondizi's Unión Cívica Radical Intransigente (UCRI) and Balbín's Unión Cívica Radical del Pueblo (UCRP).[26] In order to defeat their former party members in the election, Frondizi and his advisers decided to appeal to Peronist voters, whose party was prohibited from participating in the election. They needed a more dynamic rhetoric to attract the Peronist and leftist vote. Frondizi found this in Rogelio Frigerio and his team at *Qué* magazine.

A primary mouthpiece of anti–Liberating Revolution sentiment was the weekly news magazine *Qué sucedió en siete días* (or simply *Qué*), edited by Rogelio Frigerio. Frigerio was a self-taught economist and businessman who became the most influential and controversial figure in the Argentine developmentalist movement. He read broadly in political philosophy and economics, preferring the classical economists Smith, Ricardo, and Marx. This study, together with his practical experience as an entrepreneur, were the primary influences on this thought. Frigerio had been a Marxist in his youth. When he experienced the conversion from Marxism to developmentalism, he continued to think of himself as a revolutionary, but his new revolutionary goal was to reaffirm and renovate capitalism in Argentina. *Qué* magazine was one of his vehicles for spreading the new doctrine. *Qué* adopted a polemical editorial style in favor of its main themes of industrialization and protectionism and in opposition to its favorite targets: British interests in Argentina, the Aramburu government, and Raúl Prebisch. *Qué* brought together a group of young intellectuals and industrialists from the Left and from the Peronist party, and also attracted support from rightist Catholic nationalists who favored the pro-industrialization line of the magazine.[27]

During the 1956–1958 period *Qué* sharply criticized the Prebisch Plan and the economic policy of the Aramburu government. Referring frequently to Prebisch's historical involvement with conservative governments and the Sociedad Rural, *Qué* portrayed Prebisch as the em-

---

26. For more on the division of the Radical party, see Gallo, *1956–1958 Balbin, Frondizi y la división del radicalismo*.

27. Rouquié, *Radicales y desarrollistas*, p. 103. Interview with Oscar Camilion, Buenos Aires, June 12, 1985.

bodiment of monetarist economic policy, the representation of British imperialism in Argentina, and the scion of the agro-export elite.[28] As Frigerio and the team at *Qué* grew closer to Frondizi and his wing of the Radical party, this negative reaction to Prebisch (and hence to CEPAL in general) was incorporated into the doctrine of the Frondizi wing of the party.

The merger of thought and political action resulting from the union of the Frondizi wing of the Radical party and the young intellectuals surrounding Rogelio Frigerio and *Qué* magazine led to the formation of the desarrollista movement in Argentina. Thus in Argentina the term desarrollismo took on a political meaning somewhat different than in the rest of Latin America, where developmentalism is a more generic term. In Argentina desarrollismo refers to one specific political party, the Frondizistas, which was often at odds with the ideas of Prebisch and CEPAL.

Why did the desarrollistas oppose Prebisch and CEPAL despite a number of similarities between their economic ideas? By 1956 many members of the Radical party and those from the Left who would later become desarrollistas had tempered their earlier anti-Peronism. They began to advocate reintegrating the Peronists into political life and resurrecting certain aspects of Peronism without Perón. Aramburu, on the other hand, represented the extreme view that only the destruction of Peronism could lead to the healthy development of Argentina. The desarrollistas and the supporters of the Liberating Revolution were divided over the fundamental political issue of what position the government should take on political incorporation of the Argentine working class, as represented by the Peronist party.

Because Prebisch had written a plan for Aramburu, he was identified with the anti-Peronist point of view. The political context within which the Prebisch Plan was conceived and applied, a context of repression against the majority political party and the Argentine working class, understandably colored all interpretations of the plan. Prebisch became a target for nationalists and desarrollistas wishing to attack the political and economic order. The fleeting desarrollista coalition of 1958 temporarily allied the Argentine working class with sectors of the national industrial bourgeoisie, the middle class, students, and intellectuals, and it was built on the opposition to all that the Liberating Revolution stood for, and in particular its economic policy and the politics of exclusion.

28. During the years 1956 and 1957, Prebisch appears in photographs in *Qué* more frequently than any other single figure, even though he was physically in Santiago much more than in Buenos Aires during this period.

Implementation of the Prebisch Plan

A series of problems converged to complicate the implementation of the Prebisch Plan, difficulties arising from context, process, institutional infrastructure, and presentation. In the political context of the Liberating Revolution, economic policy took a backseat to higher political priorities, especially the "de-Peronization" process and the strengthening of non-Peronist parties and unions to prepare for a transition to limited democracy.[29] Also, the regime's transitional status made it difficult to undertake any major restructuring of the economy.

Many of the provisions of the Prebisch Plan were never put into effect. Others were implemented but did not yield the anticipated results.[30] Many of the longer-range recommendations of the Prebisch Plan, which were its most developmentalist aspects, aimed as they were at developing and revitalizing basic industries, never got off the ground.[31]

But even if the Aramburu government had had the political will to implement the developmentalist aspects of the Prebisch Plan, the Argentine state did not possess the institutional infrastructure or the cadre of trained personnel to implement a long-range development plan. No central planning institution existed, nor any organ for the coordination of development policy. The institutions of the Peronist government were dismantled, but no lasting state institutions were created in their place to take responsibility for economic development. The absence of state institutions to guarantee policy and ideological continuity left the Prebisch Plan and the corresponding CEPAL report in a void. The main long-term recommendation of the Prebisch Plan which was adopted and had an important effect over time was also one of the few institution-building efforts of the Aramburu government: the establishment of the Instituto Nacional de Tecnologia Agropecuaria, the National Institute of Agrarian Technology (INTA).[32]

29. For example, the average real wage increased during this period; by the end of 1957, it had risen 8.5 percent above the average real salary during the period 1950–1955. This surprising result of a government policy perceived as antiworking class was due in part to Aramburu's attempt to "de-Peronize" the unions. Marcelo Cavarozzi, *Sindicatos y política en Argentina* (Buenos Aires: Estudios CEDES, 1984), p. 90.

30. According to Pablo Gerchunoff, "The Liberating Revolution did not privatize public enterprises, fire public administration employees, eliminate consumption subsidies, price controls or quantitative import restrictions. It did not cancel low-cost housing construction projects, nor did it carry out a policy aimed at reducing real wages." "Política económica de la Revolución Libertadora," Instituto Torcuato di Tella, no date, p. 2.

31. E. Eshag and R. Thorp, "Economic Policies in Argentina in the Post-war Years," Oxford University, Institute of Economics and Statistics, *Bulletin* 27 (February 1965), 14.

32. Carlos Diaz Alejandro argues that INTA activities led over time to technological improvement and productivity gains in the rural sector. *Essays in the Economic History of the Argentine Republic* (New Haven: Yale University Press, 1970), pp. 190–91, 194.

83

Some of the short-term measures that were adopted, such as devaluation, did not produce the anticipated expansion of agricultural production or export earnings. This was largely the result of an adverse international situation for Argentine exports.[33] Prebisch's theory of declining terms of trade was perfectly equipped to explain the dilemma in which Argentina found itself. Prebisch, however, had failed to mention the problem of declining terms of trade in his report, and he thus failed to warn of the possibility that such a decline could cause gains in export volume to evaporate. Only Prebisch's critics, using his own theoretical framework, pointed to the terms-of-trade problem.[34] In this sense, Prebisch's ideas were influential in introducing concepts into the debate, even if they were used by his opponents to attack his policy recommendations.

Adoption of Developmentalism during the Frondizi Administration

Although the Prebisch Plan presaged some of the developmentalist policies of the Frondizi administration, developmentalism was not fully adopted in Argentina until after Frondizi took office. Frondizi was elected in only semidemocratic elections, in which the electorate was not fully informed of the economic program that the government intended to carry out. Thus, the adoption of the developmentalist program cannot be presented as the result of the demands or the decisions of the electorate.[35] A review of the Frondizi electoral speeches reveals that the desarrollistas were far from candid in sharing the specifics of their economic program with the electorate.

Although foreign investment and petroleum policy were to be the centerpieces of the Frondizi economic program, there are only a few general references to these aspects of economic policy in his campaign speeches and documents.[36] In his most pointed specific reference to

33. The international terms of trade fell rapidly during this period, and in 1957 they were 13 percent below the 1955 level, 36 percent below 1950, and 44 percent below 1948. Gerchunoff, "Política económica de la Revolución Libertadora," pp. 4, 6.

34. For example, see Jauretche, *El plan Prebisch*; and Tomas Economicus, *Radiografía del informe Prebisch* (Buenos Aires: Realidad Económica, 1955), pp. 11–12, 19.

35. Later, faced with charges that they had switched policy after they took office, the desarrollistas argued that "one cannot in good faith sustain that we did not do exactly what we said the country needed and proposed before and during the electoral campaign that brought Dr. Arturo Frondizi to the presidency." Rogelio Frigerio, written answers to interview questions, received July 15, 1985.

36. This discussion is based on a survey of all the campaign speeches and documents available at the Frondizi archives, the Centro de Estudios Nacionales. This includes the

foreign investment policy in the campaign speeches, Frondizi said, "The country needs, in many of its sectors, the contribution of foreign capital which has the announced guaranties. Naturally, we will not permit any attempt to feudalize our economy and retard our progress."[37]

But at the same time, in his campaign speeches Frondizi used a vocabulary and common to nationalist discourse in Argentina. "Our triumph will be a great step forward in the struggle against colonialist imperialism and native oligarchies who throughout the continent have always blocked national development and the fraternity of the people of the Americas."[38] This language gave the impression to many of the electorate that Frondizi would follow more nationalist policies advocated by his wing of the Radical party.

In none of these speeches or campaign documents was there ever any specific reference to a proposed policy to sign contracts with foreign firms for the exploration and exploitation of Argentine petroleum. To the contrary, Frondizi made statements that gave the impression he firmly supported the continued total monopoly of Yacimentos Petrolíferos Fiscales (YPE) over petroleum exploration and production. In his last campaign speech Frondizi said, "For us, petroleum has only one name . . . it is called Yacimentos Petrolíferos Fiscales. We will defend it and exalt it for what it is: a piece of the sovereign homeland, a guarantee of progress and liberty."[39]

In spite of this defensiveness, the tone of Frondizi's speeches was generally positive and buoyant, stressing the future, democracy, progress, and reconciliation of Argentines. Just like Juscelino Kubitschek in Brazil, Frondizi emphasized that he had carried out a "campaign of ideas, around a program of concrete achievements and effective solutions."[40]

While Frondizi was engaged in the last months of his campaign, Rogelio Frigerio traveled to Caracas to meet with Juan Perón and ne-

---

most important campaign speeches, such as the "Mensaje para veinte millones de argentinos," a radio speech on January 14, 1958; "El gobierno que el país necesita," radio speech of February 19, 1958; "Nuestro compromiso con el pueblo," the speech that closed the campaign on February 21, 1958; as well as "Mensaje a los trabajadores argentinos," radio speech of February 5, 1958; "Proposiciones para la integración del país," a press conference by Frondizi on January 28, 1958; and a series of undated campaign documents and speeches: "Un gobierno de todos los argentinos para todos los argentinos," "Una cultura de raíz popular," "Un programa de realizaciones concretas," "Desarrollo del interior de la república," "Mensaje a las familias argentinas," and "Mensaje a las mujeres argentinas."

37. Frondizi, "Mensaje para veinte millones de argentinos."
38. Frondizi, "Nuestro compromiso con el pueblo," p. 11.
39. Ibid.
40. Ibid.

gotiate a secret pact by which Perón agreed to instruct Peronists to vote for Frondizi.[41] Under electoral rules set up by the provisional military government, the Peronist party was prohibited from running candidates in the 1958 elections. It was assumed that Perón would instruct his followers to vote a blank ballot, as he had during the previous elections for a constitutional assembly in 1957.[42] With Peronism prohibited from running candidates, the Radical party could have commanded a comfortable margin over any competitor, including the blank votes, if the party had not divided. Once the Radical party divided, however, Frondizi's wing of the party, the UCRI, decided after the 1957 elections that they would not be able to defeat their former party members without the support of Peronist votes. Publicly Frondizi denied the spreading rumors of a secret electoral pact with Perón: "There are no secret pacts, no electoral alliances, nor any commitments except the one we have publicly contracted before the Argentine people."[43]

Perón's instructions calling on his followers to vote for Frondizi were sent to Buenos Aires only two weeks before the elections. The order was apparently effective: Frondizi won the election with 41.8 percent of the vote, as compared to 25.4 percent for Balbín. Blank votes accounted for only 8.8 percent of the vote, a striking decrease from the 24.5 percent in the 1957 elections.[44] This swing of Peronist blank votes to Intransigent Radical votes secured Frondizi's victory.

Whatever the specific content of the pact, its existence cast a shadow over the Frondizi administration from the moment he took office. Winning an election that excluded one of Argentina's parties eroded Frondizi's legitimacy. But the secret pact undermined his legitimacy with both Peronists and anti-Peronists. When Frondizi failed to legalize the activities of the Peronist party, the Peronists felt that they had been betrayed. At the same time, as news of the pact surfaced, anti-Peronists

41. According to historian Robert Potash, it is already an accepted fact that Rogelio Frigerio and Juan Perón negotiated an agreement before the February 1958 election. *El ejército y la política en la Argentina 1945–1962* (Buenos Aires: Editorial Sudamericana, 1984), p. 359. Indeed, in recent interviews, even Frigerio and Frondizi have abandoned their ritualistic negation that the pact ever existed. "There is no doubt that the agreement with Perón existed. Essentially the so-called pact was a political alliance for the conjuncture that the country confronted." Arturo Frondizi, in Alberto A. Amato, *Cuando fuimos gobierno: Conversaciones con Arturo Frondizi y Rogelio Frigerio* (Buenos Aires: Editorial Paidos, 1983), p. 31.

42. In the 1957 elections 24.5 percent of the voters had complied and turned in blank ballots, 23.2 percent had voted for the Unión Cívica Radical Popular (UCRP), and only 21.2 percent had voted for Frondizi's Unión Cívica Radical Intransigente (UCRI). Peter Snow, *Political Forces in Argentina* (Boston: Allyn and Bacon, 1971), p. 29.

43. Frondizi, "Nuestro compromiso con el pueblo."

44. Snow, *Political Forces in Argentina*, p. 29.

denounced Frondizi for having negotiated with a man they considered the source of all of Argentina's problems. The pact, necessary for Frondizi's election, served to exacerbate hostility and fatally weaken the government before it could even begin to implement its program.

Origins of the Frondizi Economic Program

Apparently neither the Prebisch Plan nor the CEPAL study was used by the desarrollistas to design their policies. The study that Prebisch had urged Lonardi to invite CEPAL to undertake was turned over to the newly elected Frondizi government.[45] Frigerio claims that "this CEPAL report didn't have any influence on the policies we applied. I didn't even remember that a report of this origin had been presented to Dr. Frondizi. Surely it was an attempt of monetarism to influence the government."[46]

Why did a study of this size and scope, produced by a large and prestigious team, have so little impact on policy making? In Brazil during the same period a joint CEPAL–National Development Bank study is often credited with serving as one of the bases of the Kubitschek government's Targets Program. As with all studies by international organizations, the impact of the report rested on the degree to which it influenced policy makers in key positions in the Argentine government. After Frondizi's victory, Argentine government counterparts to the CEPAL team were removed from office and with them the "institutional memory" of the accomplishments and recommendations of the CEPAL study. The lack of continuity of personnel within the Argentine state meant that previous experience was not incorporated into the economic policy program of the Frondizi government.

Based on the anti–Prebisch Plan position adopted by *Qué* magazine, we would not expect the Prebisch program to have exerted much influence on the Frondizi economic program. The Prebisch Plan, however, contained many similarities with the policies the desarrollistas advo-

---

45. The CEPAL team that came to Argentina was an impressive assembly of CEPAL skill and new Argentine talent. This group produced the most extensive study of the Argentine economy that had ever been made. The three-volume report served as a model for other CEPAL country studies and a gold mine of statistics for academics. Using the projection technique then being introduced at CEPAL, it refrained from actual recommendations, but rather projected outcomes based on hypothesized levels of investment and growth. Implicit recommendations, however, abounded, in favor of expanded investment in basic industries, infrastructure, and transportation, along a classic CEPAL line.

46. Rogelio Frigerio, written responses to interview questions, received July 15, 1985, p. 11.

cated, and even more similarities with the policies they adopted while in government. In many important areas, the Frondizi policy was more similar to the Prebisch Plan than to the policies advocated by Frondizi's party only two years earlier. A striking similarity existed in the emphasis on the need to expand petroleum production in order to decrease foreign exchange bottlenecks, their concentration on creating and expanding basic industries, and their promotion of technical advances in the rural sector.[47]

To stress the similarities between the economic programs is not to suggest that the Frondizi-Frigerio program directly "borrowed" from the earlier plan. To the contrary, Frigerio vehemently denied that CEPALian ideas, which he portrayed as monetarist, commercialist, and voluntarist, had any influence on the desarrollistas' program.[48] Since Frigerio's analysis is based on a notion of declining terms of trade which was clearly derived directly or indirectly from Prebisch, one cannot blindly accept the desarrollistas' claim that CEPAL and Prebisch had no influence on their thinking. But developmentalist ideas were "in the air" in Argentina at this time. As one person put it, "We were all developmentalists then."[49] Prebisch himself argued, "These were ideas that were emerging in Latin America. CEPAL's merit was to demonstrate that theoretically they were correct. So I am very careful about saying, 'This is due to the influence of CEPAL.'"[50]

Other divisions of what could be called the potential developmental-

47. Important differences also existed between the Prebisch Plan and the Frondizi-Frigerio program. Whereas Prebisch emphasized the need to increase agricultural production and secure more balanced development of the industrial and agricultural sectors, the Frondizi-Frigerio program stressed the channeling of investment into basic industry. During the Frondizi government, the policies toward foreign investment were more favorable than those recommended by either the Prebisch Plan or by CEPAL and Prebisch in general.

Another policy difference between Prebisch and the desarrollistas evolved around the issue of regional integration. By the mid-1950s, CEPAL and Prebisch were advocating regional integration as a means of overcoming the limits of small domestic markets. Frondizi and Frigerio, on the other hand, argued for more extensive "national integration" as a prior step to regional efforts.

48. "CEPAL's ideas didn't have any influence on our formation. . . . CEPAL's propositions ignore the modifications necessary in the productive structures of underdeveloped countries, and fall into voluntarist exhortations and commercialist formulas that do not modify the terms of trade, and thus, do not impede the perpetuation of underdevelopment." Frigerio, written responses to interview questions, received July 15, 1985.

49. Interview with Alberto Petrecolla, Buenos Aires, July 2, 1985.

50. Interview with Raúl Prebisch, Buenos Aires, October 23, 1985. The level of actual diffusion of CEPALian ideas was minimal before 1956; CEPAL did not run its first course in Argentina until 1958 and developmentalist ideas were not being taught at the

ist coalition, such as the division of the Radical party in 1957 and internal fractures within the Frondizistas, further reduced the potential influence of CEPAL and Prebisch on economic policy under Frondizi. Within the Frondizi wing of the Radical party, a group of young economists connected to Aldo Ferrer were most closely indentified with CEPAL's ideas. But once in office, Ferrer's team was excluded from the federal government, perhaps because its members were not disciples of Frigerio. Ferrer became provincial minister of economics for the Province of Buenos Aires, where he formed an innovative Planning Council. The "exile" of CEPALinos to the Province of Buenos Aires limited the arenas for the direct influence of CEPALian ideas.[51] The individuals who stayed to work with the economic policy of the Frondizi administration were either those associated with Frigerio and *Qué*, and thus either hostile or indifferent to CEPAL and Prebisch, or other Radical and independent economists without extensive exposure to CEPAL's ideas. Later, to win confidence from military and industrial circles, Frondizi invited noted liberal economists to join the government.

IMPLEMENTATION OF DEVELOPMENTALISM DURING THE FRONDIZI ADMINISTRATION

The Frondizi administration can be divided into three stages. The first, from May 1958 to June 1959, was the period when the government adopted the bulk of its new policies. The second, from June 1959 to April 1961, was a period of retrenchment, when monetary and political stabilization were top priorities. During a third period, from May to March 1961, the government took some new developmentalist initiatives, but political instability overshadowed all other activities, until the government was overthrown by a military coup on March 29, 1962.[52]

---

economics school at the university. Contact between desarrollistas and CEPALinos was scarce prior to 1956 and largely conflictual after that.

51. The Planning Council undertook an ambitious program of study and reform, focusing on an area within their jurisdiction, taxation of land in the province. The early articles discussing agrarian reform and land tax reform by the Planning Council were published in a journal that formed the initial volumes of *Desarrollo económico*, one of the most prominent journals in Latin America and a forum for CEPALian ideas. After the Planning Council was disbanded, a number of its members went to work for CEPAL in Santiago.

52. Marcelo Luis Acuña, *De Frondizi a Alfonsin: La tradición política del radicalismo 1* (Buenos Aires: Centro Editor de América Latina, 1984), p. 115.

*Stage 1. May 1958–June 1959: The Developmentalist
Program*

The first year of the Frondizi presidency was beset by military crises, civilian protests, and labor unrest. Political turmoil complicated the implementation of the desarrollista economic program. The government's severest critics were its former Radical colleagues who had broken off to form the UCRP. The UCRP took up a position of unrelenting opposition almost from the day Frondizi took office.[53]

Nevertheless, the first year of the Frondizi administration was the most fecund; during this period the greatest number of new government initiatives were introduced and the government took an offensive, rather than a defensive, position. Frondizi was still surrounded by his closest advisers, especially Rogelio Frigerio, who occupied the key position of special secretary for economic and social relations of the presidency.

The Frondizi administration never made public any formal plan or even a listing of quantitative targets similar to the Targets Program in Brazil. Nor did a planning institution exist in Argentina during this period to draw up such a plan.[54] Still, it is possible to establish the government's economic and industrial priorities from Frondizi's speeches and the government policy. The main priority in this first period was to rapidly expand investment in key industrial areas. To pursue this goal, the government engaged in negotiations with foreign petroleum companies to sign risk contracts to explore and exploit Argentine petroleum reserves, cleared up a series of long-standing investment disputes with foreign companies in order to project its intention to provide a good investment climate, passed a new foreign investment law to clearly define investment policy, and set up an executive committee to review and make recommendations on investment requests.

The political strategy designed by Frigerio for this first stage was based on the military analogy of engaging in battle on all fronts simultaneously. By this Frigerio meant that the government should initiate as many of its programs as possible at the same time. Aware that many of the new programs would provoke strong opposition, by initiating many simultaneously he hoped that opposition forces would cancel one

53. Frondizi took office on May 1, 1958. By May 12 the UCRP had published a document of severe criticism of the government. By July 1, the UCRP had already begun secretly to discuss its support for an impending military coup.

54. The ministerial reform law passed shortly after Frondizi came to power called for the executive to create an organism for study and planning of national development, but such an organism was not created until three years later, under pressure from the Alliance for Progress.

another out, since different oppositional alliances would form around different issues. This strategy was based on the assumption that the policies the government intended to implement would be controversial, and the alliance that brought the government to power was rapidly disintegrating and could not be counted on to provide support for government initiatives.[55] Since the desarrollistas believed that the primary way to expand support for their program was to begin to produce concrete results, it followed that they needed to implement the new policies as rapidly as possible, regardless of domestic opposition. Once the policies produced positive results, new space and time could be won. The centerpiece of the "all-fronts" strategy was the new petroleum policy, which was part of a more general policy on foreign investment.

Foreign investment. The government, well aware of new, more favorable trends in international capital flow, hoped to attract large amounts of public and private investment from U.S. and European sources.[56] One of the first priorities of the Frondizi administration was to create a stable environment and clear rules for foreign investors.[57] In late 1958, the Congress passed a new law governing foreign investment, which provided a legal framework for treatment of private foreign investment fundamentally on an equal footing with domestic investment. Under this law, the government offered special incentives for investments in basic industrial activities which directly or indirectly contributed to substitution of imports, expansion of exports, and the rational and balanced development of the Argentine economy. In order to obtain these benefits, foreign investment proposals had to be submitted in advance to the Argentine authorities and approved. Once approved, the inves-

55. See, for example, Arturo Sábato, *Historia de los contratos petroleros* (Buenos Aires: Cogtal, 1963), pp. 10–11.
56. Presidencia de la República, Secretaria de Relaciones Económico-Sociales, "Tendencia de los corrientes de capital en los últimos años," no date (probably 1958), pp. 1–3.
57. Before taking office members of the Frondizi government had received suggestions from a number of sources on the types of measures necessary for creating improved conditions and opportunities for domestic and foreign investors. These suggestions stressed the need for a stable political environment and clearly defined rules governing the incorporation of foreign investment. One document, "Sugestiones para una política de industrialización del país," produced by Concord, Sociedad Anónima Industrial Comercial and dated 15 January 1958, from the Frondizi archives files on foreign investment, offered the following general guidelines: "General guarantees and conditions: 1) Stability of the political order; 2) Existence of a clearly delineated industrial policy; 3) Irremovability of the norms that govern foreign capital investments; 4) Prior authorization of foreign capital investments; 5) Abandonment of all policy orientation that, in whatever form, advocates economic nationalism. There is no way more certain to distance foreign capital than to preach, or allow the preaching of economic nationalism, which always threatens, even if only potentially, nationalization or expropriation of foreign firms located in the country."

tors were guaranteed that they would be able to transfer profits abroad through the free exchange market and repatriate capital without limitations, although preference was given to investors who reinvested profits in Argentina. In addition, authorities could grant other incentives such as reduced or eliminated customs duties, import charges or other taxes, preferential credit treatment, or protection through import duties and charges.[58]

At the same time, Congress passed the Industrial Promotion Law, enabling legislation that established guidelines for the promotion and encouragement of both foreign and domestic private investment.[59] The Industrial Promotion Law was designed to benefit primarily domestic industry. While the government enacted implementing regulations immediately for the foreign investment law, it did not pass similar regulations for the Industrial Promotion Law, leaving it in a kind of juridical limbo. Small and medium-sized national industrialists interpreted the government's failure to implement the Industrial Promotion Law as evidence of bias in favor of international investors.[60]

These laws gave the executive broad power to extend incentives, or to decide whether to extend incentives at all. The Frondizi government interpreted them liberally and encouraged the installation of a variety of industrial projects. A document by a U.S. consulting firm on foreign investment possibilities in Argentina gave a glowing account of the government's attitude toward business.

> By word and deed, Argentine governments since 1955 have indicated a positive attitude toward private foreign investment in the country. More than that, specific steps have been taken to provide incentives for the attraction of foreign investors. . . . Against this background, it is clear that the government sincerely and actively believes in the desirability of a large volume and number of private foreign investments in Argentina, so that the supplementary injection of technological, managerial, and capital

58. Foreign Capital Investment Law 14.780, ratified December 4, 1958, *Leyes nacionales, año 1958* (Buenos Aires: Imprenta del Congreso de la Nación, 1959), pp. 241–46.

59. In order to qualify for special incentives, industrial projects had to contribute one or more of the following: (1) the equilibrium of the international balance of payments; (2) the full utilization of the present and potential resources of the country; (3) the decentralization of industry; (4) the improvement, expansion, and diversification of industrial production; (5) the promotion of improved technology in manufacturing; and (6) the requirements of national defense and of public health and security. Second, the law enumerated the types of incentives that the executive was authorized to offer to industrial projects that met the above criteria. These included exemption of duties, customs, and taxes; preferential exchange and supply treatment; as well as the possibility of limiting the import or imposing duties on imported products that competed with the locally produced products. Industrial Promotion Law 14.781.

60. "Vale la pena ser industrial?" *La razon*, December 13, 1960.

resources from abroad can aid the process of industrial growth in the country.[61]

Among the attempts to improve the general environment for private investment, the Frondizi government took measures to resolve some long-standing foreign investment disputes. In a controversial decision, Frondizi reversed his earlier position in favor of nationalization of a private electric company, Compañía Argentina de Electricidad (CADE), and organized the formation of a mixed enterprise between CADE and the state, on favorable terms to the private company. Frondizi was eager to resolve CADE's legal status in order to expand electrical production in Buenos Aires.[62] The Frondizi government also privatized a group of enterprises confiscated during the Second World War which had been operated by a department of the Industry Secretariat (DINIE).

To make decisions about which foreign investment projects to offer incentives to, the Frondizi administration set up the National Commission on Foreign Investment as part of the Secretariat for Socioeconomic Relations of the Presidency. Although the commission saw the encouragement of foreign investment as its fundamental task, it was not indiscriminate in approving investment projects.[63] Among the top priorities of the commission were investments in the automobile industry, petrochemicals, paper, and transportation. The encouragement of the automobile industry was one of the basic components of the Frondizi-Frigerio development plan.[64] The rules governing the installation of automobile plants in Argentina were similar to those set forth in Brazil two years earlier. According to one Argentine policy

61. Henry W. Laurant, *Factors Affecting Foreign Investment in Argentina*, Investment Series 5 (Menlo Park: Stanford Research Institute, International Development Center 1963), p. 27.

62. The checkered history of CADE is traced in Miguel Angel Scenna, "CADE: El escándalo del siglo," *Todo Es Historia* (August 1971). Although the intricacies are difficult to follow, the issue raised nationalist sentiment, and many felt the Frondizi "compromise" was a sellout of national interests. For the nationalist position, see Jorge del Rio *Electricidad y liberación nacional: El caso SEGBA* (Buenos Aires: A. Peña Lillo Editor, 1960).

63. A review of a few of the projects denied approval shows that the commission was guided by some of the criteria set out in the foreign investment and industrial promotion laws. For example, a proposal by the Haim Company to produce plastic products was rejected because it would not manufacture basic inputs in Argentina but only make consumer items with imported inputs, and thus brought no technical benefits or savings of foreign exchange. "Memoradum para informacion del S.E. el Excmo. Señor de la Nación, Dr. Arturo Frondizi, producido por el Señor Presidente de la Comisión Asesora de Inversiones Extranjeras, Dr. Nestor Grancelli Chá, October 2, 1958." Frondizi archives.

64. The policies for the promotion of the automobile are outlined in Decree 3693, starting point for the Argentine Automobile Industry Promotion Regime.

maker, this was the one area where Brazilian policy served as a clear inspiration for Argentine developmentalists.[65]

"The battle for petroleum." Arturo Frondizi built up his political image as a political leader and nationalist intellectual with the 1954 publication of his book *Petroleum and Politics*, a historical defense of the national oil monopoly. Thus, it was a surprise to his enemies as well as many of his supporters when, once in office, he adopted a new policy of signing contracts with foreign oil companies for exploration and exploitation of Argentine petroleum. The ambitious goal of the Frondizi administration was to achieve self-sufficiency in petroleum production by the end of the term. To achieve this goal, the government sent a bill to Congress which nationalized Argentine petroleum wealth and made the YPF responsible for purchase and sale of all petroleum, but allowed risk contracts with foreign firms for the exploration and exploitation of petroleum fields, the production of which would then be sold to YPF at prenegotiated prices.

Sometime in late 1957 or early 1958 Frondizi and Frigerio had altered their position on petroleum policy.[66] This change of position may have been a result of their analysis of the failures of previous economic policy, including the Prebisch Plan, to expand export earnings and thus provide adequate funds for industrial expansion. This fueled the belief that the capital accumulation process could not continue without major foreign assistance, since export expansion had apparently run up against structural limits that could be only slowly overcome.[67] It seems likely that this lesson was responsible for the turnaround of Frondizi and Frigerio on the increased need for foreign investment, including in the petroleum sector. They were worried, as Prebisch had been, by the percentage of the import bill accounted for by petroleum, in a country with large potential capacity to produce petroleum domestically.[68] Al-

65. Interview with Roberto Aleman, Buenos Aires, July 29, 1985.

66. According to Arturo Sábato, a change in policy came between the election and the assumption of power. As Frondizi and Frigerio undertook the traditional visits to the ministries, they apparently decided to switch the number-one priority of their economic program from steel to petroleum. They came to believe that it would be necessary to work even more rapidly than they had previously assumed, and an increase in petroleum production offered a faster way to reverse the balance-of-payments deficit. Sábato, *Historia de los contratos petroleros*, pp. 9–10.

67. Gerchunoff, "Política económica de la Revolución Libertadora," p. 37.

68. Frondizi justified his change of position on the state petroleum monopoly for the following reasons: "When I took office, I encountered a reality that did not correspond to that theoretical position [that of *Petróleo y política*] for two reasons. First, because the state did not have the necessary resources to exploit our petroleum by itself; second, because the immediate, urgent necessity to substitute our fuel imports did not leave any

though Frondizi got advice from foreigners connected with the petroleum companies,[69] the change in his petroleum policy must be seen as a result of evolving ideas of the president and his top advisers rather than of a succumbing to foreign pressures.

Immediately upon assuming the presidency, Frondizi instructed Rogelio Frigerio and Arturo Sábato, as his personal representative in charge of YPF, to begin negotiating contracts with foreign firms for the exploration and exploitation of Argentine petroleum. Because they were so controversial, the initial negotiations were carried out secretly. It was not until the first contracts had been signed that Frondizi made a speech on July 24, 1958, announcing the new petroleum policy to the public.

This new policy set off a storm of protest from within the president's party, as well as from outsiders. Frondizi was accused of being an *entreguista*—of selling out to foreign interests. Large protests were arranged by the newly formed Movement for the Defense of Argentine Petroleum. YPF workers declared a strike in protest against the contracts. The president denounced the strike as insurrectional and declared a state of siege.[70] As a result of his petroleum policy, adopted in the early months of the administration, Frondizi lost much of his initial support from the Left as well as from nationalist groups in his own party and in the military. Nationalists also opposed Frondizi's favorable policy toward foreign investment and what were perceived as concessions to foreign interests.

In addition to lost nationalist support, the petroleum policy created a difficult political image for the Frondizi administration. Although the desarrollistas claimed that they had openly described their policies during the campaign, the general political impression of people both inside and outside the party was that Frondizi had misled, even lied to, his followers on his positions on petroleum and investment. This impression created a sense of disillusionment, a profound bitterness, and an

---

margin of time for the government to pull together technical and financial resources." Arturo Frondizi, *Petróleo y nación* (Buenos Aires: Transición, 1963), p. 8.

69. Henry Holland, former assistant secretary of state for interamerican affairs, and then representative of various U.S. petroleum firms, prepared a draft text for Frondizi of a speech outlining a more positive policy toward foreign investment and a list of suggestions to encourage international investment, in April 1958, before Frondizi took office. "Sugerencias para un programa para fomentar inversiones internacionales," from the private archive of Nicolas Babini.

70. Arturo Frondizi, "Libertad, democracia y orden," radio and television speech, November 9, 1958. In *Mensajes presidenciales, 1958–1962*, Vol. 1: 1958 (Buenos Aires: Ediciones Centro de Estudios Nacionales, 1978), pp. 207–14.

aura of deception that colored much of the rest of the Frondizi admin-istration. For his party and for some men who had worked closely with him, the ideological transformation and the new association with Fri-gerio was seen as a betrayal, both politically and personally.[71]

The government was increasingly besieged. In response to vocal criti-cism of "parallel government," aimed at him, Frigerio resigned as the secretary for Socioeconomic Relations of the Presidency. He continued to serve, however, as Frondizi's closest personal adviser. Vice-president Alejandro Gomez, insulated from policy decisions and strenuously op-posed to the government's petroleum policy, called for formation of a coalition government to meet the crisis. Frondizi and his loyalists ac-cused Gomez of conspiring with the opposition to encourage a military coup and forced him to resign.

On the economic front, the situation was also discouraging. The bal-ance-of-payments situation continued to worsen. By late 1958 the gov-ernment decided to take strong measures to deal with this problem by adopting a stabilization program recommended by the International Monetary Fund.

Stabilization program. Some authors consider the stabilization plan to be the antithesis of the Frondizi development program and thus see the adoption of this plan as the act of a government giving up its ideals to implement a pragmatic policy under pressure from international lend-ing agencies. Indeed, as with much of the Frondizi program, the stabi-lization plan ran counter to the ideas Frondizi supported before 1958. It was not, however, in direct conflict with the basic outline of the de-velopment program that Frondizi and Frigerio adopted once in office.

The centerpiece of the development program was a massive increase in investment in basic industry and energy, primarily from private for-eign sources. Many of the early policies of the Frondizi government were designed to facilitate this policy by increasing investor confidence in the Argentine economy and government. In this sense, the stabiliza-tion plan can be seen as a continuation of these policies to increase

---

71. "Imagine, you have followed a man with a certain conduct and set of ideas, hear him say these ideas, repeat them, fight for them, win a position in the party for these ideas, and just before he arrives at the presidency, you find that he's talking in a different language. Sometimes I give a somewhat crude example of a betrayed wife. You've lived all your life with someone, and all of a sudden you discover that this man, your husband, has a second home. For us, it was a surprise of this type. Everyone asked me, what happened? Not just that he had changed, but how had he gone off with this guy?" Inter-view with Nicolas Babini, Buenos Aires, July 15, 1985. One of the most bitter attacks on the Frondizi petroleum policy was written by his vice-president, Alejandro Gomez, after he was forced to resign. See Gomez, *Política de entrega* (Buenos Aires: A. Peña Lillo, 1963).

investor confidence.[72] By attacking inflation and the public deficit, and by remedying the balance-of-payments crisis, the stabilization plan, if successful, would enhance Argentina's reputation and attract both foreign and domestic investors. An IMF-sponsored plan, while stringent, offered added guarantees for foreign investors and improved Argentina's chance of attracting additional loans and financing as well as foreign investment.

There is no indication that Frondizi and Frigerio saw the stabilization plan as incompatible with their development objectives, although they understood that it would be politically unpopular. It was only later, after Frigerio had resigned and the new economics minister, Alvaro Alsogaray, began implementing the stabilization plan while deemphasizing aspects of the development plan, that a conflict arose between the two goals of development and stabilization. Until that time, the stabilization plan was seen as short-term medicine that the economy needed to attract investment and resume rapid growth.

Initial negotiations with the IMF began shortly after Frondizi took office. An IMF delegation visited Buenos Aires in July 1958 and filed a report with the government recommending a number of changes in economic policy.[73] The Argentine government argued that the IMF had failed to recognize that the initial economic measures adopted by the Frondizi administration were short-term emergency efforts that should be viewed in the context of a broader development program, which included policies designed to correct long-range disequilibria in the balance of payments and in the economy. "The Argentine government is very conscious of the serious short-term problems that the country must confront. And it is convinced that these problems will not be solved unless progress is made in the area of the fundamental solutions that make up the economic policy plan of the Argentine government."[74] Even as the Frondizi government negotiated with the IMF for the adoption of short-term stabilization measures, it continued to es-

72. A similar argument is made by Alberto Petrecolla in "Desarrollo desequilibrado, 1958–1962," Instituto Torcuato Di Tella, Argentina, May 4, 1984. Petrecolla suggests that the stabilization plan was a component of the larger Frondizi-Frigerio development plan, and that both plans form an inseparable whole and were viewed as such by the main protagonists (pp. 1–2).

73. Banco Central de la República Argentina, Gerencia de Investigaciones Económicas, "Informe de consultas de 1958 del Fondo Monetario Internacional. Síntesis de las recomendaciones," September 4, 1958, from the private archive of Nestor Grancelli Chá.

74. Banco Central de la República Argentina, Gerencia General, memoradum no. 003/68, September 8, 1958, "Proyecto de contestación," addressed to Señor Director Ejecutivo del Fondo Monetario Internacional, Doctor Rodolfo Corominas Segura, pp. 4–5, from the private archive of Nestor Grancelli Chá.

pouse a structuralist approach to inflation, which saw the roots of infla-tion in long-range disequilibria in the economy.

The draft response outlined the government's goals:

> The economic policy of the current Argentine government is clear. The government is resolved to promote orderly economic development with-out inflation. The fundamental goal is to expand investment, mainly pri-vate, in the basic sectors of the Argentine economy. This will help pro-mote the harmonious expansion of agriculture and industry and remedy the balance of payments, whose intrinsic weakness is one of the most serious factors limiting the growth and the internal and external stability of the country's economy.[75]

Argentina eventually reached an agreement with the IMF in Decem-ber 1958, and President Frondizi announced the new stabilization plan on December 31 of that year. It was a fairly classic IMF stabilization plan, under which the double exchange system was unified into a single exchange rate. Export surcharges were instituted for agricultural goods, however, and import charges remained to protect national in-dustry. Certain items carried an import charge of up to 300 percent. The government adopted a program to eliminate the fiscal deficit, in-cluding personnel reductions and an increase in public utilities fees to make up for the losses suffered by public enterprises. Internal price controls were gradually eliminated.[76] The result of the policy was a drastic reduction in real wage levels.

The stabilization plan had the desired international effect of increas-ing the available credit for Argentine industrial development.

> Broad monetary support was obtained, and the total amount of credits obtained in December 1958 reached $328.5 million, of which $125 mil-lion was for long-term development loans. But this was not the only ex-ternal collaboration secured, since as a result of the general agreement, international confidence in the Argentine economy was reborn and thus private and official banks and institutions and industries had their possi-bilities of obtaining foreign credit increased substantially, which permit-ted the extraordinary capitalization which took place in the years 1959, 1960, and 1961.[77]

75. Ibid., p. 2.
76. Nestor Grancelli Chá, "El Fondo Monetario International y los convenios con La República Argentina," informe para el Centro de Estudios Nacionales, from the private archive of Nestor Grancelli Chá, no date, p. 6.
77. Ibid., p. 7.

Stage 2. June 1959–April 1961

This second stage of the Frondizi program, corresponding to the tenure of Alvaro Alsogaray as minister of economics, is characterized by an attempt at political and economic stabilization. Alsogaray was not a desarrollista or even a developmentalist, broadly defined. He was active in a small conservative political party and was a strong supporter of free enterprise and free trade. Alsogaray, an aeronautical engineer, had a close relationship with the Argentine military, having taught at the Army Superior Technical College, the Navy Superior College, and the National War College. Alsogaray had served as a second lieutenant in the army, and his brother, Julio Alsogaray, was a general. During the government of the Liberating Revolution, he had served as the minister of industry.[78]

At a time when the government was besieged by opposition, Frondizi chose Alsogaray as his minister of economics and minister of labor in the hope that his presence would reassure key elements of the military and the business community. In late March and early April 1959 the Frondizi government confronted a military crisis that Potash called "concrete plans for a military coup, instead of just salon conversations."[79] The *golpistas* were made up of a hard-line group of military and civilian anti-Peronists and anti-Communists, who accused the government of opening the doors to Communist penetration. Loyalists urged Frondizi to try to improve the public image of his government. The government began to take a more anti-Communist position to pacify the opposition. A number of public officials associated with Rogelio Frigerio were replaced, and in May Frigerio resigned as personal adviser to the president, although he continued to make secret visits to advise the president.

To complicate the situation, in early June representatives of Juan Perón distributed photocopies of the text of the secret pact between Perón, Frondizi, and Frigerio. Although Frondizi categorically denied that he had ever signed such an agreement, the episode heightened the governmental crisis. Frondizi decided to use a dramatic change in his cabinet to improve the government's image. Frigerio approved of the appointment, since he felt that Alsogaray was the person to carry out the stabilization plan that had been announced in December 1958.

78. Juan Carlos de Pablo, *Los economistas y la economía Argentina* (Buenos Aires: Ediciones Macchi, 1977), p. 33.
79. Potash, *El ejército y la política en la Argentina*, p. 406.

Frigerio and Frondizi also believed that Alsogaray would support and continue the developmentalist policies.

Alsogaray's appointment did placate some of the opposition. He brought in an entirely new economic team, replacing top-level people in the economics and labor ministries as well as in the official banks. But while Alsogaray pursued the stabilization program energetically, he did not support the government's developmentalist policies and often worked to undermine policies with which he disagreed. In particular, Alsogaray did not support a number of large infrastructural and mining projects considered essential by the desarrollistas. Frondizi was caught in a bind. He could not remove Alsogaray without provoking the opposition, but he was conscious that his economics minister had accumulated much power and was distorting the desarrollistas' economic program. Frondizi hoped to blame Alsogaray for the harsh and politically unpopular stabilization program, while disassociating himself to preserve his image. Later, with both economy and polity stabilized, Alsogaray could be discarded and the developmentalist experiment continued on a more stable base.[80]

Although Frigerio had originally approved the appointment of Alsogaray as minister of economics, when it became clear that Alsogaray was not implementing the development program as he had promised, Frigerio wrote various public attacks on the minister, apparently with Frondizi's knowledge and approval.[81] Thus the desarrollistas were caught in the peculiar situation of being out of control in their own government, forced to criticize it publicly from the outside. This situation could not continue indefinitely.

Although Alsogaray's appointment had somewhat placated the opposition, military unrest continued. One crisis followed another, as Frondizi continued to shuffle his military secretaries in an attempt to find a team that was loyal to him and could maintain discipline in their branches. The most open affront to Frondizi's authority came in September 1959, when his secretary of the army removed General Carlos Toranzo Montero as commander in chief of the army. Toranzo Montero holed up in the Army Mechanical School in defiance of the government. Frondizi attempted a negotiated solution to the crisis and eventually agreed to reinstate Toranzo Montero as commander in chief and to remove the loyalist army secretary. Although this arrangement restored peace, it undermined Frondizi's future relationship with loyal

80. Wynia, *Argentina in the Postwar Era*, p. 96.

81. Isidro Odena, *Libertadores y desarrollistas* (Buenos Aires: Ediciones La Bastillo, 1984), p. 165.

sectors of the military, because he had essentially rewarded a successful defiance of his authority and punished a loyalist follower in the military.[82]

By this time, Frondizi had lost most of his support in the armed forces. Nationalists in the military opposed Frondizi because they objected to his oil policy. Anti-Peronists in the military distrusted him as a result of the pact with Perón. One military figure who was a junior officer at the time claimed that an official who appeared to be sympathetic to Frondizi always ran the risk of appearing to support or accept the pact between Frigerio and Perón.[83] Frondizi's last bastion of support in the military consisted of the legalists, who supported him not because they agreed with his policies but because he was the constitutionally elected president. After his handling of the Toranzo Montero episode, much of his support in the legalist group evaporated.

Frondizi's authority and control continued to erode. By late 1959 he was saddled with a minister of economics and a secretary and commander in chief of the army not of his own choice, who had significant autonomous power. Toranzo Montero continued to use his position to try to instigate opposition to Frondizi among the military. It was not until after another military crisis, in March 1961, that Toranzo Montero's position in the military was weakened and he resigned. With his military flank protected, Frondizi felt sufficiently strengthened to request the resignation of Alsogaray and once again take charge of his government.

Stage 3. The Beginning of the End

Frondizi named Roberto Aleman to succeed Alsogaray as minister of economics. Aleman, like Alsogaray, was not a desarrollista, but he was more willing to follow Frondizi's directives on economic policy. Aleman, a professional economist, was one of the few individuals who held an important position in both the Frondizi government and the government of the Liberating Revolution. He is also one of the few economic policy makers who held a position in government throughout most of the Frondizi administration, serving first as adviser to the minister of economics, then as subsecretary of economics, adviser to the secretary of finance, financial adviser in the United States, and then as minister of economics.[84]

---

82. Potash, *El ejército y la política en la Argentina*, pp. 425–26.
83. Interview with General Isaias J. Garcia Enciso, Buenos Aires, November 7, 1985.
84. Juan Carlos de Pablo, *Los economistas*, p. 9.

During Aleman's tenure as minister of economics, developmentalist policy once again came to the forefront. The government signed a number of new petroleum contracts. Because of past public outcry, the negotiations were handled through public biddings rather than through private negotiations. In addition, new executive decrees were issued to implement the Industrial Promotion Law for specific sectors.[85]

During this period Frondizi also engaged more actively in foreign policy. Military concern heightened in August 1961 when Frondizi held a secret meeting in Buenos Aires with Ernesto "Ché" Guevara, who had attended the Inter-American Social and Economic Council meeting in Punta del Este, Uruguay. Frondizi's penchant for secrecy turned a relatively minor four-hour meeting into a national military crisis. It was particularly disconcerting for Frondizi's military secretaries, who had not been previously informed of the meeting.[86] Military unrest over the Guevara meeting was exacerbated when Argentina joined Brazil, Mexico, Chile, Bolivia, and Ecuador in abstaining on a vote to exclude Cuba from the OAS in the Foreign Ministers' Consultation in January 1962. The vote, consistent with a long Argentine tradition of independence from the United States in regional bodies, provoked yet another crisis in the military. Under strong pressure, Frondizi eventually agreed to break off diplomatic relations with Cuba.

Although these issues weakened the government's strength, it was the Peronist victory in gubernatorial and legislative elections held in March 1962 that finally led to the military coup. Frondizi had decided to permit the Peronists to present their own candidates in the elections, apparently because he believed his party was capable of defeating the Peronist candidates in key races. Faced, however, with a Peronist victory in ten of the fourteen provinces, including the politically key Province of Buenos Aires, Frondizi intervened and called for new elections, thus annulling the results of the March elections. But even this move was not sufficient to head off the impending military coup. By this time Frondizi's government had lost much of its organized civilian

85. During this period, the executives issued decrees extending investment benefits to private companies installing new steel-making capacity, establishing or expanding basic petrochemical plants, installing plants for the production of cellulose, paper, and cardboard, and to companies installing or expanding industrial plants in Patagonia and northwest Argentina. These regimes gave the investor certain benefits such as tax postponement or permission to import duty free the machinery they needed which was not produced in the country. Although these regimes led to investment in the priority areas, Aleman believes that for the investor the expanding market and the climate of stability were more important than the actual benefits received from the executive decrees. Interview with Roberto Aleman, Buenos Aires, July 29, 1985.

86. Potash, *El ejército y la política en la Argentina*, p. 454.

support, although his party had not done disastrously in the elections. His few remaining supporters among the military were not prepared to fight to defend the president. On March 29, 1962, Frondizi was arrested and imprisoned on the island of Martín García in the Rio de la Plata.

The transitional government of José María Guido stayed in office for over a year before holding elections. The Peronists were not allowed to participate, and Frondizi was still imprisoned, so victory went to UCRP candidate Arturo Illía, with only 26 percent of the vote. One of the first moves of the new government was to cancel the oil contracts that Frondizi had signed with foreign oil companies. To direct his new economic policy, Illía brought in a team of Radical party economists to the National Development Council (CONADE), the planning agency set up late in the Frondizi administration. A number of these economists had been trained by CEPAL, or drew their inspiration from CEPALian ideas.[87] They began to write a five-year development plan, which was completed in 1965 and was beginning to be implemented when Illía was overthrown in mid-1966. None of the members of the Frondizi desarrollista team was asked to work on the Illía economic program, and the desarrollistas were bitter opponents of the new government's policies. Frondizi advocated and supported the military coup against the Illía government. After the experience of his administration, Frondizi had begun to believe that it was almost impossible to reconcile development and democracy, concluding that only a more authoritarian government could undertake the developmentalist economic program.[88]

The new military government led by General Juan Carlos Onganía undertook an economic program that in some ways attempted to complete the industrialization program initiated by Frondizi with the help of foreign capital. If, however, Frondizi and his desarrollistas had hoped that they would provide the brain behind the brawn of the military government, they were mistaken. The desarrollistas were not invited to hold important positions in the military government headed by Onganía.

The Results of the Frondizi Economic Program

It is difficult to evaluate the Frondizi economic program sector by sector because most of the objectives were not quantified in the manner

87. Marcelo Luis Acuña, *De Frondizi a Alfonsín: La tradición política del radicalismo 2* (Buenos Aires: Centro Editor de América Latina, 1984), pp. 143–51.
88. Mario Barrera, *Information and Ideology: A Case Study of Arturo Frondizi* (Beverly Hills: Sage Publications, 1973), p. 44.

of the Targets Program in Brazil. The government priorities that emerge from speeches and documents included attaining petroleum and steel self-sufficiency, expanding the mining of coal and iron, and establishing an automobile and a petrochemical industry. The centerpiece of the government program was its ambitious goal of self-sufficiency in petroleum production, which was virtually reached during the Frondizi administration. Domestic petroleum production almost tripled, from 5.7 million cubic meters in 1958 to 15.6 million cubic meters in 1962 (see figure 2).[89]

The success of another governmental goal, the expansion of steel production, was less clear. Frondizi had also hoped to reach self-sufficiency in steel production (which would involve 4 million tons per year), but by the time the government left office production was still less than half that amount. The government inaugurated the first integrated steelworks and promoted steel production by a mixed public-private steel enterprise. Steel production tripled between 1958 and 1961, while pig iron production increased from 29,000 tons to 397,000 tons in the same period.[90]

Both the automobile and the petrochemical industry were established during this period. The automobile industry accounts for three-quarters of the industrial growth rate during the period 1958–1961 in Argentina.[91] By 1961 Argentina produced 137,000 automobiles and 20,229 tractors. Seven large petrochemical projects were approved during this period, for a value of $140 million. In the area of basic infrastructure, the desarrollistas' program called for the construction of 15,000 kilometers of new roads, of which 10,000 were constructed before the government was overthrown.[92] The government also carried out an ambitious program of expansion of electrical energy, increasing installed capacity for the generation of electric energy from 1958 to 1962 by 73 percent, exactly the same amount that installed capacity increased in Brazil during the Kubitschek government.[93] In the end, the development accomplishments of the Frondizi administration were substantial, but this did not help them win the support of a broad segment of the Argentine population.

89. Antonio Iglesias, *Política petrolera Argentina* (Buenos Aires: Leonardo Impresora, 1980), annex 2 (see chart 4.2).

90. Odena, *Libertadores y desarrollistas*, pp. 145–46.

91. Alberto Petrecolla, "Desarollo desequilibrado 1958–1962," Instituto Torcuato Di Tella, May 4, 1984, p. 19.

92. Odena, *Libertadores y desarrollistas*, pp. 144–50.

93. Calculated from information provided by Lorenzo Juan Sigaut, *Argentina-Brazil: Prejuicios y realidad* (Buenos Aires: La Tecnica Impresora, 1972), p. 29.

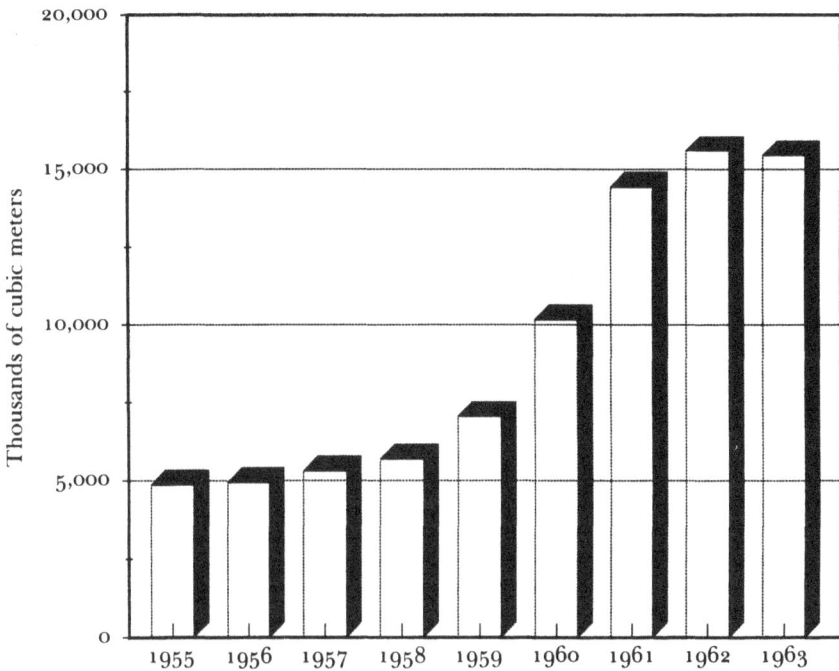

Figure 2. Argentine crude petroleum production, 1955–1963

THE CONSOLIDATION OF DEVELOPMENTALISM IN ARGENTINA

Industrialists in Argentina

Frondizi believed that domestic and international entrepreneurs needed unequivocal signals of improvement in the investment climate, and he provided these signals by adopting the new petroleum policy, resolving long-standing investment disputes, and passing the new Foreign Investment Law. Domestic and international entrepreneurs responded well to the economic incentives offered by the Frondizi government program, increasing their level of investment and their capital goods imports. In spite of the adamantly pro-industrialization position of the Frondizi administration, however, Argentine industrialists never gave strong political support to the government, never actively defended it against attacks from other opponents, and were often party to the kinds of attacks and rhetoric that undermined the government's position.

Frigerio wanted to be a representative of the Argentine industrial bourgeoisie and surrounded himself with a small group of industrialists who identified with the project he and *Qué* magazine outlined. Most of the industrialists, however, seemed impervious to this self-styled vanguard. "*Qué* magazine attempts to be the theoretical and programmatic expression of the Argentine industrial bourgeoisie. The difficulties it encounters in making those it represents understand this role and its importance, point out once again the limitations of the industrial bourgeoisie and its demonstrated historical impotence."[94]

When the industrial policies the government adopted did not illicit the unanimous support of industrialist associations, developmentalists argued that the Argentine ruling class lacked a vision of true national interests. Frondizi said, "The measures we took made possible a positive average profit rate. The doubling of the internal investment in capital goods in only three years reveals our success and the confidence our policies generated. The absence of more solid support from entrepreneurial sectors who benefited from this policy was due to the contradiction between the ideology the leaders of social sectors defend and the concrete interests of those they represent."[95]

The Argentine industrialists during the Frondizi period were divided between two organizations, the Argentine Industrial Union (UIA) and the General Economic Confederation (CGE). The CGE, set up under Perón as the representative of industrial interests, had been abolished during the Aramburu government and the UIA resurrected in its place. When Frondizi permitted the reestablishment of the CGE and the Peronist-dominated General Labor Confederation (CGT), he engendered the adamant opposition of the UIA, which considered the organizations of the Peronist period expressions of corporative totalitarian interests. In response, the representatives of large entrepreneurial groups formed a new confederation, the Coordinating Association of Free Enterprise Institutions (ACIEL), made up of the UIA, the Sociedad Rural, the Stock Market Association, the Chamber of Commerce, the Grain Exchange, and the Bank Association. ACIEL had no organizational structure and mainly existed as a vehicle for the expression of the shared liberal world view of the member groups and as an opposition front to the CGE.[96]

In the first stage of the Frondizi administration, for the most part the

---

94. *Qué Sucedió en Siete Dias*, April 1957, pp. 122–25.

95. Arturo Frondizi, written responses to interview questions, Buenos Aires, November 22, 1985.

96. Dardo Cúneo, *Comportamiento y crisis de la clase empresaria* (Buenos Aires: Centro Editor de América Latina, 1984), p. 220.

industrialist associations were not consulted and were on the margin of the policy-making process. For example, the UIA commented favorably on the stabilization plan but underscored that the organization had not participated in the elaboration of the plan.[97] The government did not attempt to gain industrialists' support for its economic policies, since the desarrollistas believed that as long as the government acted in the interests of industrialists, it would receive their support.

In the second stage of the Frondizi administration, Alvaro Alsogaray included many industrialists on his economic team, and he worked individually to lobby industrialists. One researcher found that 61 percent of the top officials in the Frondizi administration were members of one of Argentina's private entrepreneurial groups, such as the UIA, the Sociedad Rural, the Chamber of Commerce, or the stock market.[98] Many of these were individuals appointed by Alsogaray during his term in office. Not surprisingly, many entrepreneurs felt reassured by his presence in government. But since Alsogaray never shared the government's developmentalist ideology and Frondizi had named Alsogaray minister as a result of military and business pressures, this period should not be seen so much as a time of collaboration between government and industrialists as a "colonization" of the state apparatus by civil society, to use a phrase from O'Donnell. Industrialist loyalty was to an individual, Alsogaray, who served as a vouchsafe for their interests in government. Once Alsogaray was removed from office, much industrial support for the administration evaporated.

Argentine industrialists did not offer consistent opposition to the Frondizi government. The documents of their associations reveal that they supported some policies and opposed others, and that their support for the government's program varied over the years 1958–1962, depending on the particular policies and on the configuration of the economic team in power. The UIA was particularly supportive of the stabilization plan of 1958, though later argued that it had failed because it had not been carried out completely or effectively.[99] Even when the large industrialists supported government policy, their most positive political action was to renounce attempts to encourage the military to overthrow the government, rather than to endorse the government program as their own.[100]

97. Unión Industrial Argentina, *Memoria y balance, 1958*, p. 24.
98. Jorge Niosi, *Los empresarios y el estado argentino (1955–1969)* (Buenos Aires: Siglo XXI, 1974), pp. 218–19.
99. Unión Industrial Argentina, *Memoria y balance, 1961–1962*, pp. 19–20.
100. Thus in the end of 1958, when the government had repressed petroleum strikers and declared a state of siege, the ACIEL responded by announcing "there is not a rap-

The CGE also supported the stabilization plan but criticized "excessive credit restriction," which would act as a "brake on production." The smaller domestic business organizations associated with the CGE were very critical of the government's failure to enact implementing regulations for the Industrial Promotion Law of 1958, which they saw as an indication of the government's indifference to the problems of small domestic industry. But the influence of the CGE was minor compared to that of the UIA and ACIEL.[101]

Why did industrial groups not provide more active support for a government so firmly committed to industrial development? The political and economic ideologies of Argentine industrialists made them less responsive, and even suspicious of the policies of the Frondizi government, and the government's political strategies often further alienated industrial associations. Very few Argentine industrialist shared developmentalist ideas. The interests of Argentine industrialists and their interpretation of national interests were filtered through the lens of the prevalent ideology of Argentine entrepreneurial groups. For large industrialists associated with UIA this ideology stressed free market economic ideas and was adamantly antistatist. The president of the UIA expressed this distrust clearly: "If the state goes further than its function of supervising general interests . . . it is going down the road of error, corruption, tyranny and ruin. Experience has shown us that there is no room in the world for an economy that is half state controlled and half free."[102]

Argentine business associations were structured and behaved more like political movements and less like organizations. They lacked strong institutional and organizational structures.[103] Argentine industrialist groups did not have a technical bureaucratic apparatus, as did the groups of industrialists in Brazil. Their permanent staffs consisted of the presidents, some secretaries, and a few assistants. Often these institutions could not even provide minimal statistics and information on

---

prochement [between entrepreneurs and government], but rather a patriotic understanding. . . . The entrepreneurs defend the democratic system, as well as free enterprise." *La Nación*, December 19, 1958, as cited in Cavarozzi, *Sindicatos y Política en Argentina*, p. 122.

101. Niosi, *Los empresarios y el estado argentino*, pp. 83–84.

102. Pascal Gambino, cited in Cúneo, *Comportamiento y crisis de la clase empresaria*, p. 220.

103. Giorgio Alberti, "The Movement-oriented Organization and the Question of Political Stability in Argentina," paper presented at the ILF 920 Colloquia, Department of Organization Behavior, Cornell University, September 24, 1987.

their own institutions,[104] much less maintain a sophisticated research staff, like the Economics Department of the National Industrial Conference (CNI) in Brazil. The absence of an organizational capacity for research, analysis, and mediation of interests may have contributed to the rigidity of their economic viewpoints.

The economic ideas of the large industrialists grouped in the UIA and ACIEL were complemented by a political ideology that tended to identify Peronism with increased power of the labor movement and the worst excesses of state intervention. Thus, the biggest stumbling block for industrialists' support of Frondizi's policies was the conciliatory position the government adopted toward the labor movement. Frondizi's decision to permit reestablishment of the CGE and the CGT was unacceptable to key industrial leaders. Frondizi's pact with Perón frightened many industrialists. "We had fought for ten years against Perón, and then many felt as if Perón had come back into the government through Frondizi."[105]

Industrialists were also concerned with the supposed infiltration of the government by Communists. One industrial leader explained that "Frigerio was the bête noir for the Argentine industrialist. It was believed that he had too much influence over Frondizi. I don't know whether he was a Communist or not, but there was a lot of distrust."[106] At one point ACIEL publicly denounced the "infiltration of an authoritarianism destructive of our Western and Christian world view. The danger is more alarming every day."[107]

Industrialists associated with the CGE did not advocate the free market ideology of the UIA, but their ideas were closer to national populism than they were to developmentalism. They embraced strongly protectionist ideas and called for protection of all national industry against foreign competition. When the government decreased import taxes on a number of manufactured items from 300 percent to 150 percent, one domestic industrial association accused it of provoking the deindustrialization of the country and of "mutilating Argentine industry in order

---

104. Giorgio Alberti, Laura Golbert, and Carlos Acuna, "Intereses industriales y gobernabilidad democrática en la Argentina," *Organización Techint Boletin informativo* 235 (October–December 1984), 117–18. Alberti et al. make these observations on the organizational weaknesses of industrial organizations in Argentina based on research carried out in the early 1980s, but there is no evidence that the organizational structure of these groups was any stronger in the 1950s.

105. Interview with a leader of the Unión Industrial Argentina, November 1985.

106. Ibid.

107. Cited in Cúneo, *Comportamiento y crisis de la clase empresaria*, p. 238.

to receive credits from abroad."[108] Thus they were unreceptive to the desarrollista program of equal or privileged treatment for foreign investment in basic industrial sectors.

The political divisions of the period might have had less influence if there had been greater convergence between the economic ideas of the majority of Argentine industrialists and the Frondizi government. Except for a small circle of industrialists connected to Frigerio, Argentine industrialists did not act as protagonists or leaders of developmentalism. Neither the free traders of the UIA nor the ardent protectionists of the CGE favored a developmentalist policy based on extensive government support for basic industries, whether foreign or domestically owned.

The Argentine Military

Desarrollismo also found surprisingly little support among the Argentine military. According to one military desarrollista, there were very few "pure" desarrollistas in the army, those who understood the necessity of the economic transformation of the country.[109] Another claimed that "in the navy, there was not even one desarrollista," even among those who served as government ministers during the Frondizi government.[110] Even in the air force, the branch of the armed forces that gave the most support to the Frondizi government, there were very few desarrollistas.[111] These observers use the exclusionary definition of desarrollismo, which implies support of the economic and the political project of Frondizi and Frigerio, including rapprochement with Peronism. Another military observer, using a broader definition of desarrollismo, argued that there were developmentalists in the armed forces, but they were not in harmony with Frondizi's political positions and thus did not support him. As explained earlier, the support Frondizi received from the military came not from individuals who agreed with his economic or political program but from legalist groups in the armed forces who supported his administration because it was the constitutionally elected government.[112]

The Argentine armed forces were less concerned with the problems

---

108. Statements by the Camara de Fabricantes de Produtos Quimicos Farmaceuticos, "A la desindustrialización del país?" *La razon*, January 22, 1960.

109. Interview with General Manuel Rodriguez, Buenos Aires, November 1, 1985.

110. Interview with Capitan Carlos Borzone, Buenos Aires, November 1, 1985.

111. Interview with Commodore Roberto Huerta, Frondizi's first secretary of the air force, Buenos Aires, November 21, 1985.

112. Interview with General Isaias J. Garcia Enciso, Buenos Aires, November 7, 1985.

of national economic development in the 1950s than was the Brazilian military. One developmentalist argued that traditional liberal sectors in the military always controlled the teaching of economic topics in the superior colleges of the three branches of the military, and thus industrialization was never incorporated as a doctrine or goal of the Argentine military, as it was in Brazil.[113] A survey of the main military journals of the period in Argentina supports this argument. The *Revista de la Escuela Superior de Guerra*, which frequently reprinted lectures from the Superior War College, and the *Revista militar* have very few articles dealing with economic topics in general and virtually none that focus on the economy from a developmentalist perspective. Of the twenty to thirty articles per year published by the *Revista de la Escuela Superior de Guerra*, on average only one article per year from 1952 to 1962 dealt with economic topics. The lack of attention to economic topics was constant during the ten-year period, which contradicts a common assumption that more attention was devoted to economic development concerns in the military during the Peronist period.

Although the lack of pro-industrialization sentiment in the Argentine armed forces meant they did not enthusiastically embrace the government's economic program, neither did they strenuously oppose any particular economic policy of the government.[114] The position of the military toward the Frondizi government focused instead on three issues: the government's policies toward military institutions themselves, especially reincorporation of retired officers; its positions toward Peronism; and the supposed problem of Communist infiltration in the government.

The most dramatic change in the topics of the *Revista de la Escuela Superior de Guerra* came with the introduction of articles on Communist infiltration and guerrilla warfare in the late 1950s.[115] If the contents of these journals are an accurate reflection of the ideological concerns of the Argentine military, it is not surprising that the military's primary

113. Interview with Oscar Camilion, Buenos Aires, June 12, 1985.

114. Among the exceptions were the small group of nationalists who opposed the Frondizi petroleum policies and another group connected to Fabricaciones Militares, who opposed the attempts to encourage private business initiative in sectors that were already covered by Fabricaciones Militares.

115. Before 1954 only one article on these topics had appeared, whereas beginning in 1958 the *Revista* averaged four articles per year on guerrilla warfare and internal subversion. This increase appears to be primarily the result of the presence of French advisers at the school who stressed the French experience in Indochina and set forth theories of subversive warfare. See, for example, "Una teoria para la guerra subversiva," by a lieutenant colonel of the French army, Patrice Roger J. L. de Naurois, military adviser at the Escuela Superior de Guerra, *Revista de la Escuela Superior de Guerra* 329 (April–June 1958).

concern about the Frondizi administration was not its economic priorities but rather its supposed Communist infiltration. Anticommunism was, and would continue to be, the most stable element in the world view of the Argentine military in this period.[116]

Unlike the situation in Brazil, where the concerns with national security were linked to a project of rapid industrialization, the anticommunism of the Argentine military was not strongly connected to an alternative economic program. The Argentine military was not well informed on the issues of economic development, so it occasionally saw Frondizi and Frigerio's prioritization of heavy state-led industrialization as evidence of the government's pro-Communist leanings.[117]

Argentine Rural Producers

Of all the economic groups in Argentina and Brazil, the Argentine landed elites embraced the purest ideology of the free market. Over and over again in their publications, the Sociedad Rural stressed that state intervention was one of the main reasons for the decadence of agricultural production in Argentina, and that the only way to facilitate economic development of the country was to remove all arbitrary restrictions to the economic activities of producers.[118]

In spite of the differences between the ideas of the rural elite and the desarrollistas, the position of the Sociedad Rural toward the Frondizi administration was not one of extreme suspicion and opposition throughout the entire tenure of the government, as one author suggests.[119] Instead, there were points of agreement as well as conflict between rural producers and the government. The extreme opposition of the Sociedad Rural during this period was directed not against the national government but against the agrarian reform and taxation reform

116. Tulio Halperin Donghi, *Argentina: Democracia de masas* (Buenos Aires: Editorial Paidos, 1983), p. 29. In his remarks to the graduating class of 1961, the director of the Superior War College urges the recent graduates to disseminate their newly acquired knowledge on the dangers of communism and use all their efforts to combat it. "Palabras pronunciadas por el Señor Director de la Escuela Superior de Guerra, General de Brigada Carlos J. Turolo, con motivo de la quinta promoción de oficiales de Estado Mayor," *Revista de la Escuela Superior de Guerra* 343 (October–December 1961), 663.

117. In an interview, Oscar Camilion recalled that when he spoke to the Superior War College and stressed that the promotion of economic development was one of the main goals of the Frondizi government, he was asked whether this implied a Marxist-Leninist world view. Interview with Oscar Camilion, Buenos Aires, June 12, 1985.

118. See, for example, Sociedad Rural Argentina, *Memoria de la Sociedad Rural Argentina, 1959–1960*, 94 (August 1960), 18, and *Anales de la Sociedad Rural Argentina* 43 (May–June 1959), 178.

119. Niosi, *Los empresarios y el estado Argentino 1955–1969*, pp. 77–78.

efforts in the Province of Buenos Aires, which they believed threatened their basic interests more directly than did the national development program.

The Sociedad Rural Argentina (SRA) received the Frondizi economic stabilization plan favorably. According to the president of the SRA, the plan "interprets the position of the Sociedad Rural Argentina in its constant struggle for free trade." The support was short-lived, however, because the SRA disagreed with the government over the implementation of the plan, as well as over a series of other measures adopted by the government, such as the establishment of the National Agrarian Council to oversee colonization of public lands. During the last two years of the Frondizi administration, relations between the government and the Sociedad Rural improved. The rural producers applauded the removal of exchange retentions on meat, congratulated the government on the administrative rationalization plan, and maintained cordial relations with the secretary of agriculture and livestock, a member of the Sociedad.[120]

The most important point of conflict between the rural sector and the developmentalists during this period was the attempt to modify the tax system of the Province of Buenos Aires and to initiate a modest agrarian reform program, inspired by the economists of the Economic Planning Council under the provincial minister of economics, Aldo Ferrer. The Province of Buenos Aires represented a large proportion of national agrarian production. The provincial gross domestic product in crops accounted for 24.8 percent of the national total, while in livestock it reached 41 percent of the national figure.[121] Thus policy changes in the province had important repercussions on the national economic scene and were watched carefully by agricultural producers.

The Economic Planning Council proposed a new series of tax measures to encourage rural producers to introduce certain improvements in rural property, and thus increase agricultural production at the same time as it increased the tax earnings of the province. They also produced a study calling for an agrarian reform using an "index of the general economic utilization of rural holdings" as an instrument to de-

120. In the annual speech opening the Rural Exposition in 1961, the president of the Sociedad Rural referred to the removal of export taxes on meat: "The rancher greets with frank enthusiasm this measure, which will benefit our foreign trade. Argentine cattle farms in this occasion cannot silence their applause for the executive branch, nor quiet their thanks to the secretary of agriculture, Dr. Urien." *Anales de la Sociedad Rural Argentina* 95 (October 1961), 10.

121. Junta de Planificación Económica, "La utilización del 'índice de aprovechamiento económico-social de la explotaciones agropecuarias' en el plan agrario de Buenos Aires," *Revista de desarrollo económico* 2 (January–March 1959), 194.

cide which private holdings would be targets for expropriation or purchase.[122] The rural associations reacted violently against the tax and agrarian reform proposals. "It is sufficient to skim the works of the Economic Planning Council on the tax system of the Province of Buenos Aires to reach the conviction that the ultimate goal of this reform is the destruction of the existing landholding system, the confrontation of the distinct Argentine rural classes and sectors, and the encouragement of Marxist-type economic systems."[123]

Land reform proposals initially received the energetic support of Governor Oscar Alende, who referred to the United Nations, CEPAL, and FAO as legitimizing sources for the necessity of land reform. Frondizi and Frigerio, on the other hand, claimed that the problem of Argentine agrarian productivity was unrelated to the question of land ownership.[124] In contrast to the national government's policy, Alende argued that the increased mechanization and technicalization of the agricultural sector would not lead to the desired increase in productivity without a simultaneous change in the agrarian structure.[125]

Alende and the técnicos of the Economic Planning Council felt they had developed a modern Western tax and reform program that would encourage rational rural producers to increase productivity without increasing their sense of insecurity.[126] The rural producers responded, through their organizations and publications, with an all-out attack against Communist infiltration in the government. Under a banner headline that said simply *"THE COLOR RED"* the Sociedad Rural denounced the advances made by Communists, their "road companions," and their "useful idiots." Another editorial on the tax program was titled "The Path to Sovietization."[127]

The rural producers tried to play the national government off against the provincial government, thus driving a wedge between the

122. Ibid., p. 202.

123. Sociedad Rural Argentina, *Anales de la Sociedad Rural Argentina* 94 (February 1960), 64.

124. Fanor Diaz, *Conversaciones con Rogelio Frigerio* (Buenos Aires: Hachette, 1977), p. 29.

125. Oscar E. Alende, "La reforma agraria," speech given at an agrarian meeting in Rojas, Province of Buenos Aires, March 8, 1959, reprinted in *Revista de desarrollo económico* 2 (January–March 1959), 245–57.

126. A weakened version of the land reform proposal was adopted by the provincial government, and a modest program involving colonization on state-owned lands was implemented. In addition, the real estate tax base of the province was brought up to date, providing a large increase in provincial tax revenues. Interview with Aldo Ferrer, Buenos Aires, November 27, 1985.

127. Sociedad Rural Argentina, *Anales de la Sociedad Rural Argentina* 43 (April 1959), 123–24.

two groups of developmentalist policy makers. The producers stressed their support for the national government's stabilization program, with which they were prepared to collaborate, "in spite of the sacrifices it demands." They suggested, however, that agrarian groups would back off their support for national economic policy unless Frondizi took measures to limit or reverse provincial agrarian policies.[128]

The pressure campaign of the Sociedad Rural and its allies eventually bore fruit when Alende, under pressure from the national government, accepted the resignation of Ferrer and the entire Economic Planning Council. The rural groups had scored a victory. According to Ferrer, the agrarian reform and taxation schemes "were not a negotiable item for these sectors."[129]

In spite of the modest nature of the agrarian reform plan, the rural elites felt that their basic interests were threatened, and they took the offensive effectively to block those policies they opposed. But the vehemence and energies that the Sociedad Rural exerted to bring about the downfall of the Ferrer team in the Province of Buenos Aires were not repeated at the national level. Agricultural producers had points of disagreement with the Frondizi government, and they did not share its developmentalist ideology, but they did not work to undermine the government directly. Neither did they take any measures to actively support the government. Frondizi and the desarrollistas did not inspire the trust of the rural elites. But in spite of Frigerio's protestations that desarrollismo was threatening to the agro-import structure in Argentina, there is no clear indication that rural groups were responsible for the failure of the desarrollista program, or the downfall of the Frondizi government.

The Argentine Labor Movement

The bulk of the Argentine labor movement during this period consisted of Peronists who embraced national populist ideas on economic policy. In the political realm, their primary allegiance was always to the return of Perón and restoration of the legality of the Peronist party. Temporary alliances between labor and the desarrollistas were judged by their efficacy in furthering these economic and political goals. In addition, the faction of Peronism that held ideological predominance over the Peronist labor movement in this period accentuated the revolutionary and antibourgeois content of Peronism and thus increased

128. Letter dated December 30, 1959, reprinted in the *Anales de la Sociedad Rural Argentina* 94 (January 1960), 9–10.
129. Interview with Aldo Ferrer, Buenos Aires, November 27, 1985.

ideological opposition to the capitalist development program put forth by the Frondizi government.[130]

In the first months of his term, Frondizi made a series of important concessions to labor, both in response to the promises in the electoral pact with Perón and in an attempt to win labor support for the economic program of the government. Shortly after his inauguration in May 1958, Frondizi decreed a 60 percent pay increase to wage earners and presented to Congress for its approval a new "law of professional associations," which permitted the reestablishment of a national labor association, the CGT, under Peronist control. Nevertheless, from early in his administration Frondizi faced a wave of labor unrest, including a national medical strike, a postal workers strike, a railroad strike, and a general strike.

Labor began to take a position of open opposition in late 1958, in response to the government's petroleum policy. Workers of the state petroleum company in Mendoza went on strike to protest the oil contracts the government had signed with foreign oil companies. Frondizi, supposedly in response to reports that workers tended to set fire to petroleum fields, imposed a state of siege. He made a dramatic speech claiming that the strike was part of a plan of insurrection organized by Communists, who "for global strategic reasons don't want us to achieve petroleum self-sufficiency," and by Peronists, who "following instructions from abroad, try to create chaos at YPF."[131] Along with the state of siege, Frondizi also put into action the Plan Conintes (Conmoción Interna del Estado), which permitted the arrest and detention of several hundred workers and labor leaders throughout the country.[132]

Relations between the government and the labor movement worsened after the economic stabilization plan was put into effect in 1959. The confrontation between workers and the government over the plan came to a head over a relatively minor aspect of it. As one part of the effort to decrease the government deficit, the government decided to privatize the national meat packing plant. Workers occupied the plant and later declared a work stoppage. The government responded with force; it took control of certain trade unions, arrested hundreds of workers, and fired half of the workers at the plant.[133]

130. Cavarozzi, *Sindicatos y política en Argentina*, p. 108. For a detailed account of Cooke's position during this period, see his letters to Perón in *Correspondencia Perón-Cooke II* (Buenos Aires: Ediciones Parlamento, 1984).
131. Frondizi, *Mensajes presidenciales, 1958–1962*, Vol. 1, pp. 208–9.
132. Cavarozzi, *Sindicatos y política*, p. 119.
133. Donald Hodges, *Argentina 1943–1976: The National Revolution and Resistance* (Albuquerque: University of New Mexico Press, 1976), p. 37.

Table 1. Industrial disputes in Argentina

Year	Number of disputes	Workers involved	Working days lost
1955	21	11,990	144,120
1956	50	853,994	5,167,294
1957	56	304,209	3,390,509
1958	84	277,381	6,245,286
1959	45	1,411,062	10,078,138
1960	26	130,044	1,661,520
1961	43	236,462	1,755,170
1962	15	42,386	268,749

The height of working-class opposition to the economic policies of the Frondizi administration came in 1959, in response to implementation of the stabilization plan, as is evident from the upsurge of strike activity charted in table 1. Working-class opposition, however, was not able to block implementation of the plan or to modify significantly any of its components. "Facing the combination of stabilization (and recession) on one side and selective repression and negotiation on the other, the reactions of workers could not block the most drastic fall in real wages in contemporary Argentina until 1976."[134]

The most serious labor conflict in the last years of the Frondizi administration was a railroad strike in opposition to the government's administration rationalization program. The railroad workers' unions adamantly opposed the program, which called for ending the deficit of the railway system primarily by reducing personnel and privatizing certain auxiliary parts of the system. They initiated strikes in May 1961, which continued intermittently throughout the rest of the year with support from the CGT, opposition political parties, and the leftist press. An end to the strike was eventually negotiated when the government renounced part of its rationalization plan.[135] These concessions, perhaps the clearest example of labor union activity blocking the implementation of aspects of the government program, were probably the result of the government's desire to appease labor as the elections of 1962 drew near.

Working-class opposition led to failure of the initial political project of the desarrollistas, which called for integration of labor into the developmentalist coalition. Labor opposition to the government peaked in 1959 and declined significantly during the last two years of the Frondizi administration. The relations between government and labor

134. Cavarozzi, *Sindicatos y política*, p. 134.
135. Odena, *Libertadores y desarrollistas*, p. 263.

moved from tacit alliance during the initial months of the administration to outright confrontation in 1959, as workers opposed the measures of the economic stabilization plan, and finally to a modus vivendi during the last two years of the administration based on negotiation and government acceptance of Peronist predominance in the union movement.[136]

Workers were able to block the political project of developmentalism by refusing to play the role of junior partners, but they were not able to block most of the economic policies they opposed. In spite of large-scale labor mobilization in 1958 and 1959, workers were not able to block a stabilization policy that led to a drastic decline in real wages, nor were they successful in undermining the petroleum contracts that they opposed. Labor mobilization did, however, create a climate of disorder, fueling opposition military and political figures' claims that the country was in a state of chaos. In response to labor opposition toward the end of Frondizi's administration, the desarrollistas began to try an alternative political tactic, with Frondizi profiling himself as the new leader of an anti-Peronist alliance. But his conversion came too late to win him broad support, and it may have only reconfirmed the general belief that he was untrustworthy. Working-class votes contributed to the Peronist victory in 1962, which eventually provoked the military coup that overthrew the Frondizi government.

The adoption of developmentalism in Argentina was largely the result of new ideas held by individual policy makers who were responding to a set of perceived constraints and opportunities. The economic ideas held by Prebisch, Frondizi, and Frigerio help explain the content of developmentalist policy choices. These policy makers, however, operated within a set of perceived constraints and opportunities that limited and focused their choices. Prebisch admits that, faced with the crisis of the Depression and World War II, he saw little alternative but to industrialize. Some constraints, like the balance-of-payments crisis, had a powerful influence on policy. But policy makers were also constrained by their imagination and the ideas of the public. When they thought of industrialization, they could only imagine import-substituting industrialization.

The implementation of policy, on the other hand, depended much more on the institutional capacity of the state and on the ability of the government to mobilize financial, technical, and political resources. The fragility of the Argentine state, the lack of strong institutions and

---

136. Cavarozzi, *Sindicatos y política*, p. 125.

personnel continuity, hampered implementation of the developmentalist program from its onset. No clear plan was ever drawn up because no planning institution existed. Frondizi was not able to maintain a qualified cadre of staff to help implement the program.

But the most serious problem facing developmentalism in Argentina was its failure to become consolidated, to gain broad support from groups in society, and to become embedded in the state. By the time the Frondizi government fell, it had lost much of its initial political support. One by one, the groups that had supported or tolerated the Frondizi administration began to move to the opposition, leaving the government increasingly isolated and vulnerable.

This loss of support was not inevitable. If we take a pure economic interest group explanation, the actions of key groups in Argentina toward the Frondizi government are not easy to explain. In this framework, it is not surprising that the working class opposed many Frondizi policies. As a result of the stabilization program of 1958, this group suffered a major decline in real wages. But the actions of Argentine industrialists, the military, and the middle-class groups represented by the UCRP are almost impossible to understand from the point of view of "pure interests."

Only if we recognize that each of these groups interpreted their interests and the Frondizi government's actions through the lens of their historically formed ideologies, can we comprehend their actions. The ideological basis for developmentalist policies was thinner in Argentina than it was in Brazil. The ideological terrain was occupied by a struggle between national populism and liberalism, leaving less space for the developmentalist alternative.

The behavior of Argentine industrialists in particular challenges economic interest group theories that explain state action favoring these interests as a result of industrial group pressure. For the most part, industrialists were absent from the formulation and support of policies that proved to be some of the most favorable to industrialization ever adopted in Argentina. Because the developmentalist program depended on heavy investment, Frondizi and his advisers were obliged to create a positive business climate. Industry responded to government incentives by increasing investment levels but never offered significant political support for the government.

Each group interpreted its interests, including its economic interests, through the prism of powerful political ideologies. Three issues were particularly crucial to determining political support for the Frondizi government: petroleum, Peronism, and communism. Each of these issues represented a broader political debate about the political future of

Argentina. The debate over Frondizi's petroleum policy was a debate over nationalism. Frondizi's choice of a petroleum policy lost him support early in his administration from the Left, and from nationalists in the traditional parties and in the military.

The electoral pact with Perón generated opposition from a very different group in Argentine society. Many individuals and groups who would have supported Frondizi's economic policies were put off by his connections with Peronism. Thus many industrialists and anti-Peronist military figures failed to support Frondizi because they distrusted his intentions regarding Perón and the working class. Indeed, some could literally not "see" what Frondizi was doing in the economic realm because they were so obsessed with his supposed pro-Peronism. But even as the pact with Perón alienated many sectors, it failed to win Frondizi support from the Peronists except in the 1958 election and the early months of his administration. Peronists turned to Perón for leadership; they sought the return of Perón to Argentina not the substitution of Frondizi for Perón.

The accusations against Frondizi for his leftist leanings were just one more sign of the distrust that undermined his government's legitimacy. Frequently these stories were spread and elaborated by rightist elements in the armed forces in the hope of discrediting the government, but Frondizi sometimes proved his own best enemy in providing ammunition for the rumors, as when he met secretly with Ché Guevara in 1961.

Nor can we understand Frondizi's situation through the lens of political survival. The concessions that Frondizi had to make to the labor movement in order to gain their temporary support during the early months of 1958 sowed distrust among industrialists and the military, whose collaboration he needed for his economic program. At the same time, the concessions and gestures he made to convince foreign and national capitalists to invest alienated labor.

The political atmosphere in Argentina during the Frondizi administration moved from a moment of high hopes during and shortly after the election to increasing disillusionment and frustration, as apparently erratic and contradictory policies surprised the electorate. The ideologically bound sense of congruence of each sector of Argentine society was violated by a series of activities that made sense within the intricate reasoning of desarrollista thought but appeared contradictory to those not immersed in this thought. It could only be explained as the result of Machiavellianism, infiltration (of the Left or the Right, depending on one's point of view), and payoffs and corruption. What seemed only rational survival politics to Frondizi was condemned as machinations and conspiracy by the Argentine public. Survival strategies, as I have pointed out, cannot be understood separately from the substantive preferences of politicians and the public.

The economic results of the developmentalist program were substantial, even if they did not meet the initial high expectations of the desarrollistas. But the political decisions on policy making show a perverse consistency that contributed to the final undermining of the Frondizi presidency. It seems unlikely that if the economic policies of the government had succeeded more dramatically it might have overcome much of the political resistance it faced. In the one area in which the government had an undisputed economic success—petroleum policy—it continued to face its most vocal political opposition.

Nevertheless, the Frondizi administration left an important political and economic policy legacy. The push for development of the basic heavy industries in Argentina gained new force and would be attempted by other Argentine governments in the future. Perhaps Frondizi's most enduring legacy was a political one: the idea of integration, which encompassed the belief that Argentine politics could not succeed without the reincorporation of Peronism. Frondizi failed in his own attempts to reincorporate Peronism, but Argentine political actors in the future would be forced to come to the same conclusion.

CHAPTER FOUR

Developmentalism in Brazil, 1954–1961

On August 24, 1954, President Getúlio Vargas shot himself in the heart, leaving behind an extraordinary letter to the public explaining his motives. By this act, Vargas recaptured the political offensive for his supporters and altered the political climate for the emergence of developmentalism in Brazil. With Vargas dead, Juscelino Kubitschek became political heir to the populist tradition. The last trip out of Rio made by Vargas before his suicide was a visit to Governor Kubitschek in Minas Gerais to inaugurate the newly installed Mannesmann steelworks there. Kubitschek, a member of the pro-Vargas forces in Minas Gerais, had been mentioned as a possible successor to Vargas when his term expired in 1956. Vargas had told his closest associates that he was favorably inclined toward Kubitschek's candidacy.[1]

One of the key differences between the Kubitschek and the Frondizi administrations was that in Brazil developmentalism merged with populism, increasing its possibilities for mass appeal and limiting the challenges it faced from the Left. In Argentina Perón opposed Frondizi's attempts to have developmentalism subsume populism. The continuity between Vargas and Kubitschek also revealed itself in the economic policies adopted by the Kubitschek administration. Many of the individuals, institutions, and policies of the Vargas government played an important role in the formulation and implementation of Kubitschek's policies.

Kubitschek was born in a small town in the state of Minas Gerais. His father died when he was young, and his mother, a schoolteacher,

1. Ernani do Amaral Peixoto, *Ernani do Amaral Peixoto (depoimento, 1977–84)* (Rio de Janeiro: Fundação Getúlio Vargas/CPDOC-História Oral, 1985), p. 865.

worked to support her two children. He entered the medical school in Belo Horizonte in 1922, working as a telegraph operator to support himself while at the university. Among his colleagues in the telegraph office in Belo Horizonte was Jose Maria Alkmin, a law student who later served as Kubitschek's first minister of economics. After graduation, he practiced medicine until 1930, when he traveled to France to take an advanced course in urology. While in Europe, Kubitschek traveled widely around the continent and also visited the Middle East and North Africa. According to an early biographer, this trip had a profound influence on Kubitschek, awakening in him a new awareness of social problems.[2]

In one of his autobiographies, Kubitschek credits the trip to Europe with changing his views on development. "It was then that I became convinced that no countries are condemned irremediably to poverty. . . . It is no longer impossible to be victorious over any type of natural obstacle. There are, however, countries that know better than others the secret of producing more and better, and at a lower price."[3]

Kubitschek's training as a doctor influenced his approach to political and economic problems. His career as a physician spanned a period of great technical innovation in the field of medicine. Enormous strides were made which gave doctors new control over disease. Kubitschek's practical hands-on approach, his optimism about the possibilities of human and technical victory over natural obstacles, derived in part from his medical background. He often used medical metaphors, referring to a "diagnosis" and "remedy" to the problems of underdevelopment, for example. "To attempt to solve the national crisis with remedies prescribed only to achieve stability . . . is like trying to treat the crises of puberty with medicines designed to alleviate senility."[4]

Upon his return to Brazil, he became involved in politics, serving as a national deputy from Minas Gerais and as the mayor of Belo Horizonte during the authoritarian Estado Nôvo government of Getúlio Vargas. His tenure as mayor marks his first involvement in public administration. It was during this period that his fascination with public works was first evident. He supervised the construction of new streets and the paving of existing ones, and he expanded the sewer and water systems.

2. Jose Moraes, *Juscelino: O homen, a candidatura, a campanha* (Belo Horizonte: Imprensa Oficial de Minas Gerais, 1955), p. 27. On Kubitschek's life before his presidency, see Francisco de Assis Barbosa, *JK: Uma revisão na política brasileira* (Rio de Janeiro: José Olympio, 1960).

3. Juscelino Kubitschek, *A marcha do amanhecer* (São Paulo: Importadora de Livros, 1962), p. 17.

4. Ibid., p. 50.

In a small version of the ambitious construction projects he initiated as president, he teamed up with architect Oscar Niemeyer to build a new modern neighborhood in the city. Kubitschek later claimed, "The mayorship was my first large-scale direct administrative experience, which served to solidify my confidence in planned action, in a program."[5]

In 1945 Kubitschek was active in the formation of the new Social Democratic party (Partido Social Democrático, PSD), but with the fall of Vargas, he was removed from his position as mayor of Belo Horizonte. In the elections held that same year, however, he was elected a delegate to the Constituent Assembly and a federal deputy. During this period, Kubitschek made his first trip to the United States and to Canada, visiting Quebec, Montreal, Detroit, Chicago, Washington, and New York. Kubitschek found his second trip abroad significant. "In 1948, contemplating the North American civilization . . . I understood the part that Brazil could play in the world, if our development were oriented toward industrialization."[6]

In 1950 Kubitschek was elected governor of the state of Minas Gerais on the PSD ticket. His government concentrated its administrative efforts on two crucial bottleneck areas in the state: electric energy and roads. Kubitschek saw these two infrastructure sectors as prerequisites for transforming the state from a primarily agricultural area into a center of industry. The Kubitschek administration constructed major dams and electric energy plants, expanded road construction, and arranged for the installation of a steel plant by the German company Mannesmann. In short, the Kubitschek governorship of Minas Gerais presaged on a smaller scale many of the policies of the Kubitschek presidency.

Three major influences seemed to have played an important role in the development of Kubitschek's ideas: his travels abroad, his association with Vargas's development program, and his long administrative experience. He was not an intellectual and had had no formal training in economics. But he had a strong interest in building public works and a clear vision of the kind of future he desired for Brazil, based on his exposure to developed countries while traveling abroad. Kubitschek's political and ideological trajectory shows significant continuity with his work as mayor, governor, and president. His views on development and the way he put them into practice, however, increased in complexity, from the simple road and sewer building projects in Belo Horizonte, to the energy and transport projects in Minas Gerais, to the multifaceted Targets Program. This process was continuous and gradual,

5. Ibid., p. 25.
6. Juscelino Kubitschek, *Meu caminho para Brasília: A escalada política* (Rio de Janeiro: Bloch Editores, 1976), p. 153.

without any major shift or change such as the one Frondizi experienced in the mid-1950s.

The Café Filho administration, which held power between Vargas and Kubitschek as a transitional, caretaker government, lacked authority to carry out any drastic changes in economic policy.[7] In this sense, it was similar to the transitional government of the Liberating Revolution in Argentina. Compared to the Argentine transitional government, however, which attempted a cosmopolitan developmentalist economic program with the Prebisch Plan, the Brazilian transition government did not propose any new developmentalist initiatives. On the other hand, the Café Filho government did not dismantle the bulk of the economic policies and institutions inherited from the Vargas government, as did the Liberating Revolution government with the institutions and policies of the Peronist government. This facilitated Kubitschek's efforts to continue and consolidate the economic initiatives of the second Vargas administration.

One economic measure taken by the Café Filho government which was important for Kubitschek's economic policies was a regulation on foreign investment called Instruction 113. Issued by the Superintendency for Money and Credit (SUMOC), a powerful semiautonomous branch of the Banco do Brasil responsible for monetary policy, Instruction 113 was designed to attract foreign capital to Brazil. One of the origins of the new policy may have been the new Eisenhower government's insistence that investment-receiving countries create an appropriate climate for foreign investment.[8]

Instruction 113 allowed the Department of Foreign Trade (CACEX) of the Banco do Brasil to grant benefits to attract foreign investment into priority industrial sectors. The most important provision of Instruction 113 authorized CACEX to issue import licenses for industrial equipment without exchange cover. In other words, capital goods imports were treated as additional foreign investment and would not have to be paid for in foreign currency. These provisions were attractive to foreign investors since they raised the rate of return on investment. For Brazil, they permitted a rapid increase in capital goods imports without expenditure of foreign exchange.[9] Since these imports could only be

7. Thomas Skidmore, *Politics in Brazil: 1930–1964* (New York: Oxford University Press, 1986), p. 161.

8. Regis Bonelli and Ricardo Tolipan, "Industrial Policies in Brazil: A Summary of Two Decades," Instituto de Planejamento Econômico e Social, no date, p. 22.

9. Carlos Lessa, "Fifteen Years of Economic Policy in Brazil," *Economic Bulletin for Latin America* 2 (December 1964), 173.

made by foreign companies, however, domestic firms were at a considerable disadvantage. Although Instruction 113 was vigorously attacked by Brazil's business associations, it was incorporated later into the Kubitschek economic program, becoming one of the principal measures used to attract foreign investment.

Even before Kubitschek's party, the PSD, nominated him as its presidential candidate in 1955, individuals in military, government, and political circles began working to undermine his candidacy. The primary political party in opposition to Kubitschek was the Union Democrático Nacional (UDN), a group of individuals with varied political viewpoints who had been united by their militant anti-Vargas position. Generally, UDNistas were civil libertarians with antistatist, free market ideas about economic policy. The UDN and military figures associated with the party thought that Kubitschek was too much an heir of the Vargas tradition and too far to the left to be an acceptable candidate. Key military figures suggested that if Kubitschek were elected, he would not be allowed to take office.

Nevertheless, in early 1955 the PSD convention nominated Kubitschek as its candidate and entered into negotiations with the Brazilian Labor party (PTB) about the possibility of an electoral alliance. Both of these parties traced their roots back to Getúlio Vargas, and they had jointly supported the Vargas government. They had done well in congressional elections, together representing a solid majority in the National Congress. By April the two parties decided to jointly support the ticket of Kubitschek for president and João (Jango) Goulart for vice-president. The nomination of PTBista Goulart, with his strong connections to organized labor, did nothing to reassure the military.

SOURCES OF THE TARGETS PROGRAM

The value of the Targets Program was less in its originality or uniqueness than in its success in bringing together a number of previous policy initiatives and giving them new coherence and impetus.[10] Many of the ingredients of the Targets Program had been proposed in previous administrations and were already in place when Kubitschek took office. As one policy maker who worked with both Vargas and

10. The classic study of the Targets Plan, Celso Lafer, *The Planning Process and the Political System in Brazil: A Study of Kubitschek's Target Plan* (Dissertation Series 16, Cornell University, 1970), stresses the continuity of the Targets Plan with earlier Brazilian planning efforts, especially with the work of the Joint U.S.-Brazil Economic Development Commission.

Kubitschek pointed out, "The Targets Program was a coordination, a sum, a collage of various programs, many of which had been initiated during the Vargas government: the reequipping of the merchant marine, the automobile industry program, the electric energy program."[11]

Nevertheless, although the Targets Program drew on a variety of sources and made use of policy instruments that were already in place, it was still something new. Kubitschek's team brought together disparate policies into a single program for the first time. While the Targets Program fell short of a full-scale plan, some efforts were made to coordinate the various targets.

Much of the economic program Kubitschek presented during the campaign was an expanded national version of the projects he had undertaken as mayor of Belo Horizonte and governor of Minas Gerais. The most important source for his program was his direct experience in expanding the energy and transportation systems in the state of Minas Gerais while he was governor. His advisers convinced Kubitschek to expand his program beyond energy and transport. Kubitschek wanted a program made up of quantifiable objectives, which he captured with the word *metas*—targets or goals—and began to use in his speeches in reference to his economic program.[12] The Targets Program did not emerge full-blown at the beginning of the campaign. It began to be elaborated during the campaign by a group of técnicos headed by Lucas Lopes in consultation with Kubitschek, and continued to develop during the campaign and the first two years of the Kubitschek government.[13]

In late 1954 Kubitschek first met a group of intellectuals who would later form the think tank called Instituto Superior de Estudos Brasileiros (ISEB). Since ISEB is frequently credited with being one of the intellectual forces behind the Kubitschek economic program, it is important to understand the role played by this group. ISEB was composed of intellectuals who shared a common commitment to national industrialization and development. They came from a variety of backgrounds: some were from the Left; others had initially been involved with the Integralists, the Brazilian version of the European Fascist movements. Made up of economists, philosophers, historians, sociolo-

11. Cleantho de Paiva Leite, *Cleantho de Paiva Leite (depoimento)* (Rio de Janeiro: Fundação Getúlio Vargas/CPDOC-História Oral, 1986).
12. Speech by Lucas Lopes, "JK e o Programa de Metas," Kubitschek Memorial, Brasília, May 14, 1986.
13. The basic economic document for the campaign was Juscelino Kubitschek de Oliveira, *Diretrizes gerais do plano nacional de desenvolvimento* (Belo Horizonte: Livraria Oscar Nicolai, 1955).

gists, and political scientists, the group founded an institute, which later became ISEB and was incorporated as part of the Ministry of Education during the Café Filho government.

Kubitschek met with this group of intellectuals during the electoral campaign.[14] But the actual contribution of ISEB to formulation of the Kubitschek economic program was limited.[15] Despite this minimal contribution, Kubitschek's contacts with ISEB helped generate support for his candidacy and program in nationalist intellectual circles.[16]

Lucas Lopes was the central figure in the formulation of the Kubitschek economic program. Lopes, an engineer, had worked with Kubitschek in Minas Gerais formulating and carrying out an electrification plan for the state. Later he had served on the Joint Brazil–United States Economic Development Commission, which was an important source of ideas for the initial documents drawn up by Lopes for Kubitschek during the campaign.[17] The main economic campaign document was compiled by Lopes in collaboration with Kubitschek and others. This document was written for politicians, not for economists. It responded to some specific attacks made on Kubitschek by his opponents. For example, in response to those who said that the Kubitschek government was going to be socialistic, it stressed that the state was primarily to serve as a "manipulator of incentives" for private initiative.

The major source material for the campaign document came from the Report of the Joint Brazil–United States Economic Development Commission and from the National Development Bank (BNDE). Roberto Campos was Lopes's "right arm" in the formulation of the Kubitschek economic program. It was his ideas of "bottlenecks" and "growing points," outlined in the Joint Commission report, which provided the theoretical basis for the priority projects of the future Targets Plan.

---

14. Roland Corbisier, *JK e a luta pela presidência: Uma campahna civilista* (São Paulo: Livraria Duas Cidades, 1976), p. 19. The author recalls that he left the meeting convinced that Juscelino, who had won their sympathy, would be invincible in the presidential race.

15. Interview with Roland Corbisier, Rio de Janeiro, June 25, 1986. Lucas Lopes, the author of the main economic campaign document, understood that the first six chapters of this document given to him by Kubitschek had been written by individuals from ISEB. But the bulk of the document, and all the concrete policy proposals, were not of ISEB origin. Interview with Lucas Lopes, Rio de Janiero, May 19, 1986.

16. For a discussion of the role of ISEB, see Caio Navarro de Toledo, *ISEB: Fábrica de ideologias* (São Paulo: Atica, 1982). Roland Corbisier, who later served as director of ISEB, made a series of almost sixty radio speeches in favor of the Kubitschek candidacy. *JK e a luta pela presidência.*

17. Interview with Lucas Lopes, Rio de Janeiro, May 19, 1986.

ITAMARATY GROUP

One small group of diplomat-economists from the Brazilian Foreign Service greatly influenced economic policy making of the 1950s. The importance of this group has been almost entirely overlooked by historians of the Kubitschek period. Their influence was the result of the unique skills and training acquired as part of their experience in the Foreign Service, as well as the job stability and educational opportunities associated with the diplomatic profession in Brazil. The nature of the Brazilian Foreign Service as a state institution, and the nature of the diplomat's job in the postwar period, led to the emergence of an elite group that exercised great power over economic policy in the 1950s.

Then located in the graceful palace of Itamaraty, the Brazilian Foreign Service is most often referred to simply as "Itamaraty." Itamaraty was long considered one of the most elite and professional branches of the Brazilian bureaucracy.[18] The Foreign Service traditionally focused on diplomatic problems of a political or juridical nature. In the late 1930s and the early 1940s a cohort of young men entered the Brazilian Foreign Service through the traditional competitive exams. Although they shared the Foreign Service ethos of professionalism and cosmopolitanism, they charted new territory by gaining advanced economics training in U.S. universities in preparation for the new tasks of postwar economic diplomacy. Many also participated in the postwar U.N. conferences on the creation of new international economic institutions.

Most young diplomats still considered an assignment in the political department a plum appointment. The new diplomat economists were looked down at as "merchants," and the economics department was jokingly referred to as the "Wet and Dry Goods Department."[19] Their training and experience were later tapped by the Kubitschek government when they moved into key economic policy positions.[20] At the

18. Alexandre de S. C. Barros, "The Formulation and Implementation of Brazilian Foreign Policy: Itamaraty and the New Actors," in *Latin American Nations in World Politics*, ed. Hernaldo Munoz and Joseph S. Tulchin (Boulder: Westview Press, 1984), p. 31.

19. Interview with João Batista Pinheiro, Rio de Janeiro, June 19, 1986.

20. Members of the Itamaraty group were called on to participate in the Kubitschek government largely because they possessed economic training and skills that made them valuable for the formulation and implementation of the new developmentalist policies. In an interview, Lucas Lopes referred to a basic informal group that oversaw the elaboration and implementation of the Targets Program, which included himself and three members of the Itamaraty group as the principal members: Roberto Campos, João Batista Pinheiro, and Octavio Dias Carneirno. Interview with Lucas Lopes, Rio de Janeiro, May 19, 1986.

same time, these diplomat-economists contributed to changes at the Foreign Service, elevating the prestige of economic tasks and improving the economic training of future diplomats.[21]

Roberto Campos was the most important member of the Itamaraty group, and his career is a good example of the career paths of the new group of economists within Itamaraty. When Campos was posted in the commercial section in the Brazilian embassy in Washington, D.C., "out of despair" he decided to study economics to prepare himself for his work, eventually earning a B.A. and a master's degree in economics. But what had been a "path of despair" turned into a "path of prescience." With the upsurge in international economic diplomacy, his skills were soon in demand. When the Brazilians were putting together a delegation for the Bretton Woods Conference in 1944, Campos was one of the only people in the Foreign Service with some economic training; he was named secretary of the Brazilian delegation. The experience was "dramatically important" for him.[22] Campos was a cosmopolitan developmentalist who favored foreign investment and believed the state should limit its intervention to indicative planning, where the plan serves to guide or coordinate development rather than control it. Although he would later devote greater attention to the problems of inflation and exchange rate policy, during the 1950s he was a firm advocate of industrialization and planning.[23]

According to Lucas Lopes, the initial work on the Targets Program was not concerned with theory. The targets seemed obvious, beyond

21. The 1951–1953 entrance exam for the Instituto Rio Branco included for the first time a section on economics. Also in 1951 and 1952, economics became a required course in both the first and the second year of the Diplomatic Training Course at the Instituto Rio Branco, and the refresher courses for diplomats began to include a course called "Treaties and Political Economy of Brazil." Ministerio das Reláões Exteriores, *Anuario do Instituto Rio Branco 1952*.

22. Campos served as an adviser to the Brazilian delegation at the International Conference on Trade and Employment, held in Havana in November 1947, and participated in the GATT Conference in Geneva in August 1948. Campos took part in negotiations with the Export-Import Bank and the IBRD on the possibility of increasing U.S. investment in Brazil, which led to setting up the Joint U.S.-Brazil Commission on Economic Development in 1950. He participated in plans for creating the National Economic Development Bank (the BNDE), formed in 1952, and then served as its first economic director. In this position, he initiated contacts with CEPAL, helping to organize a Joint CEPAL-BNDE study group, under the direction of Celso Furtado. In 1955 he returned to the BNDE as its superintendent-director. Interview with Roberto Campos, Rio de Janeiro, June 20, 1986.

23. For an overview of Campos's economic thought, see Ricardo Bielschowsky, "Brazilian Economic Thought 1945–1964: The Ideological Cycle of Developmentalism" (Ph.D. diss., University of Leicester, 1985), pp. 146–79.

discussion.[24] This only underlined the degree of consensus that existed on certain economic policy issues among important groups of técnicos and politicians. Over the years a series of economic commissions and study and planning groups had built upon each other to create technical and political support for certain kinds of development projects. Later Targets Program documents would all contain a recitation of the prior steps leading up to the creation of the Program:

> When the Second World War ended, the governments of most of the underdeveloped countries, encouraged by the action of the United Nations in the economic sphere, by the emancipation of the previously colonized countries, and by the unprecedented boom of new technical advances in the industrialized countries, resolved to prioritize economic programs and plans for their respective national economies. The government of Brazil requested the U.S. government to send the Cooke, Abbink, and Kleine-Saks missions; instituted in 1948 the SALTE plan; created, in 1951, the Joint Brazil–United States Economic Development Commission, and in 1952, the National Development Bank; financially supported research of the joint group made up of employees of the Economic Commission for Latin America (CEPAL) and the National Development Bank, and last, in 1956, established the Development Council in the Executive Office.[25]

This lineage is essentially correct and serves to emphasize the significant, self-conscious continuity of Brazilian development policy in the postwar period, with various efforts building on and contributing to one another. It fails to distinguish, however, which of these previous development study and planning efforts were most directly responsible for and connected to the elaboration of the Targets Plan. The Kubitschek administrative experience in Minas Gerais, the work of the Joint Brazil–United States Economic Development Commission, and the early work of the National Development Bank were the most important sources of inspiration, ideas, and data for the formulation of the Targets Program. Likewise, the BNDE's work with CEPAL under the supervision of Celso Furtado was not an important influence in the initial elaboration of the Kubitschek economic program.[26] As the BNDE took control of implementation of the economic program, CEPAL's in-

---

24. Interview with Lucas Lopes, Rio de Janeiro, May 19, 1986.

25. Presidência da República, Conselho do Desenvolvimento, *Programa de Metas: Relatório das atividades do Conselho do Desenvolvimento em 1958* (Rio de Janeiro, 1959), pp. 13–14.

26. Interview with Lucas Lopes, Rio de Janeiro, May 19, 1986.

fluence increased, because CEPAL ideas had been disseminated widely among técnicos in the BNDE through the work of the joint BNDE-CEPAL group and CEPAL training programs.

THE IMPLEMENTATION OF DEVELOPMENTALISM

The initial stages of Kubitschek's presidency were plagued with instability and the threat of a military coup. But even before he took office, he had faced increasing opposition to his candicacy from conservative forces after the Communist party had urged its voters to support the PSD-PTB alliance. Although Kubitschek won a plurality of the votes, he received only 36 percent of the total national vote. The opposition claimed that Kubitschek's victory was illegitimate, since he had failed to gain an absolute majority and had won with support from the votes of the Communists. The Superior Electoral Tribunal had declared in 1951 that an absolute majority was unnecessary to win an election, and although the Communist party had been outlawed in 1947, there was nothing to stop individual citizens who had been party members from casting their votes for another candidate. Nonetheless, these arguments carried weight in many military circles.

Talk increased of a military coup to prevent Kubitschek and his vice-presidential running mate, Goulart, from taking office.[27] In the midst of coup rumors, General Henrique Lott, the minister of war, made it clear that he would respect legality and assure that the government was turned over to the elected candidates. Lott was a member of the nationalist group within the army, as opposed to the more cosmopolitan Grupo da Sorbonne, which was associated with the Army Superior War College. Kubitschek's main opponent in the 1955 election, UDN candidate General Juarez Tavora, was one of the Superior War College group. On November 11, 1955, to prevent a coup in the making, Lott staged a "countercoup," or preventive coup, to insure that the elected candidates would be allowed to take office. The president was forced to resign and was replaced by the speaker of the Senate. Congress, following the urging of the military ministers, imposed a state of siege. The

27. To discredit the new administration, an opposition newspaper published a document, the so-called "Brandi letter," which appeared to show that Goulart had purchased arms from Perón in 1953 to arm worker militias. An official investigation by the military found the letter to be a forgery, but the episode testifies to the powerful fear produced by Perón in military circles in Brazil. Any association with Perón could be used to discredit Brazilian politicians.

new government oversaw the inauguration of Kubitschek and Goulart on January 31, 1956.

The November 11 preventive coup was fundamentally important to the stability of the Kubitschek government. It undermined the power of the Grupo da Sorbonne forces aligned with the UDN.[28] Prior to the coup, important groups within the Brazilian military had opposed the Kubitschek-Goulart ticket almost as firmly as the Argentine military would oppose the Frondizi candidacy two years later. After the preventive coup, the nationalist and loyalists in the army gained the upper hand and provided a stability that facilitated the implementation of the Kubitschek economic program.[29] The nationalist group generally supported Kubitschek's economic policy, as long as he did not interfere with basic nationalist issues, such as the oil monopoly under Petrobras. During the electoral campaign, Kubitschek spoke out in favor of Petrobras, a position he adhered to when he took office.

To reward Lott, Kubitschek named him minister of war in the new government, a position he held for most of the Kubitschek administration. Lott was a firm believer in military discipline; throughout the Kubitschek administration he punished any military behavior he regarded as disloyal or political. Kubitschek gave him a free hand in military matters and thus was spared major responsibility for disciplinary problems in the army.[30] Although Kubitschek was faced with military unrest during his government, this came primarily from the air force and the navy. Shortly after he took office, Kubitschek faced a rebellion of Brazilian air force officials who occupied an air base in the Amazon in the hope of inciting a wider coup against the government. Although the rebellion was put down easily and the president granted amnesty to the participants, discontent in military circles continued to fester, encouraged by members of the UDN who stressed the illegitimacy of the Kubitschek government.

28. Alexandre de Souza Costa Barros, "The Brazilian Military: Professional Specialization, Political Performance, and State Building" (Ph.D. diss., University of Chicago, 1978), p. 173.

29. Mario Victoria Benevides stresses the importance of the military support as one of the fundamental bases of stability of the Kubitschek government. *O governo Kubitschek: Desenvolvimento econômico e estabilidade política* (Rio de Janeiro: Paz e Terra, 1979), pp. 147–50.

30. Lott himself stated, "President Kubitschek . . . as regards the army, confided in me and left to me the initiative and the orientation of the activities of the Ministry of War, without any interference on his part." Henrique B. Duffles Teixeira Lott, *Henrique Teiseira Lott (depoimento, 1978)* (Rio de Janeiro: Fundação Getúlio Vargas/CPDOC-História Oral, 1982), p. 148.

From the first moments of his presidency, Kubitschek's actions underscored the importance he accorded his development program. At 7:00 A.M. on his first day in office, Kubitschek called a meeting of his cabinet at which he outlined his government program and gave his ministers responsibility for various aspects of the program. Later that day he signed the decree creating the Development Council, the body responsible for controlling and overseeing implementation of the development plan.[31] Kubitschek also signed a decree abolishing press censorship. A week later, the state of siege was suspended. With these early measures, Kubitschek hoped to convey an image of dynamism and communicate the priority his administration would place on development planning and the restoration and maintenance of democratic freedoms. True to these early impressions, the Kubitschek administration ushered in a unique period of Brazilian political life, noted for its respect for political and civil liberties.[32] A state of siege was never reimposed during the next five years, as it was in Argentina in response to striking petroleum workers.

The Targets Program

Between the election and the inauguration, Lucas Lopes and Roberto Campos worked with a group of técnicos to further elaborate the Targets Program. Campos argued for a set of three programs: a monetary and budget program, an exchange reform, and an investment plan. But Kubitschek and Minister of Finance Alkmin were enthusiastic only about the investment plan, which would become the Targets Program. While the team was working to elaborate the economic program, Kubitschek made a pre-inaugural trip to the United States, the Netherlands, the United Kingdom, Belgium, France, Germany, Italy, Spain, and Portugal. During the trip Kubitschek discussed his economic program with government officials and industrialists. Upon his return he had new suggestions and information for the economic team.[33]

Even before the new government took office, formulation of the Targets Program became the responsibility of the Development Coun-

31. The Development Council had very few staff members or facilities and was staffed mainly by BNDE employees. Since the Development Council also functioned in the same building as the BNDE and had the same president, they were for all practical purposes merged into a single identity.

32. The main exception to the political freedom of the period was that Kubitschek never reinstated the legality of the Communist party, although it was allowed to function openly during much of this period.

33. Lopes, "JK e o Programa de Metas."

cil and the BNDE. Of the six broad objectives discussed in the campaign document, three had been dropped: valorization of the worker, education for development, and regional and urban planning. They were more difficult to formulate in quantifiable goals, and they were not the main concerns of Kubitschek and his top advisers. Of the three broad areas that remained—expansion of basic services of energy and transport, basic industries, and rationalization of agriculture—the bulk of the program focused on energy, transport, and basic industries. For the first time, the targets began to be discussed in quantitative terms, listing both quantity and expenses.[34]

Also in early 1956 a number of study and working groups were set up to work on the different target areas and make recommendations about how to achieve the goals. Each group generally had one person who was a member of the informal coordinating group of the Development Council. In some cases, all the study groups had to do was update the studies of the Joint Brazil–United States Economic Development Commission; in other cases, they developed new reports and programs. Some working groups were transformed into executive groups to help implement their recommendations. The working group on the automobile industry recommended establishment of an executive group for the automobile industry, which would implement the program recommended by the working group.[35] This executive group, the Grupo Executivo da Indústria Automobilística (GEIA), established in 1956, served as a model for future executive groups in other sectors.

Executive groups were not established for all or even most of the targets, nor were all executive groups as successful in accomplishing their goals as was the GEIA. Nevertheless, the working groups and executive groups were useful administrative innovations that facilitated policy implementation for some of the more important aspects of the Targets Program. The informal groups, with firm backing from the executive, helped speed up the policy process.[36]

34. This early document lists sixteen main targets and twenty-eight subtargets, but there are significant differences between this list and the heralded thirty-one targets of the final Targets Plan. Presidência da República, Conselho do Desenvolvimento, "Documento de trabalho no. 3: Metas do Programa de Desenvolvimento," no date, but must be from late 1955.

35. Presidência da República, Conselho do Desenvolvimento, "Relatório do Grupo de Trabalho sobre indústria automobilística," document no. 6, 1956.

36. Executive groups were made up of representatives of the ministries and government agencies and those in the private sector who were interested or involved in the formulation or implementation of an investment target. Thus GEIA, for example, included representatives from the Ministry of Finance, the Bank of Brazil, SUMOC (the monetary authority), CACEX (the agency that granted import permits), as well as técnicos and representatives of the Brazilian auto parts industry. This format speeded policy

Table 2. The Targets Program's goals[37]

I. *Energy sector*

Target 1. *Electric energy*—Increase installed capacity from 3 to 5 million kilowatts by 1960 and undertake works that will permit an increase to 8 million by 1965.

Target 2. *Nuclear energy*—Install a pioneer atomic plant of 10,000 kilowatts and expand nuclear mineral metallurgy.

Target 3. *Coal*—Increase production from 2 to 3 million tons per year from 1955 to 1960.

Target 4. *Petroleum (production)*—Increase from an average of 6,800 barrels per day at the end of 1955 to 100,000 barrels per day at the end of 1960.

Target 5. *Petroleum (refining)*—Increase refining capacity from 130,000 barrels per day in 1955 to 330,000 barrels per day at the end of 1960.

II. *Transport sector*

Target 6. *Railroads (reequipment)*—Invest U.S. $239 million and 39.8 billion cruzeiros.

Target 7. *Railroads (construction)*—Construct 2,100 kilometers of railways, 280 kilometers of branch lines to 320 kilometers of gauge widening.

Target 8. *Roadways (paving)*—Complete asphalt paving of 5,000 kilometers of roadways by 1960.

Target 9. *Roadways (construction)*—Construct 12,000 kilometers of new roads and improve 3,800 kilometers.

Target 10. *Ports and dredging*—Reequip and enlarge ports and acquire a dredging fleet, involving investments of U.S. $32.5 million and 5.9 billion cruzeiros.

Target 11. *Merchant marine*—Enlarge coastal and long-range fleet by 300,000 tons and petroleum tankers by 330,000 tons deadweight.

Target 12. *Airline transport*—Renovate the commercial airline fleet with the purchase of 42 airplanes.

III. *Food sector*

Target 13. *Agricultural production (wheat)*—Increase production from 700,000 to 1.5 million tons.

Target 14. *Warehouses and silos*—Construct warehouses and silos for a static capacity of 742,000 tons.

Target 15. *Cold-storage warehouses*—Construct cold-storage warehouses for a storage capacity of 45,000 tons.

Target 16. *Industrial packing houses*—Construct packing houses with a daily capacity of 3,550 head of cattle and 1,300 swine.

Target 17. *Agricultural mechanization*—Increase the number of tractors in agricultural use from 45,000 to 72,000.

Target 18. *Fertilizers*—Increase production of chemical fertilizers from 18,000 to 120,000 tons.

IV. *Basic industries sector*

Target 19. *Steel*—Increase production capacity of steel ingots from 1 to 2 million tons per year in 1960 and to 3 million tons per year in 1965.

---

making and improved coordination. For example, the working group on the automobile industry completed its preliminary work in thirty days.

37. Presidência da República, Conselho do Desenvolvimento, *Programa de Metas. Tomo I: Introdução* (Rio de Janeiro: Gráfica Editora Jornal do Comércio, 1958), pp. 11–13.

Target 20. *Aluminum*—Increase production to 18 million tons in 1960.

Target 21. *Nonferrous metals*—Expand production and refining of nonferrous metals (copper, lead, tin, nickel, etc.).

Target 22. *Cement*—Increase production capacity from 2.7 to 5 million annual tons in 1960.

Target 23. *Alkali*—Increase alkali production from 20,000 annual tons in 1955 to 152,000 annual tons in 1960.

Target 24. *Paper and cellulose*—Increase cellulose production from 90,000 to 260,000 tons and newsprint from 40,000 to 130,000 tons between 1955 and 1960.

Target 25. *Rubber*—Increase rubber production capacity from 22,000 to 65,000 tons, with the outset of synthetic rubber production.

Target 26. *Mineral exports*—Increase the export of ferrous minerals from 2.5 to 8 million tons and prepare for the export of 30 million tons in the next five-year period.

Target 27. *Automobile industry*—Establish an industry to produce 170,000 vehicles nationally in 1960.

Target 28. *Naval construction*—Establish a naval construction industry.

Target 29. *Mechanical and heavy electrical industry*–Establish and expand mechanical and heavy electrical industry.

V. *Education sector*

Target 30. *Technical personnel*—Intensify training of technical personnel and orient education system for development needs.

By 1958 the Targets Program had taken its final form. It consisted of thirty targets divided into five sectors: energy (targets 1–5), transport (6–12), food (13–18), basic industries (19–29), and education (30). (See table 2.) For most target areas, a specific quantitative goal was set, although some were stated in more general terms. The goal for naval construction, for example, was simply to establish a naval construction industry, whereas the goal for education called for only the intensification of the training of technical staff and the orientation of education for development, without giving any specific numbers.

The notion of thirty targets is misleading; some were considered more important than others and received greater attention and resources; others were relegated to the sidelines. Particular attention was devoted to those areas of special concern to the president: steel, petroleum production and refining, road building and paving, and automobile production. Kubitschek followed the implementation of the Targets Program with great interest. Economic officials responsible for the various goals recalled early-morning phone calls from the president to inquire on progress in meeting the targets and to make suggestions and give encouragement.

The dedication and interest of other powerful members of the administration contributed to progress in certain areas. Admiral Lucio Meira served first as minister of public works and later as president of the BNDE. More than any other Brazilian policy maker, he was a man obsessed with an idea: Brazil as a great producer of automobiles. His passionate concern for the automobile and the naval construction industries gave a special impetus to work in this area. His passion for naval construction is more understandable in a navy man than his obsession with automobiles. But, then, Meira is better understood as a developmentalist who happened to be in the navy than as a military developmentalist. Due in part to Meira's special interests, the two executive groups in this domain, GEIA and Grupo Executivo da Industria da Construção Naval (GEICON), are generally considered the most successful of the executive groups.

Brasília

Much as Frondizi and Frigerio would do in Argentina two years later, Kubitschek felt the need to initiate his program vigorously on various fronts at once. At the same time that he was launching the Targets Program, Kubitschek requested that Congress approve transfer of the national capital to Brasília. The construction of Brasília and the implementation of the Targets Program became Kubitschek's two grand passions during his presidency.

Kubitschek called for the construction of the national capital in the interior state of Goias as part of his campaign platform. Once he took office, he moved quickly to initiate the implementation of this dream. In September Congress created the Companhia Urbanizadora da Nova Capital (NOVACAP), the public company responsible for construction of the new capital.[38] The date for the transfer of the capital was set for April 21, 1960. Kubitschek was convinced that if the transfer did not take place during his administration, it might be postponed indefinitely by future presidents. The president involved himself in the day-to-day planning of the new capital, traveling to Brasília frequently to oversee construction.

For Kubitschek, Brasília was not just part of the developmentalist program; it was its physical and symbolic culmination. The construction of the new capital symbolized Brazil's integration of its national territory and its movement into the future. Kubitschek called the construction of Brasília the "synthesis goal" of the Targets Program.

38. The transfer of Brazil's capital to the central part of the country was called for in a provision of the Brazilian constitution. The opposition agreed to the creation of NOVACAP because provisions called for opposition representation in the new company. Some believe that the opposition supported the early Brasília legislation because they thought it impossible that the new capital would ever be completed.

Brasília required intense construction of new transportation and communication networks, linking the interior of the country more closely with major urban centers near the coast. Kubitschek's opponents, and some of his allies, argued that Brasília was a white elephant that would lead to inflationary pressure and diverted resources from more productive activities. Cosmopolitan developmentalists' opposition to the construction of Brasília was a point of friction between them and the president. For example, Roberto Campos had never sympathized with the idea of Brasília and had worked to sabotage the plan in a number of ways. For example, Brasília was never included as part of the Targets Program in the documents published by the BNDE. So although Kubitschek insisted that Brasília was the "synthesis target" of the entire plan, the very concept of Brasília was absent from BNDE presentations of the program.[39] But the idea of Brasília captured the imagination of much of the population of Brazil. Photos of the futuristic buildings designed by Oscar Niemeyer rising from the bare backland of Brazil figured on magazine covers, and visitors arrived from around the world to witness the emerging city.

International Support for the Development Program

International collaboration in the form of loans and foreign investment was essential to the successful implementation of Kubitschek's economic program.[40] Thus the World Bank's refusal to provide major financing for the program disappointed and angered Brazilian developmentalists. Relations between Brazil and the World Bank had cooled in 1952 when Vargas imposed restrictions on profit remittances of foreign firms. Total loans declined in 1953–1954, and except for a few exceptions in 1958 and 1959, the World Bank granted no new loans to Brazil during the 1955–1964 period.[41] This was a blow to Brazilian development plans, since the whole program of the Joint Brazil–United States Economic Development Commission had been predicated on World Bank financing.[42]

39. Interview with Roberto Campos, Rio de Janeiro, June 20, 1986.

40. An early memo from the Brazilian government to the United States stressed that "the entire administrative program of the Brazilian government hinges upon the specific measure of cooperation it can obtain for the solution of its urgent and serious financial and economic problems." "Memorandum" (confidential), annex 1, Presidência da República, Conselho do Desenvolvimento, "Cooperação econômica entre os Estados Unidos e o Brasil," vol. 3, document no. 11, p. 1.

41. Edward Mason and Robert Asher, *The World Bank since Bretton Woods* (Washington, D.C.: Brookings Institution, 1973), pp. 657–59.

42. In 1951, the bank had agreed to $300 million over five years as an appropriate planning figure for Joint Development Commission projects. Brazilian officials consid-

Faced with the World Bank's intransigence, Kubitschek turned to the U.S. government to secure needed financing. The first phase of negotiations between the United States and Brazil began when President-elect Kubitschek met with President Eisenhower during his pre-inaugural tour. Eisenhower "liked Kubitschek but badly underestimated him, doubting 'his stamina if he gets into a real battle.'"[43] Later, Vice-President Richard Nixon, who represented the United States at Kubitschek's inauguration, was presented with a preliminary document outlining the Kubitschek economic program and discussing the possibility of obtaining loans from the United States. Shortly after taking office, Kubitschek traveled with Nixon to the large steelworks at Volta Redonda, built with Export-Import Bank assistance during the Second World War. Nixon announced that the Export-Import would grant a new loan for $35 million to the National Steel Company, a joint state-private enterprise responsible for the Volta Redonda works.[44]

The first two years of the Kubitschek program were a period of relative collaboration between the United States and Brazil. Although Kubitschek never received the amount of support he had anticipated from U.S. public sources or from international agencies, the bulk of the support he did receive came under the Lopes-Campos team, before the government broke with the IMF. A special informal working group was set up within the National Development Council to discuss economic cooperation with the United States. This group, composed mainly of diplomat-economists on loan from Itamaraty to the Development Council and the BNDE, engaged in informal discussions with the U.S. embassy.[45] But earnest negotiations with the United States did not begin until Vice-President João Goulart traveled to the United States in May 1956 at the invitation of Nixon.

The bureaucrats at the Foreign Ministry, who saw João Goulart as a rough-and-ready politician not known for his diplomatic skills or his

---

ered this a commitment for financing projects up to this amount. After 1952, however, the World Bank did not consider Brazil creditworthy until it controlled inflation and solved other basic problems of its economy. Instead of $300 million, Brazil received only slightly over $50 million in the five years following the completion of the Joint U.S.-Brazil Commission report. Mason and Asher, *The World Bank since Bretton Woods*, pp. 657–58.

43. Stephen G. Rabe, *Eisenhower and Latin America: The Foreign Policy of Anticommunism* (Chapel Hill: University of North Carolina Press, 1988), p. 97.

44. Since 1941, when the Export-Import Bank had financed the construction of the Volta Redonda plant, it had taken "a fierce proprietary interest in Brazil's steel industry," according to *Business Week* (February 13, 1971), cited in Mason and Asher, *The World Bank since Bretton Woods*, p. 532.

45. Conselho do Desenvolvimento, "Cooperação econômica entre os Estados Unidos e o Brasil," vol. 3, pp. 1–2.

sympathy for the United States, were nervous about the trip. Kubitschek requested that diplomat-economist João Batista Pinheiro, a member of the Itamaraty group, accompany Goulart as a technical adviser. Goulart shared with Pinheiro his private intention to "put Eisenhower against the wall." During the meeting, however, Goulart was a model of diplomatic discretion; he limited himself to stressing the realistic nature of the ambitious new economic program.[46]

During this visit U.S. officials told Goulart that the United States was prepared to initiate negotiations with Brazil on financial assistance. An official mission, headed by Lucas Lopes and composed of three members of the Itamaraty group, arrived in Washington to carry out negotiations. U.S. economic training of the Itamaraty group served them well in these sessions, allowing them to speak with U.S. policy makers in a language they understood and to reassure them on various points of the Targets Plan.

President Eisenhower was planning on attending the Congress of American Presidents in Panama in July 1956 and he wanted to be certain that Kubitschek would also attend. Kubitschek let it be known that he hoped for some concrete indication of U.S. financial support as a gesture of goodwill before he made his trip to Panama.[47] Kubitschek was following in the tradition of Vargas by negotiating for economic assistance in exchange for Brazilian support for U.S. political and diplomatic objectives.

The principal outcome of these negotiations was a decision by the Export-Import Bank to approve $151 million of assistance to Brazil. In addition, the bank signaled its willingness to help finance the dollar requirements of Kubitschek's development program without setting any specific limitations as to amount. This commitment covered projects in the fields of power, air and surface transportation, industry, mining and agriculture, including projects elaborated by the Joint Brazil–United States Economic Development Commission which had been previously submitted to the World Bank.[48] These Export-Import Bank

46. Interview with João Batista Pinheiro, Rio de Janeiro, June 19, 1986.
47. Juscelino Kubitschek, *Meu caminho para Brasília: cinqüenta anos em cinco* (Rio de Janeiro: Bloch Editores, 1976), p. 59.
48. Letter from Samuel C. Waugh, president of the Export-Import Bank, to Lucas Lopes, dated July 20, 1956, annex 4, "Cooperação econômica entre os Estados Unidos e o Brasil," vol. 3, p. 1. Export-Import Bank loans were tied to the purchase of materials and equipment produced in the United States and the technical services of U.S. firms and individuals. In the late 1940s and early 1950s some competition had developed between the World Bank and the Export-Import Bank, because the World Bank felt that Export-Import Bank long-term lending in Latin America tended to supplant World Bank lending. The World Bank was trying to use its position to influence the macro-

credits, both long- and medium-term, became the primary international financial support for the Targets Program.

Brazilian técnicos complained that the attitude of international financial organizations created a vicious cycle for Brazilian development; financial entities conditioned loans on a series of requirements that were difficult to meet without having the security of future financing. The Export-Import Bank's prior commitment to finance economically viable projects helped break this cycle.[49]

Tariff Policy

In early 1957, when it passed the Tariff Law of 1957, the government put into place another piece of its economic program. The Targets Program was based on three measures: the financing policy of the BNDE, SUMOC's Instruction 113, and the Tariff Law of 1957.[50]

The new tariff law replaced the tariff rates of 1937 with strongly protectionist but flexible new rates. In addition, the five import categories established in 1953 were reduced to two, general and specific. Multiple exchange rates were maintained only for certain luxury goods.[51] To implement the new tariff policy, a Council on Customs Policy (CPA) was set up; it was composed of representatives of business, workers, and the government. The CPA had the power to classify goods into import categories and modify the tariff rates within a range for any particular subgroup of products.

The new tariff law was designed both to facilitate the entry of capital goods and inputs necessary to the industrialization process and to protect new domestic capital goods industries. It did so first by granting a 50 percent reduction of tariffs for those capital goods imports that the industrial association could prove were unobtainable from domestic producers. But once the CPA determined that a domestic industrial sector was capable of satisfying domestic demand for a particular product, no further exchange or tax concessions could be granted for imports of that product.

The establishment of the CPA thus transferred significant discretionary power over tariff policy to the executive and provided a flexible

---

economic policies of countries like Brazil, and it sometimes felt that Export-Import Bank loans undermined their position by lessening pressure on governments for policies changes. Mason and Asher, *The World Bank since Bretton Woods*, pp. 197, 496–98.

49. Conselho do Desenvolvimento, "Cooperação econômica entre os Estados Unidos e o Brasil," p. 6.

50. Bonelli and Tolipan, "Industrial Policies in Brazil," p. 37.

51. Lessa, "Fifteen Years of Economic Policy in Brazil," p. 193.

and pliable economic instrument that could be easily modified to reflect changing economic developments. According to Carlos Lessa's classic study of economic policy making during this period, the combination of the tariff and the CPA constituted "the most precise and well adjusted instrument of economic policy existing in Brazil."[52]

Petroleum Policy

Petroleum policy and a stabilization plan, two of the issues that had led to a breakdown of the tactical alliance between cosmopolitan and nationalist developmentalists in Argentina early in the Frondizi administration, contributed to a similar division in the Kubitschek government in 1959.

Although Kubitschek had settled the petroleum issue early in his administration by his support for the state oil company, divisions emerged later over the form of Brazilian exploitation of Bolivian oil fields. Under the Roboré Agreement, Bolivia granted Brazil the right to explore and exploit petroleum deposits in a large sub-Andean region of Bolivia.[53] A provision of the new Bolivian petroleum code, however, excluded the national petroleum company, Petrobras, but permitted investment by Brazilian private firms. The BNDE took responsibility for the selection of firms and the provision of credit for the undertaking. Roberto Campos believed that Brazilian firms did not have the necessary capital or technology to exploit the Bolivian oil fields, so he allowed Brazilian firms contact with private foreign firms with which they could contract for the actual exploration and exploitation of oil in Bolivia. Although similar to the risk contracts Frondizi was signing with foreign oil companies in Argentina, the Brazilian contracts were somewhat different in form. "I had put together a less obvious, less frank arrangement than the one in Argentina," Campos said. Rather than direct contracts between the state and foreign firms, fully Brazilian firms contracted to have foreign firms act as their "operating companies" in Bolivia.[54]

Although the arrangement was "less obvious" than the Argentine contracts, it provoked similar political opposition from nationalist

52. Ibid., p. 193.

53. The Roboré Agreement originated in a revision of treaties of 1938 between Brazil and Bolivia. Under the revised arrangement, Brazil agreed to construct the Corumba-Santa Cruz Railroad and to assist Bolivia in a study of petroleum deposits in an extensive region. In return, Bolivia granted Brazilian firms the right to exploit petroleum resources in a portion of the region. Jesus Soares Pereira, *Petróleo, energia elétrica, siderúrgia: S luta pela emancipação* (Rio de Janeiro: Paz e Terra, 1975), pp. 193–195, n. 52.

54. Interview with Roberto Campos, Rio de Janeiro, June 20, 1986.

groups. Campos was branded an *entreguista*, or "sellout" to foreign interests. As political opposition increased, Kubitschek began to face pressure from a number of fronts to ask for Campos's resignation. The conflict over petroleum reinforced and exacerbated existing divisions between cosmopolitans and nationalists within the Kubitschek administration. In February 1959 the students of Rio organized a demonstration against Campos and the involvement of foreign firms in the exploitation of Bolivian oil, under the terms of the Roboré Agreement. ISEB supported this demonstration, and later the director of ISEB would take personal responsibility for contributing to the downfall of Campos.[55] At the same time it was rumored that Vice-President Goulart was pressuring Kubitschek for Campos's resignation.[56] Campos had always called for a greater degree of "exchange realism" than was being practiced by the Kubitschek government. The Roboré case added a new source of tension in the already troubled relationship. As long as Lucas Lopes was in control of economic policy, Campos's position was relatively secure. But new conflicts emerged between Lopes and Campos, and between Kubitschek and the nationalists, over the implementation of the stabilization plan.

The Stabilization Plan and the Break with the IMF

From early 1958 the Brazilian economic program began to encounter increased financial difficulties. Export earnings were stagnating, primarily as a result of falling coffee prices, at the same time that the industrialization program led to increased demand for imports.[57] Multilateral credit was minimal, and the bilateral sources of finance on which Brazil had relied to finance its development program were becoming more difficult to secure.[58] While inflows of capital were decreasing, payments for servicing the external debt were increasing. The balance of payments deficit reached U.S. $280 million in 1958. At the same time inflation had increased to 9 percent for the first half of 1958 and 24

55. Interview with Roland Corbisier, Rio de Janeiro, June 25, 1986.

56. Casemiro Ribeiro, *Casemiro Ribeiro (depoimento, 1975–79)* (Rio de Janeiro: Fundacão Getúlio Vargas/CPDOC-História Oral, 1981), p. 102.

57. In 1958 import capacity fell by U.S. $300 million in comparison with 1957, largely explained by the decline in the value of coffee exports, which fell by $158 million from 1957 values. At the same time, imports fell by only U.S. $105 million. Lourdes Sola, "The Political and Ideological Constraints to Economic Management in Brazil, 1945–1963" (Ph.D. diss., Oxford University, 1982), p. 147.

58. According to one adviser to the minister of economics, "Outside credit was becoming more difficult all the time, and increasingly dependent on the IMF, whose opinion of Brazil was getting increasingly more restrictive." Ribeiro, *Depoimento*, p. 99.

percent over the whole year, as compared to 7 percent in 1957.[59] Large surplus coffee purchases, an expansion of public investment, especially for the construction of Brasília, and the drought in the northeast exacerbated the government deficit.

All of these conditions threatened the continuation of the Targets Program. The Monetary Stabilization Plan (PEM), adopted in 1958, can be seen as an attempt to ensure the continuation of the Targets Program by reestablishing international creditworthiness and by resolving the economic constraints on continued growth. In June 1958 Lucas Lopes was named to replace Alkmin as finance minister, and Roberto Campos took over Lopes's position as president of the BNDE. This was not a major ministerial change, because Lopes and Campos had been active in the formulation of economic policy since the beginning of the Kubitschek administration, but it did pave the way for the formulation and implementation of the PEM.

In its essence, the PEM was a gradual stabilization alternative to the more drastic programs advocated by the IMF. It attempted to gain the approval of the IMF while taking into account the political pressures faced by the Kubitschek administration. The plan was to be adopted in two stages: first, a period of transition and readjustment lasting through 1959; and second, a period of stricter stabilization. The gradualist strategy was aimed at deflecting domestic opposition. The PEM called for limiting monetary expansion and decreasing the federal deficit, which it identified as the principal sources of inflation. As part of the program to limit monetary expansion, the plan placed a ceiling on Banco do Brasil credit. It proposed reducing the federal deficit via cuts in expenditures, an increase in taxation, the postponement of salary increases for public servants, and increases in public utility rates. Although the plan did not advocate a cut in real wages, it called for a readjustment of wage levels below the rate expected by workers. In addition, to remedy the balance of payments, it proposed modifying exchange policies to encourage exports, reducing exchange rate subsidies, and showing greater discipline in the use of suppliers' credits to finance imports.

The PEM tried to take a middle ground between domestic political demands and the need for monetary and fiscal discipline, but it was unable to secure needed support from either the staff of the IMF or the groups that made up the developmentalist coalition supporting the Kubitschek government. Industrialists opposed the plan because of its

---

59. Sola, "Political and Ideological Constraints to Economic Management in Brazil," pp. 147–48.

restrictive credit policies and its call for increased taxation. The Economics Department of the National Industrialists Confederation proposed an alternative stabilization that called for more credit in private industry but adopted an even more restrictive position on wages than the PEM. Thus it questioned indirectly the very basis of the Kubitschek economic policy: a project of accelerated development within the framework of a social compact between capital and labor.[60] Coffee growers were primarily opposed to the plans for purchasing surplus coffee, which were less generous than in previous years, ignoring one of the overall thrusts of the plan, which aimed to benefit the export sector and expand exports. Further opposition came from nationalist groups, who viewed the PEM as a concession to foreign pressures of the IMF. Since Roberto Campos was intimately involved with both the PEM and the Roboré Agreement, there was a tendency toward issue linkage, portraying Campos as a sellout to foreign interests in both areas.[61]

As was the case with the petroleum issue, opposition to the PEM not only came from societal forces but also exacerbated divisions within the state. The president of the Banco do Brasil refused to comply with the stabilization plan's targets for the limitation of credit to domestic industries and continued a more expansive credit policy. The divisions created by the PEM, however, cannot be understood simply in terms of a division between the nationalists and the cosmopolitan técnicos. Rather, a small group of cosmopolitan técnicos led by Lopes and Campos lined up against a broader coalition made up of individuals with connections to banking and industrial circles in São Paulo, PSD politicians, and nationalists.[62] Thus, contrary to the situation in Argentina, where business and rural groups firmly backed the stabilization plan, in Brazil a similar but more moderate plan found little domestic support.

Whereas domestic groups in Brazil saw the stabilization plan as too harsh or as a sellout to foreign interests, the IMF staff refused to endorse the plan because it failed to meet their stringent standards for monetary and fiscal responsibility. Brazil depended on IMF approval in order to receive on an additional credit of U.S. $37.5 million. But another $260 million of credits from the Export-Import Bank and European banks depended on IMF approval of Brazil's creditworthiness.

60. Ibid., p. 180.

61. Demonstrators against Campos held signs referring to him as "Bob Fields," a translation of his name into English, implying that he was more at the service of U.S. interests than those of Brazil.

62. Sola, "Political and Ideological Constraints to Economic Management in Brazil," p. 188.

During the final discussions between the IMF staff and the Brazilian técnicos, Lucas Lopes sent a message to the head of the IMF delegation urging them to help the Brazilian team arrive at a compromise agreement because "we're the last bastion of rationality" in the government. He warned the fund "not to be overly purist or else we won't reach an agreement. I've already obtained the maximum I could from the president, and I'm sensing that he is prepared to break with the fund. It would be a good scapegoat, from a political point of view."[63] But the fund staff refused to accept the Brazilian proposal and pushed the team to secure further concessions from their government. Kubitschek called the negotiators back to Rio, where the government was deciding whether or not to break with the fund.

Kubitschek called a meeting of his advisers to get their opinions. Lucas Lopes, who had suffered a heart attack, was not present. Roberto Campos was not invited. One of Brazil's negotiators with the fund recalled that of the thirty people present, he was the only one to speak against breaking off with the IMF. Among the técnicos arguing against the IMF were Celso Furtado and the nationalist group within the BNDE. The fund was criticized for its lack of sensitivity to the political problems facing developing countries and its lack of concern with the structural problems underlying inflation. A number of those present, including Kubitschek himself, pointed to the example of the IMF stabilization plan being carried out by Frondizi in Argentina, which was seen as excessively rigorous and recessionary.[64]

Kubitschek made up his mind to break off negotiations with the IMF. The costs of making more concessions to the fund, both political and in terms of completion of his program, were too high and the payoffs too uncertain. Later he argued, "If I had submitted to the imposition of the fund, I would have had to give up on the Targets Program, the construction of Brasília, and the industrialization of the country, and let the people suffer from hunger."[65]

The decision to break with the fund received enormous political backing. A popular demonstration gathered in front of the presidential palace to show support for the move. In Congress, even members of the conservative PSD cheered the decision. It helped solidify the political coalition that supported the Kubitschek administration until the end of his term. But the break with the IMF complicated the already serious financial difficulties Brazil faced. To replace Lucas Lopes, Kubitschek named Sebastião Paes de Almeida, president of the Banco

63. Casemiro, *Depoimento*, p. 103.
64. Ibid., pp. 117–21.
65. Kubitschek, *Cinqüenta anos em cinco*, p. 255.

do Brasil, as the new finance minister. Lucio Meira, minister of transport and public works replaced Roberto Campos as president of the BNDE. The cabinet change, a reshuffling of existing policy makers, cannot be seem as an unqualified victory of nationalists over cosmopolitans, since neither Paes de Almeida nor Lucio Meira were clear members of the nationalist group; but nationalists did gain more influence in policy making with the exit of Campos and Lopes.

The inflexibility of the IMF in its negotiations with Brazil was clearly one of the factors that made the break nearly unavoidable, given the political conditions in Brazil.[66] The position of both the IMF and the World Bank toward Brazil during the Kubitschek government served to limit the economic options available to Brazil. The position of the U.S. government was more flexible toward Brazilian economic policy during the Kubitschek government than were the staff of the IMF and the World Bank.

THE LAST YEARS OF THE KUBITSCHEK ADMINISTRATION

By the time Kubitschek broke off negotiations with the IMF in 1959, the presidential campaign was already under way. Indeed, one of the justifications that Kubitschek gave for not continuing the stabilization program was that it was too late in his term to undertake such severe economic measures. Under Brazilian electoral law Kubitschek was not allowed to succeed himself in the presidency, although he could run for office again in another five years. The PSD nominated as its candidate General Henrique Lott, Kubitschek's minister of war and the hero of the November countercoup that had smoothed the way for Kubitschek to take office in 1956. Later Lott was also endorsed by the PTB, which nominated Goulart as Lott's running mate. Lott was a weak candidate, dry and unappealing politically. He conducted a lackluster campaign against the candidate of the UDN, the dynamic governor of São Paulo, Jânio Quadros, who was running on a conservative populist platform against administrative inefficiency and corruption.

Kubitschek's closest supporters were already beginning to plan ahead for the 1965 elections, when Kubitschek could once again run for the

66. The rigidity of the IMF can be traced to its adoption of a new set of policies in 1957, which tied standby loans to much more stringent fiscal and monetary objectives, which were quantified in the form of specific targets and ceilings. David Pion-Berlin "The Role of Ideas: The International Monetary Fund and Third World Policy Choices," paper presented at the 1985 American Political Science Association Meeting, New Orleans, August 29–September 1, 1985, p. 17.

presidency, and the concerns of the "JK-65 movement," as it was called, appear to have influenced the president's behavior during the 1960 campaign. According to some sources, Kubitschek favored the election of a UDN candidate, both to placate the "disloyal opposition" within the UDN and because a UDN candidate could be counted on to carry out the necessary but unpopular stabilization measures that Kubitschek had been unwilling to implement himself.[67] So although Kubitschek officially supported the Lott candidacy, he refrained from campaigning actively for his minister of war.

Kubitschek could also claim that the demands of his office gave him little opportunity for campaigning. In November 1959 he faced the last military challenge to his administration, a minor rebellion led by air force officers which was put down in thirty-six hours without any casualties. At the same time, Kubitschek continued to work toward the completion of the Targets Program goals and the construction of Brasília. The important new initiative in the economic realm that Kubitschek took on during these last years was the creation of a development agency for the drought-stricken northeast of Brazil.

The 1958 drought, one of the most severe ever experienced in the country, led to increased concern with the conditions of this, the poorest region of Brazil. The impact of the industrialization program could not be felt in the poor northeastern states of Brazil, where one-third of the Brazilian population lived. In response to this situation, the government asked Celso Furtado, a native of the northeast who had long been concerned with the economic problems of the region, to prepare a report and a plan of action. Furtado's impressive report advocated a comprehensive development program for the region, supervised by a new development institution, the Superintendency for the Development of the Northeast (SUDENE).

Furtado's plan received support from the Catholic bishops in the northeast but was opposed by many of the established economic and political interests in the region, including politicians from Kubitschek's party, the PSD.[68] Nevertheless, the initiative received strong government support, and the law creating SUDENE was passed by Congress in December 1959. Albert Hirschman argues that Kubitschek supported the formation of SUDENE because it corresponded to the im-

67. Renato Archer, *Renato Archer (depoimento)* (Rio de Janeiro: Fundação Getúlio Vargas/CPDOC-História Oral, 1973), p. 169.
68. For a detailed discussion of the problem of the northeast of Brazil and the creation of SUDENE, see Albert O. Hirschman, "Brazil's Northeast," in his *Journeys toward Progress: Studies of Economic Policy-making in Latin America* (New York: Norton, 1973), chap. 1.

age he wanted to project of his administration, one of modernity and large-scale development projects. His support was an affirmation of his faith in the group of nationalist técnicos who argued in favor of the project. It was these same nationalists who had sided with the president during his break with the stabilization plan and the IMF.[69] In this sense, SUDENE can be seen as one of the concrete outcomes of the victory of nationalist over cosmopolitan developmentalists during the last years of the Kubitschek administration.

Nineteen hundred and sixty was called the Year of Brasília, and much of the first part of the year was consumed by symbolic and practical preparations for the installation of the new capital. Kubitschek, with his flair for symbolic political action, organized a variety of political activities around Brasília leading up to the move. In early 1960, a Caravan of National Integration was organized as a collaborative effort between the automobile industry and the national government. Columns of cars produced in Brazil and powered by Brazilian gas departed from four corners of the country: Belém, Porto Alegre, Rio de Janeiro, and Curitiba. Traveling over the newly constructed road networks connecting Brasília to the rest of the country, they converged on Brasília, where they were greeted by the president and his ministers.[70] When President Eisenhower visited Brazil in February 1960, he and Kubitschek traveled to Brasília, where they issued a joint communiqúe in defense of democracy in the hemisphere. But it was not until April 21, 1960, the date set four years earlier by Congress, that the new capital was inaugurated in a series of ceremonies attended by Brazilians and international visitors and representatives.

The successes of the Kubitschek government, however, were not sufficient to ensure the election of his party's candidate for president. In October 1960 Quadros resoundingly defeated General Lott, receiving 48 percent of the vote as compared to Lott's 28 percent. The election results were far from a clear-cut defeat of the Kubitschek coalition, however. Kubitschek's vice-president, João Goulart, running again for the vice-presidency on the PTB-PSD ticket, defeated the UDN candidate. By a particular quirk of the Brazilian electoral rules, which allows voters to split their ballot for president and vice-president, Goulart was elected Quadros's vice-president. Thus on January 31, 1961, Kubitschek passed the presidential sash over to his successor.

But this "happy ending" was only temporary. Quadros stayed in of-

69. Ibid., p. 86.
70. In its symbolic significance, this caravan of national integration might be compared to the Golden Spike ceremony performed in the United States when the railroads from the west and the east coasts met to complete the first transatlantic railway.

fice only seven months before resigning. After a military crisis, Goulart was allowed to take office, but only after his power was drastically curtailed by installation of a parliamentary system of government. Kubitschek supported Goulart's bid for the presidency but mainly kept his eye on 1965, when he could again run for president.

As Goulart's nationalist policies and erratic political style provoked increasing internal unrest, the developmentalist coalition that had backed Kubitschek began to divide. Many continued to collaborate with the Goulart government. Celso Furtado was nominated minister of planning and asked to draw up the government's three-year plan for economic and social development. Even arch-cosmopolitan developmentalist Roberto Campos was named Brazilian ambassador to Washington, D.C., where he helped negotiate an economic aid package for the Goulart administration. Campos, however, increasingly disagreed with Goulart's policies and began to move into the ranks of the opposition. In general, the cosmopolitan developmentalists were more often associated with opposition to Goulart.

Other close Kubitschek associates became part of the "disloyal opposition" to Goulart. One of Kubitschek's closest political associates, Augusto Federico Schmidt, engaged in often virulent attacks on the Goulart government and joined organizations instrumental in the eventual overthrow of the Goulart administration in March 1964.[71] Kubitschek's first minister of economics, Alkmin, also collaborated with the activities that led to the overthrow of Goulart in 1964. After the coup, Congress elected Alkmin to serve as vice-president to General Castelo Branco. Castelo Branco named Roberto Campos minister of planning and economic coordination. Other Kubitschek policy makers continued to occupy positions in the state but were not supporters of the military coup. Some were marginalized in backwater positions in the economic apparatus of the state. Other Kubitschek policy makers resigned and moved on to the private sector or to positions in international organizations.

Many of Kubitschek's associates had set up private economic consulting firms during the 1950s to provide technical and legal advice and feasibility studies for state agencies and national and international companies. These consulting firms formed part of the "bureaucratic rings" through which private national and international interests were integrated with the state. According to René Dreifuss, these private economic consulting firms formed part of the new "block" of political

71. Augusto Frederico Schmidt, *Preludio a revolução* (Rio de Janeiro: Edições do Val, 1964); Fundação Getúlio Vargas/CPDOC, *Diccionario histórico-biográfico brasileiro* (Rio de Janeiro: Forense-Universitaria, 1984), p. 3116.

power that supported the coup and the post-1964 military government.[72]

But in spite of the extensive collaboration of men from the Kubitschek administration with the new military government, Kubitschek himself did not escape persecution. In July 1964 the new government removed the political rights of Kubitschek, then a senator for the PSD, and eventually forced him into exile. Shortly before the coup, Kubitschek had been selected to be the presidential candidate of the PSD, and the military saw him as a threat to the continuity of military rule.

The Accomplishments of the Targets Program

The Targets Program succeeded in its basic goal of stimulating investment, accelerating growth, and provoking a transformation of the Brazilian economy by establishing a more integrated industrial structure. Although not all of the targets were achieved, enough progress was made to consider the plan an unqualified success.[73]

Energy. The first target, expansion of electric energy capacity to 5 million kilowatts, was almost achieved: installed capacity reached 4.8 million kilowatts by 1960. The targets in petroleum production and refining capacity were not reached by 1960, but these areas expanded dramatically, and target levels were almost reached by 1961. Coal production, however, actually fell during this period.

Transport. The plans for road construction and paving were more successful than those for expansion of the railroad system. In the railways, less than half of the construction of new lines programmed by the target were actually made. In contrast, the road building and improvement program achieved and surpassed its goals. The target for the expansion of the merchant marine was also almost reached, although port facilities remained wanting.

Food. These targets were not actually concerned with food but, rather, with agricultural infrastructure and mechanization of agriculture. The only foodcrop target, for wheat, was a complete failure. The goals for agricultural storage and for meat packing facilities, although modest, were also not met. The wheat target was undermined by U.S. wheat shipments via the P.L. 480 or "Food for Peace" program. The

72. René Armand Dreifuss, *1964: A conquista do estado: Ação política, poder e golpe de classe* (Petrópolis: Vozes, 1981), pp. 82–89.

73. This section is primarily based on Carlos Lessa's discussion of the results of the Targets Program in "Fifteen Years of Economic Policy in Brazil," pp. 34–52.

proceeds from the sale of U.S. wheat surpluses were one important source of funds for the BNDE during this period, so the wheat target was essentially sacrificed to the higher goal of financing industrial projects. Thus, while the Targets Program did not explicitly attempt to prioritize goals, in practice an implicit prioritization took place. The goals for an increase in the number of tractors in use was reached, and although domestic fertilizer production fell short of the goal, it did increase significantly during this period.

Basic industries. It was in this area that the program had some of its most important successes. The steel target met with complete success. Domestic cement production did not reach the numerical goal of 5 million tons, but it did reach the implicit goal of cement self-sufficiency. Aluminum production reached its goal by 1961, one year after the target date, and lead, tin, and nickle production expanded as called for in the program. Alkalis production fell short when the opening of the National Alkalis Company plant was delayed. Cellulose production almost reached its goal, but newsprint reached only 50 percent of anticipated production levels, mainly due to the large concessions made for the import of newsprint, always a demand of the press.

Only three goals involved the production of capital goods: the targets for the automobile industry, naval construction, and the mechanical and heavy electrical industries, but these were among the most important targets of the program. The target for the automobile industry was almost reached, in terms of both absolute production numbers and indices of nationalization, which required that 90 percent of the automobile parts, by weight, be produced domestically. The naval construction industry was reinvigorated with the construction of two new large shipyards and a series of smaller projects. The program called for the installation and expansion of mechanical and heavy electrical industries, without quantifying the targets, so it is more difficult to evaluate; but the Development Council estimated that during the 1955–1960 period, the production of machines and equipment grew by 100 percent, and the production of heavy electrical material increased by 200 percent.

In order to finance the Targets Program and other government expenditures, the government had dramatically expanded foreign investment and foreign borrowing. But it also expanded its taxation. From 1955 to 1960 tax receipts as a percentage of GNP increased from 17.4 to 22.9 percent, most of this due to an increase in indirect rather than direct taxes. But the increase in taxation could not offset the expansion in government expenditures, which led to an increase in the government deficit. The government cash deficit increased from 0.8 percent of GNP in 1955 to 3.7 percent of GNP in 1961. This deficit was viewed as one of the chief trigger mechanisms of inflation during the period.[74]

THE CONSOLIDATION OF DEVELOPMENTALISM IN BRAZIL

Industrialists in Brazil

In Brazil the Kubitschek administration received strong support from groups of industrialists, the result of both the developmentalist ideology of the industrial groups in the 1940s and 1950s and of the direct benefits that these groups received from government policies. Although national industrialists disagreed with the Kubitschek government on important issues, in particular over the benefits offered to international capital via SUMOC Instruction 113, these disagreements did not lead industrialists to back off from their explicit support for the government and its economic plan. Indeed, Brazilian industrialists saw themselves as protagonists and leaders of the process of industrialization during the Kubitschek period. When Kubitschek's term ended, the pronouncements of industrial leaders made it clear that they saw the economic results of the period as a victory for their industrialization strategy.[75]

Rather than the image of a strong state imposing its economic program on a weak industrial bourgeoisie, or of powerful industrial interests manipulating the state for their own ends, one must see the policies of the Kubitschek period as the result of a strong convergence of interests and ideas between Kubitschek, the state técnicos, and industrial interests.

The ideology of Brazilian industrialists was more self-consciously developmentalist than their Argentine counterparts. In Brazil the hegemonic project of industrialists, present in both key industrial associations of the period, the National Industrial Conference (CNI) and the São Paulo Industrialist Federation (FIESP), was clearly developmentalist and pro-Kubitschek. Under Brazil's corporatist system, these industrial organizations were chartered and regulated by the state and so have traditionally had a closer relationship to the state than their counterparts in Argentina. Industrial associations in Brazil were among the

74. Eugenio Gudin, "The Chief Characteristics of the Postwar Economic Development in Brazil," in *The Economy of Brazil*, ed. Howard Elis (Berkeley: University of California Press, 1969), pp. 22, 16–17.

75. Maria Jose Trevisan, *50 anos em 5: A FIESP e o desenvolvimentismo* (Petropolis: Vozes, 1986), pp. 43, 196.

pioneers in advocating developmentalist ideas in Brazil. Under the leadership of Roberto Simonsen, industrial associations in the 1930s and 1940s began to advocate state support for industrialization, protectionism, and planning. Meetings of business groups in the 1950s clearly indicated that developmentalism had been assimilated by the leading industrial entrepreneurs.[76]

Although Simonsen died in 1948, the year CEPAL was founded, his ideas prepared Brazilian industrialists to be more receptive to CEPAL's ideas. It was in Brazil that CEPALian ideas had the most impact on industrial entrepreneurs. CEPAL's seminal articles appeared in the journals of CNI in the early 1950s. Prebisch was invited to speak at FIESP and CNI conferences and to visit the factories of Brazilian entrepreneurs. The head of the industrial economics department of FIESP was "one of the most vigorous disseminators of CEPAL's ideas in this initial phase."[77] Industrial leaders in Rio de Janeiro and São Paulo already had adopted CEPAL terminology in their speeches by the early 1950s. The CNI provided financial support toward organization of the 1953 CEPAL meeting held in Quintadinha, Brazil, which was than presided over by Euvaldo Lodi, the president of the CNI.[78]

CEPAL's ideas were influential among Brazilian industrialists because they dovetailed so well with the existing ideas of the entrepreneurs, while providing more convincing theoretical justifications for policies that industrialists already had been advocating. Although industrialists were developmentalists, theirs was a special brand of developmentalism which placed more emphasis on private initiative and less on state intervention.[79] Still, Brazilian industrialists, following the lead of Roberto Simonsen, were advocates of state efforts to promote industrialization, especially through indicative planning and protectionism.

Developmentalism, however, was not the monolithic orientation of all Brazilian industrialists of this period. During the 1950s a division emerged between neoliberals, who dominated the Industrialist Federation of Rio de Janeiro, and the nationalist developmentalists who controlled FIESP.[80] At the same time the composition of the national in-

76. Bielschowsky, "Brazilian Economic Thought," pp. 126–27.

77. Celso Furtado, *A fantasia organizada* (Rio de Janeiro: Editora Paz e Terra, 1985), p. 73.

78. Maria Antonieta P. Leopoldi, "Industrial Associations and Politics in Contemporary Brazil: The Associations of Industrialists, Economic Policy-making and the State with Special Reference to the Period 1930–1961" (Ph.D. diss., St. Anthony's College, Oxford, 1984), pp. 138–39.

79. For a discussion of developmentalism in the private sector, see Bielschowsky, "Brazilian Economic Thought," pp. 108–43.

80. Leopoldi, "Industrial Associations and Politics in Contemporary Brazil," p. 120.

dustrial association was beginning to change, as more national firms associated with foreign capital, which muted the positions of more nationalist sectors within industrial associations.

The ideological orientation of Brazilian industrial associations predisposed them to be receptive to the policies advocated by the Kubitschek administration. Kubitschek's choice of economic policy team reassured industrial groups that their interests would be represented in the government. The industrialists gave Kubitschek solid political support once he was elected to the presidency. In the crisis that preceded Kubitschek's assumption of power, the CNI launched an appeal urging installation of the legitimately elected president. After his inauguration, Kubitschek visited the CNI and FIESP frequently, and in 1958 he was decorated by the CNI for his service to industry. The Targets Program was received enthusiastically by representatives of industry, as was the Tariff Law of 1957.

Relations between the executive and industrialists, however, were not totally harmonious. National industrialists strenuously opposed measures such as SUMOC Instruction 113, which gave privileged treatment to international firms. Often the técnicos of the CNI's economics department attacked unfavorable government policies while the leaders of the industry courted Kubitschek.[81] Industrial associations expressed misgivings about the stabilization program in 1958, in particular with its attempt to curtail bank credit to industry. Contrary to their counterparts in Argentina, Brazilian industrialists were more tolerant of inflation than of restrictions on industrial credit. In Brazil industrialists opposed the stabilization plan, in particular because of its limitation on industrial credit. In Argentina industrialists were among the most enthusiastic supporters of stabilization. Thus Kubitschek was able to break off negotiations with the IMF and let the stabilization effort lapse without losing the support of domestic entrepreneurs. Frondizi's more severe stabilization efforts, although applauded by industrialists, did not assure him sufficient political support from industrialists for his program. These differences in their response to inflation are largely attributable to different ideas about stabilization held by industrialists in the two countries. Because of their developmentalist ideas, Brazilian industrialists believed that control of inflation should be subordinated to the overall policy of economic development and industrialization.[82]

Industrialists were able to work out a style of interaction with the state by opening up a space for direct participation in key questions

81. Ibid., pp. 298, 299, 304.
82. Trevisan, *50 anos em 5*, pp. 147–50.

related to their class interests. Cardoso has referred to this style of interaction as a system of bureaucratic rings that cut horizontally between the bureaucratic structures of the public and the private sector.[83] Industry had representatives on some of the executive and working groups that contributed to the implementation of the Targets Plan, such as the executive group for the auto industry and the executive group for heavy machinery industry. Likewise, input from industrialists was crucial for the formulation of the new tariff policy in 1957.

Brazilian Labor Movement

The Kubitschek-Goulart ticket represented a continuation of the Vargas tradition of an alliance with labor, albeit in a subordinated position.[84] Goulart, as the leader of the PTB, was seen as a guarantee that labor concerns would be represented in the government. The labor movement in the 1950s was divided between factions loyal to the PTB, the Communist party, and a new renovators group, which included Catholic unions and splitoffs from the Communists. The labor vote does not appear to have been as decisive as some authors suggest in Kubitschek's 1955 election victory.[85] In the state of São Paulo, where the largest concentrations of organized workers live, Kubitschek received only about one-eighth of the total vote, suggesting that the electoral pact with the PTB had given Kubitschek minimal help there.[86] Half of the votes in São Paulo went to populist Paulista politician Adhemar de Barros, who clearly received the bulk of the working-class vote. The Brazilian Communist party, an important force in the Brazilian labor movement, took a more active role in galvanizing labor support for the Kubitschek-Goulart ticket than did the PTB.[87] Communist support for developmentalists was the result of their analysis of Brazilian society and their strategy, which deemphasized class struggle and called for a national front of labor allied with national capital against large landowners and foreign capital.

Although working-class support was not decisive for the Kubitschek-Goulart victory, labor leaders, including Communists, perceived that the Kubitschek period was significantly better for workers than any

83. Fernando Henrique Cardoso, *Autoritarismo e democratização* (Rio de Janeiro: Paz e Terra, 1975), p. 182.
84. This section relies heavily on Timothy Harding's account of organized labor's relation with the Kubitschek administration, in "The Political History of Organized Labor in Brazil" (Ph.D. diss., Stanford University, 1973).
85. This is the position, for example, of Harding, ibid., p. 300.
86. Skidmore, *Politics in Brazil 1930–1964*, p. 149.
87. Harding, "The Political History of Organized Labor in Brazil," pp. 293–97.

previous one, including the second Vargas administration.[88] Some suggest that working-class support for the Kubitschek government was the result of rapidly rising real wage levels. But the patterns of change in real wages are difficult to ascertain. Throughout the period, indices of real wage levels show a seesaw pattern, as wage level adjustments were rapidly overtaken by inflation and then readjusted again. Labor directed its energies to struggles for periodic revisions of wages, and of the minimum wage, but they were rarely able to overcome the effects of inflation for long. One source shows that real wages increased from 1955 to 1958 and then declined from 1958 to 1960; it attributes increased politicization and radicalization of labor during the 1958–1960 period to this decline.[89] Another source shows that in spite of the zigzag pattern, the overall trend of the minimum wage in São Paulo was positive for the period as a whole.[90] Sola also argues convincingly that the Kubitschek government conformed to working-class expectations set up during the Vargas administration for continuing real increases in the real minimum wage.[91]

Whether or not real wage levels actually increased during this period, they did not experience a dramatic fall as in Argentina during the stabilization plan. One crucial difference between the response of labor to the developmentalist program in Brazil and Argentina was that in Argentina workers had a point of reference in the past—the Peronist government—in which conditions for workers had been considerably better, but Brazilian workers had no collective memory of a better past. In addition, during the Kubitschek period urban employment opportunities expanded and experienced workers moved into more skilled jobs while new workers who had recently migrated to the city received the minimum salary.[92] This may have created a perception of upward mobility, which together with the atmosphere of greater tolerance of working-class organization and protest led to labor leaders' positive evaluation of the Kubitschek administration.

It is difficult to evaluate whether workers shared the developmental-

88. Conclusion reached by Harding, based on extensive interviews with labor leaders during the period. Ibid., p. 323.

89. Ibid., pp. 311–13.

90. Edmar Bacha and Lance Taylor, "Brazilian Income Distribution in the 1960s," in *Models of Growth and Distribution for Brazil*, ed. Taylor et al. (New York: Oxford University Press, 1980), p. 324.

91. Sola, "Political and Ideological Constraints to Economic Management in Brazil," pp. 176–78.

92. Harding, "The Political History of Organized Labor in Brazil," p. 315. The number of urban workers in Brazil expanded 70 percent in the 1950s, but commerce, transport, and services accounted for more of this growth than did industry, which tended to be less labor intensive (p. 319).

ist ideas of the Kubitschek government. But a survey of more than six hundred manual and nonmanual workers in Rio de Janeiro and the provinces in 1960 provides some information on their attitudes toward two key elements of developmentalist policy: foreign investment and state involvement in the economy.[93] Sixty percent of those surveyed said that foreign capital is necessary or could contribute to development, and that the government should try to attract it—a firm endorsement of the developmentalist policies that the Kubitschek government was then pursuing. Only 25 percent said that foreign capital could be harmful or was very harmful to development. Fifteen percent had no opinion.[94] Regarding government involvement in the economy, only 6 percent said that the government should not mix in economic life and ought to leave it to private enterprise; 26 percent said that the government should not own industries but should control the activities of private enterprise; 21 percent said that the government, besides controlling private enterprise, ought to own basic industries; 23 percent said the government ought to own the majority of industries and control all economic life; and 24 percent had no opinion. These answers do not show a clear endorsement of developmentalism, which corresponds to the second position, but they do show virtually no support for the liberal economic ideas advocated by Kubitschek's main party opposition, the UDN. Most surprising is the high percentage of workers with no opinion, which, in 1960, a period of relatively little repression, would seem to indicate low levels of politicization.

Nevertheless, this was not a period of complete working-class acquiescence to government policies. The first massive work stoppage during the Kubitschek government, in October 1957, succeeded in pressuring the government for an increase in wages. Later in 1958, as the government began to implement its stabilization program, workers again organized to fight for an increase in the minimum salary. Al-

93. Joseph A. Kahl, *The Measurement of Modernism* (Austin: University of Texas Press, 1968), pp. 104–5. Kahl uses the answers to these questions to construct a measure of radical orientation, but one can also use it to understand positions vis-à-vis developmentalism.

94. Ibid., p. 104. This corresponds to the findings of another survey of attitudes on foreign investment in twelve countries in 1958, two from Asia, two in Latin America, one from Canada, and seven European. Brazilians indicated the lowest level (14 percent) of opinion regarding private foreign investment as bad for the country. The ratio of favorable to unfavorable attitudes on private foreign investment was also the highest in Brazil. The reasons most frequently cited were that foreign investment increased opportunities for employment and generated industrial progress. *New York Herald Tribune*, April 6, 1958, cited in William B. Dale, *Brazil: Factors Affecting Foreign Investment*, International Comparative Studies, Investment Series 1 (Menlo Park: Stanford Research Institute, 1958), p. 32.

though workers are sometimes credited with blocking implementation of the economic stabilization program,[95] it was more clearly the convergence of the opposition of business groups, técnicos, and workers, together with Kubitschek's own fears that the stabilization program would keep him from reaching Targets Program goals and completing the construction of Brasília, which led to the defeat of the plan.

In 1959 workers in the state of São Paulo engaged in an all-time high number of 954 strikes involving 254,215 workers and leading to a loss of 2.3 million man-hours of work.[96] A general strike called in December 1959, however, was not a success. The primary sources of worker discontent—inflation and the high cost of living—apparently contributed to labor support for UDN candidate Jânio Quadros over General Lott in the 1960 elections.

The Kubitschek government's response to increased labor agitation was a combination of concessions and sporadic repression. Goulart had control of the day-to-day labor policy and used his position to encourage harmony among the different factions within the labor movement, including the Communists. The Kubitschek government was less repressive toward the labor movement than the Frondizi administration in Argentina. It never declared a state of siege in response to labor agitation, as did Frondizi when petroleum workers went on strike. Nor were there massive arrests or imprisonment of union leaders.

The most important concession made to labor during this period was the 1960 social security law, which assured labor leaders one-third of the seats on the governing councils of all social security agencies, where previously they had no representation. This gave the labor movement a foothold in the state to use as leverage to increase their political influence.[97]

The support or acquiescence of workers to developmentalist policies made possible the temporary success of the Kubitschek political project, which called for an alliance of developmentalists and nationalists, and incorporated labor as a subordinated partner in the developmentalist coalition in a democratic polity. During the Kubitschek administration, conditions were arising that would make this political project increasingly difficult to maintain, such as the emergence of an independent

95. Harding refers to "labor's defeat of Kubitschek's stabilization plan," in "The Political History of Organized Labor in Brazil," p. 390.

96. Jover Telles, *O movimento sindical no Brasil* (Rio de Janeiro: Editorial Vitoria, 1962), p. 89. Unfortunately, there is no available data on strikes for other years to allow more complete comparison.

97. Kenneth Paul Erickson, *The Brazilian Corporative State and Working-class Politics* (Berkeley: University of California Press, 1977), p. 62.

trade union movement less beholden to the state and therefore less manageable. Many of the renovator groups in São Paulo became associated with the mayor of São Paulo, Jânio Quadros, and supported his bid for the presidency in 1960 against the PSD-PTB candidate, General Lott. While Lott's defeat can be seen as the workers' partial repudiation of Kubitschek's policies, especially the resulting high rates of inflation, Goulart's victory also signaled continuity with the populist-developmentalist tradition of the 1950s.

Brazilian Rural Sector

If industrialists and the military were generally supportive of Kubitschek's economic program, the rural producers were frequently opposed. Rural producers in Brazil did not share the developmentalist ideology of the Kubitschek government any more than their Argentine counterparts had shared the ideas of the Frondizi government. Compared to wheat and beef producers in Argentina, however, Brazilian coffee producers were only lukewarm defenders of free market economic ideas, since their well-being depended on the government coffee purchases program and minimum set prices for coffee, both of which were antithetical to a free market approach.[98]

The attitude of coffee producers toward state intervention was ambiguous largely because the special characteristics of the international coffee market had made producers dependent on government action. The government coffee purchasing and stock programs assured producers of a market for their product when world demand was low, and helped stabilize producers' incomes. Because foreign demand for coffee was relatively price-inelastic and because Brazil accounted for such a large percentage of the world coffee market, any effort by Brazilian authorities to devalue the currency in order to improve the competitiveness of Brazilian exports could depress world coffee prices and thus have the opposite effect than was intended.[99] As a result, contrary to rural producers in Argentina and elsewhere, Brazilian coffee

98. In her book on Brazilian coffee producers, for example, Verena Stolcke points out that while coffee exporters were firm free-traders, the coffee producers themselves had a more ambiguous attitude toward government intervention. For example, at the end of 1956 in a conference on foreign trade, the coffee producers were profoundly offended by the suggestion of one of the São Paulo businessmen present that the earnings of coffee producers should be stabilized not through government price fixing but through the free play of market forces. Stolcke, *Cafeicultura: Homens, mulheres, e capital (1850–1980)* (São Paolo: Editora Brasiliense, 1986), p. 164.

99. Nathaniel H. Leff, *Economic Policy-making and Development in Brazil 1947–1964* (New York: John Wiley and Sons, 1968), pp. 14–15.

growers did not tend to advocate devaluations. For the most part, Brazilian coffee producer associations understood that the government had an interventionist role to play both domestically and internationally, although some producers still urged the government to end its support for prices and let prices fall to drive out other producers and expand the volume of Brazilian exports.[100]

The main concern of most coffee producers, however, was to pressure the government to assure satisfactory prices. This made them adamant foes of the government's multiple exchange policy of the 1950s, which they considered a form of "exchange confiscation," since it effectively allowed the government to skim off part of the earnings from coffee exports and transfer them to industrial sectors. The income generated in this fashion was used to subsidize certain imports and to finance the system of purchasing coffee surpluses.[101]

In 1957–1959 coffee exports accounted for 57.9 percent of Brazil's total export earnings.[102] Coffee producers made up the largest group of rural producers negatively affected by the exchange rate policy. Coffee producers complained that the multiple exchange rate system allowed the state to appropriate profits from the rural sector. These protests increased whenever coffee prices fell. During the Kubitschek period, coffee prices reached new low levels because high prices in the early fifties had stimulated planting both in Brazil and abroad, leading to oversupply and declining prices.

When Lucas Lopes took over as minister of finance in 1958, he reduced the prices for domestic coffee purchases, hoping to discourage overproduction in a period of low international prices. Coffee producers reacted dramatically and organized a "production march" to protest government coffee policy. When the government prohibited the march and called out the army to block the progress of the caravans toward the capital, coffee producers postponed the protest. To placate coffee producers and exporters, coffee bonus levels were readjusted three times over the next few years. But it was not until Kubitschek left office that the multiple exchange rate system was totally dismantled.

At the same time as the Kubitschek government modified its domestic coffee policy, it tried to restrict international coffee output and thus to maintain or increase prices. In September 1958 Brazil and other Latin American coffee producers signed the Inter-American Coffee

100. Ibid., p. 26.
101. Lessa, "Fifteen Years of Economic Policy in Brazil," pp. 183, 187.
102. Werner Baer, *The Brazilian Economy: Its Growth and Development* (Columbus, Ohio: Grid Publishing, 1979), p. 58, table 12.

Agreement, under which each country agreed to limit exports. When these measures proved inadequate to halt declining prices, the International Coffee Agreement (ICA) was signed by the Latin American and African coffee producers, as well as a number of importing countries. The ICA assigned annual export quotas to member nations. The Brazilian quota required the Brazilian government to purchase and stockpile immense quantities of coffee, since the Brazilian coffee harvest of 1959 alone exceeded total world coffee exports that year.[103] The cost of these coffee purchases was substantial; in 1959 the cost of the coffee retention program accounted for 2.77 percent of total GDP for that year.[104] Although the government's purchase price for coffee was much lower than international prices and had fallen behind the price rise of industrial products and other agricultural goods, the internal price was still a sufficient incentive to stimulate substantial overproduction.[105] The government assured coffee growers that their entire crop would be purchased by the government at guaranteed prices. Even though these prices were lower than desired by coffee growers, the commitment to purchase the entire crop encouraged coffee production.

The Kubitschek economic program paid little direct attention to the agricultural sector. Brazil's primary export crop, coffee, was not included in the goals of the Targets Program. Although some of the targets of the Program focused on providing infrastructure to rural areas and improving supply of agricultural inputs such as fertilizers, in practice these targets did not receive the attention that other projects received. Only 3.2 percent of total investments initially planned in the Targets Program were destined for improving the production and supply of foodstuffs. In addition, the BNDE gave very little credit to agricultural projects, in line with its primary concern with industrialization and import substitution. The other state banking institutions during this period, however, expanded their credit to the agricultural sector, often at negative real interest rates. Fertilizers were also granted very favorable exchange rate and tariff treatment, which suggested an implicit subsidy to farmers.[106]

103. Pedro Malan, "Relaçãoes económicas internacionais do Brasil: As décadas de con-solidação do sistema de Bretton Woods," mimeo., p. 57.

104. Lessa, "Fifteen Years of Economic Policy in Brazil," p. 183.

105. Leff, *Economic Policy-making and Development in Brazil*, pp. 30–31.

106. During the Kubitschek period, the real value of loans to agriculture by official banks other than the BNDE rose 28.2 percent, as compared to only an 8.2 percent increase for industry. This expansion of subsidized credit was used to stimulate use of modern farm inputs. Gordon W. Smith, "Brazilian Agricultural Policy 1950–1967," in *The Economy of Brazil*, ed. Howard S. Ellis (Los Angeles: University of California Press, 1969), pp. 237–40.

The reaction of the rural sector to the Kubitschek program was based as much on what Kubitschek did not do as on what he did. He did not, for example, propose or support any revision of property relations in the countryside. Land reform, as we have seen, was not an integral part of the developmentalist ideology, and Kubitschek was no exception. His development program focused on expanding rural production primarily by extending rural infrastructure and increasing mechanization of agricultural production. Kubitschek's government took no measures to redress agrarian property relations through a program of agrarian reform. This position kept him from entering into conflict with the members of his party, the PSD, which included important landholding interests. A "ruralist block" within Congress, made up primarily of PSD deputies, worked to systematically obstruct any projects to reform the agrarian structure.[107]

Thus, although the agricultural sector was relegated to a position of secondary importance in the Kubitschek economic program, its most basic concerns were not threatened. The continuation of the coffee retention program at guaranteed prices and the substantial funds expended on this program, other subsidies for agricultural inputs, as well as Kubitschek's "tacit agreement" not to interfere with relations of production or the structure of property rights of the rural sector, compensated the large rural producers somewhat for their losses from the exchange policy.[108]

Leff argues that the hegemony of the landed elite had already been eclipsed during this period, as evidenced by their inability to veto policies that worked against their interests, such as export taxation and low prices. The failure of the 1958 "production march" is seen as further proof of the impotence of this sector.[109] Revisionist interpretations, such as that of Stolcke, attribute greater strength and autonomy to the rural bourgeoisie as an influence on government policy, pointing out that although they may not have been able to attain their maximum program, they did secure frequent adjustments of government policy and were able to block those policies they most opposed.[110]

107. Stolcke, *Cafeicultura*, p. 151. The PSD politician who headed up the Economic Committee of the House of Representatives during the Kubitschek period declared that no agrarian reform proposal would pass through his committee, and not one did. Benevides, *O governo Kubitschek*, p. 219.

108. Stolcke, *Cafeicultura*, pp. 150, 163.

109. Leff, *Economic Policy-making and Development in Brazil*, pp. 26–27.

110. Stolcke, for example, draws our attention to the existence of the "Bloco Ruralista" in the House of Representatives, formed in 1955, which was made up primarily of PSD deputies and was able systematically to block any legal reforms to agrarian structure. *Cafeicultura*, p. 151.

For our purposes, it is sufficient to understand that although the Brazilian rural elite did not share the developmentalist ideology, they were not successful in blocking the spread of developmentalist ideas or the implementation of any of the essential elements of the developmentalist economic program. This elite may have had greater strength than Leff and others give them credit for, but their actions only served as a protective blocking or holding action, not as a major influence on developmentalist policy. Brazilian rural groups were weaker vis-à-vis the state than their Argentine counterparts, since they were not able to end the "export confiscation," whereas in Argentina rural producers succeeded in convincing the Frondizi government to eliminate a number of exchange retentions on agrarian products long opposed by the rural sector.

Congressional Support for the Kubitschek Program

The alliance between the more conservative PSD party and the pro-labor PTB party is often credited with providing the underlying stability of the Kubitschek period.[111] Likewise, the situation during the Kubitschek government is often portrayed as one in which a progressive and innovative executive confronted a conservative Congress and was stymied by his opponents in the UDN party.

Wanderley Guilherme dos Santos has shown, however, that the PSD-PTB legislative coalition was not a sufficiently winning coalition to support the Kubitschek government during more than half of his term. His parliamentary coalition had to encompass more than just the PSD and the PTB.[112] Much of the Kubitschek program (43.2 percent of roll call votes) was supported by a coalition that included a majority of all four major political parties—the PSD, PTB, UDN, and Partido Social Progressista (PSP)—and another 29.9 percent of roll call votes was supported by a three-party coalition made up of the PSD, PTB, and the PSP, the populist party led by Ademar de Barros.[113]

Further analysis showed that a majority of roll call votes essential for the implementation of the Targets Program, such as decisions to increase budgets or to grant special credits to the executive, were sup-

111. This is one of the explanations offered, for example, by Maria Victoria Benevides in her classic study of the Kubitschek period, *O governo Kubitschek*.

112. Wanderley Guilherme dos Santos, "The Calculus of Conflict: Impasse in Brazilian Politics and the Crisis of 1964" (Ph.D. diss., Stanford University, 1979), pp. 133–39.

113. Maria Isabel Valladão de Carvalho, "A colaboração do legislativo para o desempenho do executivo durantes o governo JK" (masters thesis, IUPERJ, Rio de Janeiro, 1977), p. 51, table 8.

ported by all four parties.[114] Thus, in spite of much vocal public opposition from such flamboyant UDN politicians as Carlos Lacerda, the Kubitschek government received broad political support where it counted, in the legislative votes necessary for the implementation of its basic program.

In order to maintain congressional support, however, Kubitschek had to grant incentives and concession to his opponents. For example, to generate support for the construction of Brasília, the government offered the opposition opportunities to participate in the public company responsible for construction of the new capital, a new source of patronage appointments.

Brazilian Military

There was greater convergence between the views of the developmentalist government in Brazil and the economic ideas of a large sector of the Brazilian military. Benevides argues that this support was in part a result of co-optation of the military by its incorporation in prominent administrative positions in the state.[115] But the placement of military personal in key administrative positions may have been more a result of shared economic ideas than one of the causes of convergence between the military and the Kubitschek government.

A review of Brazilian military journals during this period reveals that the military was more concerned with and well informed on economic issues than its counterpart in Argentina. The Brazilian Escola Superior de Guerra (ESG) was strongly anti-Communist, but it also stressed that development and security issues were inseparable, and thus the military had the responsibility to be well informed about issues of economic development.[116] A survey of the conferences offered in the Brazilian ESG during this period reveals a totally different balance between economic, strategic, and political themes than in the Argentine ESG. In the lectures of the Brazilian ESG, economic themes at least equaled and frequently outnumbered those on other topics, such as military strategy or political relations. During the period 1951–1961, lectures on economic issues made up approximately 15 to 25 percent of the total. Al-

114. Guilherme dos Santos, "The Calculus of Conflict," p. 143.
115. Benevides, *O governo Kubitschek*, pp. 177–88.
116. Alfred Stepan, *The Military in Politics: Changing Patterns in Brazil* (Princeton: Princeton University Press, 1971), p. 186. See also Marechal Juarez Tavora, "A segurança nacional: Sua conceituação e seu estudo na ESG," Escola Superior de Guerra lecture (C-01-59).

though developmentalist speakers and themes did not dominate in the economic lectures, they were well represented.

The ESG students in Brazil were exposed to a much more varied and sophisticated range and treatment of international and domestic economic and political issues than their counterparts in Argentina. The ESG was more concerned with development themes and more exposed to developmentalist ideas than its counterpart in Argentina.[117] Because the ESG national security doctrine posited that development was linked to national security, it stressed the need for strong government and economic planning.[118] In general, the economic ideas of the ESG could be categorized as cosmopolitan developmentalist ideas, since they supported state planning to promote industrialization but emphasized the centrality of private initiative, including private foreign investment, to Brazilian development.

In spite of the developmentalism of the group of officers associated with the ESG, however, it formed one of the principal sources of opposition to the Kubitschek government. The anti-Communist position of the ESG group led them to oppose Kubitschek, whom they viewed as politically weak and excessively connected to the Vargas political tradition. This group opposed Kubitschek's political project of a coalition between nationalists and developmentalists, which involved bringing in labor as a subordinated partner in the alliance.

Other military journals, such as *A defesa nacional*, published by the War Ministry, and the *Revista do clube militar*, published by the Military Club, took a more nationalist developmentalist stance than the ESG. *A defesa nacional* changed from a journal with a few relatively simple articles on economic topics in the early 1950s, to one with detailed and extensive treatment of economic development from a developmentalist perspective in the mid- to late 1950s.[119] The *Revista do clube militar* was

117. This may be in part due to the difference in composition of the student body of the school in Brazil and Argentina. Whereas in Argentina, the ESG was primarily a training ground for military elites, with slight participation of civilians, either as students, teachers, or lecturers, in Brazil it was a self-styled organism of interelite communication. During the period 1950–1963 almost half the graduates of the Curso Superior de Guerra were civilians, and half the civilians came from the public administration and public enterprises. Vanda Maria Costa Aderaldo, "A Escola Superior de Guerra: Um estudo de curriculos e programa" (masters thesis, IUPERJ, 1978), annex 2.

118. Stepan, *The Military in Politics*, p. 179.

119. *A defesa nacional* in 1958 included articles by Raúl Prebisch, Roberto Campos, and Octavio Dias Carneiro and speeches by President Kubitschek and Lidio Lunardi, president of the National Industrial Confederation (CNI). By 1959 and 1960, however, a new, more geopolitical angle emerges in the journal, which features prominently articles by Golbery do Couto e Silva and U.S. military authors on the defense of the West and the free world.

the standard-bearer for nationalist developmentalism in the military during this period. It featured articles by prominent nationalist intellectuals from the government and from the Instituto Superior do Estudos Brasileiros. Defense of the state oil monopoly was the principal crusade of the magazine during the 1950s. The leadership of the Military Club during this period was connected to General Lott and military men who held prominent positions in the Kubitschek government.[120] Thus, military support for the economic program was conditioned on the maintenance of Petrobras' oil monopoly, which nationalists considered an "untouchable" political objective.

Brazilian and Argentine Military Compared

The bulk of the Brazilian military advocated some form of pro-industrialization developmentalist economic ideas. The divisions within the Brazilian military were not between developmentalists and liberals, but between nationalist and cosmopolitan developmentalists. This strong strand of pro-industrialization sentiment among the Brazilian military has been attributed to their function in society and their combat experience in World War II. Thus Barros argues, "The military were the single social group which was more conscious of the need for the acceleration of the industrialization process. This was so, if nothing else, because for the fulfillment of their stated professional objectives, professional soldiers needed an industrialized country."[121] Yet the Argentine military faced the same need to fulfill their professional objectives, but pro-industrialization sentiment was less pronounced in Argentine military circles. One factor that contributed to the pro-industrialization sentiment among the Brazilian military was the concrete combat experience of World War II, which forced Brazilian officers to make the inexorable link between the fulfillment of their professional objectives and the achievement of national industrialization, and to institutionalize this link in the training of future generations of military officers.[122]

In an abstract sense, the Argentine military may have been equally committed to the idea that industrialization was essential. But they did

---

120. The Nationalist military won all three elections in the Military Club during this period—1956, 1958, and 1960.

121. Alexandre de Souza Costa Barros, "The Brazilian Military: Professional Specialization, Political Performance, and State Building" (Ph.D. diss., University of Chicago, 1978), p. 291.

122. Stepan, *The Military in Politics*, discusses the influence of the Brazilian Expeditionary Force experience on the attitudes of Brazilian officers (pp. 239–45).

not have as comprehensive an idea of industrialization as the Brazilian military. They displayed not so much an opposition to industrialization as an indifference—a lack of intense concern with industrial issues. This was reflected by their failure to place economic and industrial issues at center stage in military training, balanced with political and strategic concerns, and their failure to inform themselves completely on modern currents of economic thought. This indifference may be attributable to the nonparticipation of the Argentine military in World War II, which left them unawakened to one of the central military lessons of the war: the centrality of a developed heavy industrial base as the backbone of military preparedness. Brazilian officers had seen the fruit of industrial preparedness in the battlefield.

Because industrialization issues were not central to the Argentine military mind while national security concerns were gaining increased importance in the late 1950s, the Argentine military was out of sync with the desarrollistas, who subordinated all other concerns to the overriding goal of industrial development. In Brazil the military shared a perspective that linked anticommunism and national security concerns to development and pro-industrialization sentiment. This did not ensure unified political support for the Kubitschek government. The group associated with the ESG often opposed the government's political projects, although they often agreed with its economic program. The nationalist developmentalists associated with Lott and the Military Club provided the bulk of military support for the Kubitschek administration, but their support was contingent on the handling of key issues, such as the maintenance of the state oil monopoly.

The adoption of developmentalism was not as abrupt in Brazil as it was in Argentina. Developmentalist policies showed greater continuity, especially with some of the policies of the second Vargas presidency.

The high level of institutional and personnel continuity during the Kubitschek administration facilitated coherent and consistent implementation of the developmentalist policy. Although Kubitschek had three different ministers of economics—Alkmin, Lopes, and Paes de Almeida—none of the ministerial changes represented a complete turnover of economic policy makers or a major shift away from the developmentalist policy of the government. At the top levels, as well as at lower levels, policy makers were shuffled within the economic apparatus of the state, but one economic team did not entirely replace another. Cosmopolitan and nationalist policy makers disagreed about the need for controlling inflation, but they did not differ on the essential components of the developmentalist program. Lopes and Campos left the Kubitschek administration because they lost the internal struggle over the need for a stabilization policy. Their departure signaled an abandonment of stabilization measures but not a major shift in industrialization policy.

Institutions provided important continuity during the Kubitschek years and between the second Vargas administration and that of Kubitschek. The BNDE and its organizational cluster, including the Development Council and the executive and working groups, played a pivotal role in consistently formulating and implementing the Targets Plan. These institutional characteristics are explored further in Chapter 5, which compares the state in Argentina and Brazil. Developmentalism received broader support from domestic groups in Brazil because it "fit" better with the existing ideas held by many of these groups. In particular, Brazilian industrialists and the military had a strong predisposition toward developmentalism.

CHAPTER FIVE

The State in Brazil and Argentina:
State Autonomy and Capacity Compared

The few comparative treatments of the Argentine and Brazilian states generally agree that the Brazilian is stronger than the Argentine state. Guillermo O'Donnell has characterized Argentine state-society relations as the state apparatus dancing to the rhythm of societal forces, more a battlefield than a formulator of generalized interests. At the same time, he argues that the Brazilian state apparatus has been so powerful and decisive that it has monopolized the nation's political life.[1] Although O'Donnell presents us with some tantalizing and thought-provoking contrasts between state-society relations in Brazil and Argentina, he does not clarify the precise characteristics of state strength in a way that would allow us to analyze it more carefully.

To understand the differences between the Argentine and Brazilian states one needs to move beyond vague notions of state strength and autonomy. As discussed in Chapter 1, notions of state capacity and purpose are more useful ways of understanding the differences between the Brazilian and the Argentine states, and they help explain different patterns in the adoption and implementation of developmentalist policies. In this chapter, I highlight more carefully the specific internal characteristics of state structures that contributed to or blocked the adoption and implementation of developmentalist policies.

The differences in the capacity of the state in Brazil and Argentina are not primarily related to the absolute size of the states in the two countries, nor to the number of functions the state has acquired. Although expansion of state functions in regulating and directing the

1. O'Donnell, Guillermo, "Y a mi, que me importa? Notas sobre sociabilidad y política en Argentina y Brasil," *Estudios CEDES* 10 (November 1984), 20, 33.

economy may be an indicator of increasing state autonomy, an expansion of state functions without a corresponding expansion of state capacity to carry out those functions, as was the case in Argentina, can undermine confidence in the state. The dilemma of state capacity in Brazil and Argentina is that in both cases the economic functions of the state had been expanded, but in Argentina, the disjunction between state capacity and tasks was particularly acute. The most important differences between the state in Brazil and in Argentina lie in the nature of the organizational structures in the two countries, the norms and procedures that govern the bureaucracy, and the technical capabilities of state officials.

The comparison between Brazil and Argentina shows that we need not perceive an absolute tradeoff between clientelism and meritocracy as a defining characteristic of bureaucracies. Indeed, one can argue that the Brazilian state was both more clientelistic and more meritocratic than the Argentine state during the period under study. Because the Brazilian state was more central to politics, it was the arena both for more clientelistic policies and for the more successful mobilization of technical resources. The key difference between the two states was the existence in Brazil of a small "insulated" sector of the bureaucracy.[2] This insulated sector, governed by merit hiring and efficiency criteria, was used and modified by Kubitschek to formulate and implement the main lines of his economic policy. For an insulated bureaucracy to be effective, it must not only be relatively free from political pressures but also must be governed by merit criteria to assure a high-quality staff. No such insulated bureaucracy existed in Argentina, so whereas Kubitschek was able to work through and expand existing state institutions, Frondizi had to attempt to bypass the bureaucracy in order to formulate and implement his policies.

Various writers have stressed different conditions favoring state capacity and autonomous state action.[3] Among the conditions most fre-

2. For a discussion of the insulated bureaucracy in Brazil, see Edson de Oliveira Nunes, "Bureaucratic insulation and Clientelism in Contemporary Brazil: Uneven State-building and the Taming of Modernity" (Ph.D. diss., University of California at Berkeley, 1984); and Barbara Geddes, "The Insulation of Economic Decision Makers in the Brazilian Bureaucracy, 1930–1964," paper presented at the Thirteenth Congress of the Latin American Studies Association, Boston, October 1986.

3. Among the government characteristics that engender autonomy Geddes lists: (1) technical expertise among officials, (2) coherence within the government group, (3) the existence of instruments for influencing the economy, (4) insulation of government decision makers from societal pressures, and (5) the skill of leaders in using persuasion and the manipulation of incentives to build support for the policy changes they initiate. Barbara Geddes, "The Insulation of Economic Decision Makers," p. 3.

quently mentioned are the existence of collectivities of career officials relatively insulated from ties to dominant socioeconomic interests,[4] and an extensive, coherent bureaucratic machinery.[5] Such bureaucratic machinery and collectivities of career officials are not created rapidly or in an ad hoc fashion; nor are they the product of a simple reorganization of bureaucratic structures. They are the result of a long-term historical process of institution building.[6]

The historical development of the Brazilian and Argentine states differed significantly. Of interest here are the developments in state structure involving the expansion of state capacity to intervene in the economy, the creation of institutions to supervise state involvement in the economy, and enactment of procedures governing the bureaucracy which facilitated the development of public servants capable of managing new economic tasks. Argentina and Brazil faced similar external and internal environmental changes that tended to stimulate efforts to expand governmental capacities. But qualitatively different state-building responses occurred in the two countries. In both countries state functions were expanded, but Brazil placed greater emphasis on administrative reforms, leading to greater administrative capacity.[7]

EXPANSION OF THE BRAZILIAN STATE

Many writers have emphasized the importance of the temporary residence of the Portuguese court in Brazil (1808–1820) and the tenure of the independent monarchy there in laying the bases and attitudes for later development of modern Brazilian institutions.[8] A number of other important state-building efforts also occurred during the early years of

4. Theda Skocpol, Introduction in *Bringing the State Back In*, ed. Peter Evans, Dietrich Rueschemeyer, and Theda Skocpol (New York: Cambridge University Press, 1985), p. 9.

5. Dietrich Rueschemeyer and Peter Evans, "The State and Economic Transformation: Toward an Analysis of the Conditions Underlying Effective Intervention," in *Bringing the State Back In*, ed. Evans, Rueschemeyer, and Skocpol, p. 50.

6. See ibid., pp. 51–52, 59, for a discussion of the historical character of the bureaucratic apparatus.

7. Skowronek argues that the combined impact of international crisis, class conflict, and increased complexity stimulated efforts to expand governmental capacities in the United States during the period 1877–1920. Environmental changes are, however, only stimuli for institutional development. The forms these institutional innovations take are contingent on the specific responses of government officials. Stephen Skowronek, "Building a New American State: The Expansion of National Administrative Capacities, *1877–1920* (New York: Cambridge University Press, 1982), p. 12.

8. Lawrence S. Graham, *Civil Service Reform in Brazil: Principles Versus Practice* (Austin: University of Texas Press, 1968), pp. 17–20.

the republic.[9] The Banco do Brasil, for example, which stood at the center of the national financial system, was founded in 1890, and nationalized in 1905.[10]

Most of the changes in the Brazilian state of interest to us took place after the Great Depression. Two important bureaucratic innovative strategies contributed to the state's capacity to intervene effectively in the economy. The first was a generalized process of civil service reform initiated during the Vargas government after 1930. The second was in many ways an ad hoc response to the failure of the first strategy; in the absence of universalistic reform, "pockets of efficiency" and autonomy were created outside the traditional bureaucracy, including some public enterprises and executive groups.[11] The bureaucratic protagonists of the second strategy were often the products of earlier civil service reform efforts. The second innovative strategy was dependent on a long prior process of institution building by individuals committed to installing the merit system in the bureaucracy, but who did not necessarily share the developmentalist goals to which the insulated bureaucracy would devote itself during the Kubitschek administration.[12]

The 1930 revolution that brought Getúlio Vargas to power was a major turning point for the development of the Brazilian state. Vargas moved to centralize authority in the executive by reorganizing the public administration to make it more efficient and autonomous from societal pressures. Among other reforms, he reinforced the principle that admission to the career civil service should only be through public examination.[13] After the imposition of the Estado Nôvo in 1937, Vargas created a new centralized administrative organ, the Administrative Department of Public Service (DASP), to oversee centralization of the bureaucratic apparatus. DASP, based on U.S. public administration

9. Topik argues that the Brazilian state was one of the most interventionist in Latin America well before the Great Depression. The state expanded its intervention in the economy in an effort to represent and defend the export economy. But this intervention was a response to economic crisis rather than the result of development planning, and it did not involve any major procedural changes in the state apparatus. No independent civil service or institutionalized career patterns for bureaucrats were established. Steven Topik, *The Political Economy of the Brazilian State, 1889–1930* (Austin: University of Texas Press, 1987), pp. 23, 161–63.

10. Ibid., pp. 30–47.

11. Geddes, "The Insulation of Economic Decision Makers," pp. 14, 22–23

12. The individuals and institutions connected with the public administration movement in Brazil were not necessarily developmentalist. Nevertheless, the pioneers of "scientific" public administration in Brazil helped create a merit-based sector of the Brazil bureaucracy that the developmentalists used during the Kubitschek administration to implement their economic programs.

13. Graham, *Civil Service Reform in Brazil*, p. 25.

models, resembled a combination of the U.S. Budget Office and the Civil Service Commission.[14] It had broad responsibility to budget, centralize control of personnel and material, and oversee competitive entrance exams and preservice and in-service training.

During the Estado Nôvo, DASP became "a sort of superministry" in charge of installing a new bureaucratic apparatus and creating an elite civil service.[15] Although after Vargas was removed from office in 1945 his successors limited the power and authority of DASP, its legacy continued to be felt in the Brazilian public administration. Although it did not succeed in its long-term efforts to create a modern career civil service free of political patronage, it did leave a group of technical elites that infused parts of the state with the new ideas of meritocracy. When Vargas was elected president in 1951, he worked to reinforce the administrative reforms implemented during the Estado Nôvo, placing new emphasis on competitive entrance examinations to the civil service and reinstating pay differences between permanent civil servants and temporary political appointees.

After the public administration initiatives of the 1930s, a nucleus of public administration experts and advocates emerged in Brazil. They were concentrated in two state institutions: DASP and the autonomous government foundation, the Fundação Getúlio Vargas, set up in 1945. Both had had extensive training programs, leading to the spread of their ideas and specific skills throughout the bureaucracy.[16]

The movement for administrative reform in Brazil began a full twenty years earlier in Brazil than in Argentina, gathered more influence, and had a more profound impact on the structure of the state. Although attempts were later made to dismantle some Estado Nôvo administrative reforms, the core of the system survived sufficiently intact to power the insulated bureaucracy during the Kubitschek administration.

In spite of the emphasis Vargas placed on the creation and maintenance of a career civil service, he, like later Brazilian presidents, essen-

14. Beatriz M. de Souza Wahrlich, *Administração de pessoal: Princípios e ténicas* (Rio de Janeiro: Fundação Getúlio Vargas, 1964), p. 29.

15. Graham, *Civil Service Reform in Brazil*, p. 29.

16. These institutions were given continuity of vision and leadership by Luis Simões Lopes, a key adviser to Vargas on all matters of public administration. Lopes served as president of the Federal Civil Service Council and of its successor, DASP. He proposed and supervised the formation of the Fundação Getúlio Vargas and served as its president for decades. When Vargas was removed from office in 1945, Lopes left the presidency of DASP but retained his position in the Fundação Getúlio Vargas, where he continued to exercise influence over state public administration. Lopes's story is another example of how the continuity of specific individuals in institutions gave continuity to Brazilian policy over the period 1930–1960.

tially adopted a dual approach to the Brazilian bureaucracy; he worked to reinforce the merit system in certain parts of the bureaucracy, while continuing to use other parts of the bureaucracy for political patronage. The result was a system that has been called a dual bureaucracy.[17] Some institutions and ministries were characterized by one tendency or another; for example, the patronage system dominated the personnel practices of the social security institutes, whereas the Ministry of Finance had more of a merit personnel system.[18] Dual bureaucratic tendencies also operated simultaneously within a single institution.[19]

The "insulated bureaucracy"—made up of some of the state enterprises, some state-controlled banks such as the BNDE, and the various policy-making councils and executive groups—has been primarily responsible for implementing economic policies since the 1940s.[20] The insulated bureaucracy was created when existing institutions, like the Banco do Brazil, adopted meritocratic hiring practices, while new institutions and agencies were created, such as SUMOC in 1945 and the BNDE in 1952, with the goal of creating autonomous professional centers of economic policy making.

To formulate and implement its economic policies, the Kubitschek administration both relied on existing institutions within the insulated bureaucracy and created new agencies and groups to facilitate policy coordination. The most notable insulated administration innovations of the Kubitschek administration were the Development Council and the executive and working groups that operated under its aegis. The Development Council was primarily staffed by individuals from the BNDE but provided an overarching institutional coordination development policy. In contrast with Argentina, however, it is notable that the

17. Graham, *Civil Service Reform in Brazil*, applies this term from Bert Hoselitz to the Brazilian bureaucracy, p. 170.

18. Ibid., p. 185.

19. Barbara Geddes and Edson Nunes call the dual Brazilian bureaucracy a "syncretic political model." Syncretism "entailed maintaining clientelism in certain arenas of policy making while insulating others to allow them to function separately from the traditional political system." Edson de Oliveira Nunes and Barbara Geddes, "Dilemmas of State-Led Modernization in Brazil," Instituto Universitario de Pesquisas do Rio de Janeiro (IUPERJ), *Serie estudos* 39 (July 1985), 14.

20. Ibid., p. 2. Wanderley Gilherme dos Santos also stresses the dual nature of the Brazilian state apparatus, arguing that the division is generally between the centralized state apparatus, where clientelism is rampant, and the decentralized state apparatus, which had been protected from patronage politics since its inception. Wanderley Guilherme dos Santos, "Relatorio de pesquisa, centralização burocrática e renovação de elites: Estudo preliminar sobre a administração federal descentralizada" (Rio de Janeiro: IUPERJ, 1979), p. 60.

Targets Program was primarily formulated and implemented by institutions that already existed prior to the Kubitschek administration, and in many cases by government officials and civil servants who already were in office before Kubitschek came to power. The Kubitschek administration was able to use the institutions and the personnel of the insulated bureaucracy because of previous efforts under Vargas and other administrations to create pockets of expertise and administrative autonomy within the state.[21]

EXPANSION OF THE ARGENTINE STATE

Argentina went through an intense and successful period of "state building" in the late 1800s and early 1900s, led by a group of men called the "generation of 1880," a group equivalent to the *científicos* in Mexico in their outlook and influence. During this period of national organization, a new system of centralized power was set up to replace local power embodied by regional caudillos. The generation of the 1880s established the national army, a national judiciary, and an executive bureaucracy. The motivation of this group was a liberal one; the state was to organize a juridical framework that would assure the smooth functioning of the agro-export system. The state also worked to support and stimulate commercial and financial activities, especially through the creation of a series of state-backed financial institutions such as the Banco de la Nacion and the Banco de la Provincia de Buenos Aires.[22]

After President Yrigoyen came to power in 1913, state activity took on a more nationalist and interventionist stance, as shown by the creation of the state oil company, YPF, and the state railroad company. After the conservative coup of 1930, the state continued to intervene to buffer domestic economic groups from the external shocks of the Great Depression. The government created a Central Bank and sec-

21. Like Vargas, Kubitschek simultaneously made widespread political patronage appointments at the same time that he used and modified the insulated part of the bureaucracy to implement economic policy. Shortly after taking office, it is estimated that he was responsible for seven thousand appointments, a large part of them going to his coalition partner, the PTB, in return for its support during the presidential campaign. Although the whole period 1946–1964 is marked by a gradual expansion of civil service, there is no evidence that Kubitschek engaged in more excessive patronage than his predecessors. Graham, *Civil Service Reform in Brazil*, pp. 134, 143.

22. Jorge E. Roulet and Jorge Federico Sabato, "Estado y administración pública en la Argentina: Frenos o motores del proceso de cambio social?" *Polemica* 78 (1971), 202–5.

toral boards for various agricultural products. During this period a group of state administrators called "proconsules" appeared: "brilliant administrators who managed completely and with wide decisional autonomy whole areas of the state apparatus."[23] One of the chief examples of these proconsules was Raúl Prebisch as the director of the Argentine Central Bank.

But in spite of the success of this period of state building, the early capacity of the Argentine state was not institutionalized, and the state had little autonomy from dominant classes. State institutions were often created explicitly with a voting majority of members of the directorate made up of "representatives of organizations of production," that is, of individuals from agricultural and industrial groups. State administrators were part of a gentleman's club with strong links to propertied classes, not part of a civil service with primary loyalty to the state.

The organization of a civil service occurred later in Argentina than in Brazil. Before the Peronist period there was no uniform or centralized control over selection, promotion, discipline, or dismissal of public servants in the federal or provincial governments. Only a few very general rules existed concerning government employment, such as requiring that public servants be Argentine citizens at least eighteen years old. Since there was no central agency to enforce rules, in practice every state institution had complete autonomy to "hire with or without examination and dismiss with or without acceptable reasons," leading to a large turnover of federal employees with each new government. In 1942 one writer estimated that 99 percent of Argentine government employees were chosen more or less directly for political reasons.[24]

This practice continued when the Peronist government came into power, and government departments were emptied of personnel to make way for Perón's followers. The first Argentine Civil Service Statute was enacted in December 1943 under the military government of General Ramirez, for which Perón served as the labor and welfare secretary. Among the provisions of the statute was the requirement for the first time of a primary education as a prerequisite for entry into public administration.[25]

During the first Peronist government, the functions of the state were

23. Ibid., p. 213.
24. Jean-Claude Garcia-Zamor, *Public Administration and Social Changes in Argentina* (Rio de Janeiro: Casa Vallelle, 1968), pp. 139–40.
25. Decree 16.672/43 (December 16, 1943), as cited in Pan American Union, Department of Economic Affairs, *Estudios sobre administración pública en América Latina: Argentina* (Washington, D.C.: General Secretariat of the Organization for American States, 1968), p. 63.

expanded dramatically, and the number of state employees multiplied.[26] The state assumed an active role in maintaining full employment by absorbing personnel who did not find work in the private sector. At the same time the Peronist government froze or decreased the salary levels of top-level public employees.[27] Through the nationalization of the banking system, the acquisition of the railroads and most public utilities, the expansion of executive authority through the constitution of 1949, and the provisions of the first and second five-year plans, the state extended its control over the national economy during the Peronist government.

While Perón vastly extended the size of the state and the extent of the state's functions in the economic realm, he did not insure a concomitant expansion of the state's capacity to perform those functions. The increase in the state's functions and the level of economic development put new demands on the efficiency of public administration which the system was not prepared to handle. The Peronist government experimented with a variety of institutional arrangements for the organization of executive power, but virtually none of them survived the fall of Perón in 1955.[28]

Under Peronism the state for the first time gained a high level of autonomy from the traditional Argentine dominant classes.[29] But it was perceived by these classes as a case of "inverted instrumentalism," in which subordinate groups were able to capture the state and use it for their own ends.[30] The very effectiveness and transparency of the Peronist government's efforts to use the state to redistribute income rein-

26. During the period 1943–1952 349,000 new workers (a 144.4 percent increase) were added to the public payrolls, to reach a high of approximately 600,000 national government employees in 1952. Benjamin A. Most, "Authoritarianism and the Growth of the State in Latin America: An Assessment of Their Impacts on Argentine Public Policy, 1930–1970," *Comparative Political Studies* 13 (July 1980), 182.

27. Roulet and Sabato, "Estado y administración pública en Argentina," p. 217.

28. Jose Alberto Bonifacio, "Diseno organizacional de la presidencia en la Argentina entre 1943 and 1983 (Cambios organizacionales e instituciones de fomulacion de politicas)," Direccion General de Investigaciones, INAP, 1985. Garcia-Zamor, *Public Administration and Social Changes in Argentina*, p. 109. Wynia argues that "although Perón announced many plans for the reorganization of the Argentine state, few of them were actually carried out." Gary Wynia, *Argentina in the Postwar Era: Politics and Economic Policy Making in a Divided Society* (Albuquerque: University of New Mexico Press, 1978), p. 56.

29. Carlos Waisman has argued at length that Peronist policies were an example of state autonomy because they were not in the interests of the central segments of the dominant class, nor were they imposed on Argentina by inescapable external constraints. Carlos Waisman, *Reversal of Development in Argentina: Postwar Counterrevolutionary Policies and Their Structural Consequences* (Princeton: Princeton University Press, 1987), p. 137.

30. The concept of "inverted instrumentalism" is discussed by Rueschemeyer and Evans in "The State and Economic Transformation," p. 63.

forced the vision not of a state serving general "national" interests but of one that could be wielded by groups in power against groups out of power. This perception of inverted instrumentalism on the part of dominant groups led to an increasing distrust of the state by private producers. "This legacy, combined with the expansion of state responsibility for economic management, left his successors with the near impossible task of fulfilling the state's expanded role by seeking the cooperation of citizens who distrusted their motives and were determined to avoid enforcement of their policies."[31] The Peronist period should be seen as a case of "governmental autonomy" rather than state autonomy, since there was no perception of "stateness"—of a neutral state defending national interests—and little continuity of the institutions, policies, or personnel of the state after the fall of the Peronist government. At the same time little was done to enhance the capacity of the state.

It was not until the mid- to late 1950s that the initial efforts to create a professional public administration began to be felt. The Civil Service Statute of 1943 was applied more consistently after 1957, and a centralized civil service bureau was established to oversee application of the statute. The powers and capacities of the Civil Service Bureau were much more limited than those of the DASP in Brazil, since it had no responsibility for budgeting or supervising training of civil servants.

The positions adopted by the Frondizi government toward state action were a response to the prevalent attitudes about the state in Argentina and the lack of agility of the state bureaucratic apparatus. The nature of the state was such that the Frondizi administration felt it was unable to establish control over its functions. Rather than trying to implement their program working with and through the state, as Kubitschek did (with some administration modification to improve speed and flexibility), they tried to circumvent the state.[32]

Some of the most important economic initiatives of the Frondizi ad-

31. Wynia, *Argentina in the Postwar Era*, p. 76.

32. Some authors credit the Frondizi government with institution building. William Ascher, for example, argues that Frondizi built new institutions with the goal of having técnicos in influential positions throughout the policy-making apparatus. William Ascher, "Planners, Politics, and Technocracy in Argentina and Chile," (Ph.D. diss., Yale University, 1975), pp. 44–45. But the institutions he cites, the National Development Council (CONADE) and the Federal Investment Council (CFI), were either afterthoughts or not an initiative of the national government at all. CONADE was founded at the end of the Frondizi administration, and the CFI was set up by the governors of the provinces. In my interviews with economic policy makers from the Frondizi administration, none mentioned CONADE as an important government initiative or as a center of economic policy making or coordination during the Frondizi government.

ministration, such as the petroleum and foreign investment policies, were initially carried out outside of normal bureaucratic channels. Thus Frondizi appointed his personal representative to head up the state oil company, YPF, and empowered him to carry out secret negotiations for oil contracts without involving the rest of the YPF staff. He appointed Frigerio as his personal secretary for economic and social affairs of the presidency with the intention of sidestepping the Ministry of Economics in the formulation and implementation of economic policy. In the office of the presidency, under Frigerio's control, Frondizi set up the National Commission on Foreign Investment to approve or reject foreign investment proposals. Like the executive groups in Brazil, the commission included representatives from a number of other institutions involved in economic policy decisions. The Secretariat for Economic and Social Affairs of the Presidency, however, was perceived as a personal vehicle to enhance the political power of Frigerio, a man almost universally mistrusted by Argentine elites, rather than as a bureaucratic innovation for increasing the speed and flexibility of policy making.

As a result of these measures, Frondizi's political opponents accused him of trying to set up a "parallel government." As one Frondizi collaborator explained: "Frondizi could not rely, for his government efforts, on the total control of the state apparatus. . . . As a result, he had to look for outside collaborators . . . the center of the so-called parallel government was made up of Frigerio, who was totally identified with Frondizi as regards the government's objectives."[33]

Frondizi launched a program aimed at overhauling and rationalizing Argentine public administration. The Administrative Rationalization Plan was initiated in late 1958 with the creation of the Executive Committee for the Rationalization and Austerity Plan. As the name indicates, the plan was conceived in the context of the economic stabilization plan then being implemented in Argentina, and its main thrust was to reduce the cost of public administration through privatization of state enterprises and reduction of surplus personnel. The purpose of the rationalization program was not to create an insulated part of the bureaucracy based on merit hiring practices and protected from societal pressures. The plan aimed at increasing the efficiency of public administration, but not at improving the state's capacity to implement economic policies.

The centerpiece of the rationalization plan was a frontal attack on

33. Juan Ovidio Zavala, *Desarrollo y racionalización* (Buenos Aires: Ediciones Arayu, 1963), pp. 25–26.

the administration of the state-owned railroad system. The transport sector was central to developmentalist programs in both Argentina and Brazil. And in both countries the primary emphasis was placed not on rail transport but on expanding the national road networks and on car and truck transport. In Argentina road transport was seen as more flexible and responsive to the development needs of the country. For the desarrollistas a logical outcome of the decision to emphasize road transport was a simultaneous program to reduce and rationalize the rail transport system, eliminating the uneconomical lines and superfluous personnel. Since the state railroad deficit contributed heavily to the overall public deficit, the rationalization program served both developmental and stabilization goals.

Much as was the case with petroleum policy, in his attempt to rationalize the state railroads Frondizi not only took on powerful interests, including one of the strongest unions in the countries, but he confronted a potent symbol of Argentine independence and nationhood. The railroad system, constructed by the British, had long symbolized foreign ownership of important sectors of the Argentine economy. When Perón used inconvertible British sterling accumulated during the Second World War to purchase the aging rail system, it was widely perceived as a victory for Argentine nationalism. The heated political struggle generated by the railroad rationalization program contributed to the resignation of economics minister Aleman and the secretary of transport, the chief architect of the rationalization program. It was among the crises that eventually debilitated the Frondizi administration and led to its downfall in early 1962.

The other goal of the rationalization program was to privatize state enterprises and reduce state personnel. In both these areas the program was successful. In late 1961 the administration announced to the press that the state had reduced its personnel since 1958 by 157,081 employees, primarily through a series of hiring freezes.[34] A study of the size of the Argentine public administration shows that this estimate is correct, or even somewhat low, and that the bulk of jobs the Frondizi administration eliminated were in state enterprises, probably as a result of privatization. The Frondizi rationalization program led to a decline of 12 percent of total state employment by the third year of its application.[35]

34. Ibid., p. 199.
35. Jose Alberto Bonifacio, "El empleo en la administración pública nacional entre 1958 y 1985," Direccion General de Investigaciones, INAP, August 1986, pp. 10, 25. Bonifacio shows that the Argentine public administration did not return to the size it was at the beginning of the Frondizi administration until 1976, only to fall again during the

Although Frondizi was able to impose a drastic cut in total state personnel, he was not able to maintain even some of his closest collaborators in state policy-making positions. When Alvaro Alsogaray was appointed minister of economics in 1959, he recentralized economic policy making in the ministry and appointed his own team to run key national banks and economic policy institutions. For over two years Alsogaray and his team essentially occupied the state economic policy-making apparatus, holding the president hostage in his own government.

But even after Frondizi regained some control over the state apparatus, the reforms he initiated were aimed at streamlining rather than at strengthening the capacity of the state over the long term. The bureaucracy continued to lack basic reforms and procedures that could have strengthened it and increased its autonomy.

ATTITUDES ABOUT THE STATE IN BRAZIL AND
ARGENTINA

J. P. Nettl has pointed out that recognition of the state as a significant factor in political and social life "depends not only on empirical problems relating to the activity and structure of a particular state, but also to a cultural disposition to allot recognition to the conceptual existence of the state at all."[36] Thus, he suggests that one can examine the qualities of "stateness" in particular countries by examining historical, intellectual, and cultural traditions regarding the state.

A precise examination of such traditions is more difficult than a comparison of the specific characteristics of the state, but it sheds useful insights on the differences between the Brazilian and the Argentine state.

In Brazil there is a strong intellectual tradition of interest in and concern with the state and its institutions, stretching back to the time of the empire. In the 1930s, when Vargas initiated administrative reforms, this intellectual concern with the state was transformed into a budding discourse on "scientific management" and public administration, borrowing heavily from debates in the United States and Europe. The founding of DASP and the Fundação Getúlio Vargas gave homes

---

post-1976 military regime. The cut in personnel during the Frondizi administration was the largest one between 1958 and 1976.

36. J. P. Nettl, "The State as a Conceptual Variable," *World Politics* 20 (July 1968), 566.

to the new research, teaching, translation, and publication efforts, making Brazil a regional center for public administration study.

The development of social science research in Brazil showed a concern and focus on the state that outweighed that of colleagues in the United States and elsewhere in Latin America. The weight of the Estado Nôvo and the predominance of the state in structuring societal relations led to a state-centric view of politics. Only more recently has Brazilian social science begun to experience a backlash against what was perceived as excessive concern with the centrality and power of the state, as increasingly today we see research on political parties, business associations, rural producers, peasants, and the labor movement which stresses that the degree of autonomy and maneuverability of these groups vis-à-vis the state was greater than often portrayed in the past. In spite of the new revisionism, a state-centric tradition continues to hold a powerful sway over intellectual life in Brazil.

In Argentina, to the contrary, there has been little intellectual tradition of research and writing on the state. Largely legalistic accounts of the development of state institutions were common in the 1800s, but they virtually disappeared after 1930. The field of public administration is vastly underdeveloped in Argentina compared to that in Brazil, and few studies exist outlining in detail the contours, functions, and attributes of the modern Argentine bureaucracy and the civil service.[37] So little empirical research exists on the Argentine bureaucrat that it is difficult to even put together a picture of this class of individuals. The absence of major public administration reform in Argentina made it a nonissue for academic writers, just as the administrative reform of the Vargas years in Brazil spurred the major public administration research projects. Social science research tended to concentrate on the more vital societal forces, especially political parties and the labor movement, and on distinctive types of regimes, such as populist and bureaucratic authoritarian.

In Argentina this lack of an intellectual tradition of emphasis on the state was coupled with an intense concern with the politics of nationalism. The debate over nationalism, in turn, often focused on debates over the expansion of state functions and the development of certain institutions, such as formation of the state oil company, YPF, and nationalization of the Central Bank and the railroads. Perhaps because of the very weakness of the state, some of these institutions became exces-

37. A 1971 study on the Argentine state and public administration stated baldly, "It profoundly worries us that there are so few people who do research, study, and reflect on the nature of the Argentine state, what role it plays, what it does, and what it should do." Roulet and Sabato, "Estado y administración pública en Argentina," p. 223.

sively identified with the nation, and any attempt to modify them was perceived as an attack on nationhood or sovereignty.[38] Thus Frondizi's attempts to streamline or modify the state as a part of his development program were interpreted as an attack on the very nation, which was seen as fragile and constantly threatened by certain domestic and especially foreign interests.

A reciprocal relation exists between the development of certain state structures and practices and domestic attitudes about the nature of the state. That is, the more the state is viewed as an agency favoring the general interests of the nation, the more likely action will be taken to strengthen the state apparatus. At the same time a stronger and more insulated state may take actions that reinforce the perception of the state as a protector of national interests. A weaker and less autonomous state, however, may be perceived as ineffectual, or as a vehicle for powerful societal interests, and may inhibit attempts to enhance its powers for fear of enhancing the power of the groups that dominate the state. Thus, it is possible to envision a circle by which certain state attributes and practices generate attitudes about the state, which in turn reinforce state characteristics.

Comparison between the Brazilian and Argentine cases reinforces Skocpol's argument that "various sorts of states . . . give rise to various conceptions of the meaning and methods of 'politics' itself, conceptions that influence the behavior of all groups and classes in national societies."[39] The structure and procedures of existing state institutions in Brazil and Argentina conditioned the attitudes of developmentalists toward the state and shaped the political strategies they adopted to put their economic programs into effect. These different political strategies in turn provoked dramatically different responses from societal forces, whose own vision of the state influenced their behavior.

INDICATORS OF STATE CAPACITY AND AUTONOMY

A useful typology for categorizing and comparing the attributes of the state has been presented by Stephen Skowronek, who distinguishes

38. K. H. Silvert pointed out that Argentine nationalism mainly consisted of attracting foreign countries and of the mystical glorification of the nation, but dedicated little effort to assuring the relative position of the state as the supreme institution. "Liderazgo político y debilidad institucional en la Argentina," *Desarrollo económico* 1 (October–December 1960), 164–65.

39. Skocpol, Introduction in *Bringing the State Back In*, ed. Evans, Reuschemeyer, and Skocpol, p. 22.

among the organizational, procedural, and intellectual determinants of a state's mode of operation.[40] Skowronek describes the organizational orientation of the state in terms of concentration, penetration, and centralization of authority, and specialization of institutional tasks.[41] As regards concentration, penetration, and centralization of authority, Brazil and Argentina do not differ significantly. It is at the level of specialization of institutional tasks that we see a divergence between the state structures in the two countries. By the 1950s the Brazilian state had a more complex and specialized web of state institutions to conduct economic policy. But the most striking differences between the Brazilian and Argentine states fall in the procedural and intellectual areas, in particular as recruitment, retention, and training of a core of civil servants who provide continuity to the economic policy process. The following section compares the organizational, procedural, and intellectual dimensions of the Brazilian and Argentine states.

Organizational Orientation

Total size of the public administration in Argentina and Brazil. The absolute size of the state apparatus and the number of functions that the state is expected to undertake are potential conditions favoring state capacity. It is not obvious that a large state is a strong or autonomous state, and indeed the possibility of a small strong state is very real. Nevertheless, it is valid to ask if a larger state with a broader number of functions is more capable and more likely to be autonomous than a small state.

One indication of state size is the number of public employees. It is very difficult to get reliable comparable information on the number of public employees in Brazil and Argentina, but some attempts at comparison can be made. According to a major study of Argentine public administration, in 1960–1961, Argentina had a total of 289,058 "centralized" employees of the national government, plus 140,566 employees of "decentralized" organisms, such as the Central Bank and the Industrial Bank, for a total of 429,724 national government employees.[42]

40. Skowronek, *Building a New American State*, pp. 19–24.
41. Ibid., p. 20.
42. This figure does not include state enterprises or provincial or municipal government employees. It is a summary of total positions, and thus includes even those vacant at any moment. Pan American Union, *Estudios sobre administración pública en América Latina: Argentina*, p. 67. Another study shows in 1960 a total of 296,697 employees in centralized administration, plus 209,670 employees in decentralized organisms, for a total of 506,367 state employees. In addition, 415,457 people were employed in state enterprises, for a grand total of 921,824 state employees. Bonifacio, "El empleo en la administración púb-

One source estimates that in 1960 Brazil had 273,645 positions in the "direct administration" and 142,179 total positions in the "autarquias," for a total of 415,824 federal public service positions, including vacant positions. Direct administration includes the ministries, agencies, and commissions directly responsible to the president; autarquias refer to the autonomous agencies, government corporations, and mixed enterprises.[43] Although it is difficult to be certain if these figures are comparable,[44] what emerges is a picture of a roughly similar total number of federal employees in the two countries. Given that the Argentine population is much smaller than the Brazilian, Argentine federal public employees form a larger percentage of total population than in Brazil. Thus the differences in the Argentine and Brazilian states that we are discussing are not primarily related to differences in the absolute sizes of the public administration in terms of number of employees.

Table 3, which includes only centralized public administration in the two countries, reveals that while the Kubitschek government (1956–1961) was a period of moderate growth of the direct public administration, the numbers of public employees in Argentina was cut back during the Frondizi administration (1958–1962) as part of the administrative rationalization program carried out by the government.

Institutional infrastructure. More important than the actual size of the state is the issue of the specialization of the institutional infrastructure within the state to carry out the developmentalist policies and the eco-

Table 3. Growth in public administration, 1943–1960[45]

Brazil* (direct administration)		Argentina† (centralized positions)	
1943	131,628	1943	232,987
1953	180,410	1953/54	279,447
1956	217,135	1955/56	300,151
1958	232,632	1958/59	295,722
1960	231,504	1960/61	289,058

*Excludes vacant positions.
†Includes vacant positions.

lica nacional entre 1958 y 1985," p. 10. This study points out that the level of state employment in Argentina in 1985 was still well under the 1960 levels.

43. Graham, *Civil Service Reform in Brazil*, p. 132.

44. For example, some state enterprises are included in the autarquia category in Brazil, but state enterprises are excluded from the Argentine totals.

45. Figures for Brazil from Graham, *Civil Service Reform in Brazil*, p. 132. Figures for Argentina from Pan American Union, *Estudios sobre administración pública en América Latina: Argentina*, p. 67.

nomic functions of the state. Over the years since 1943, Argentina has suffered from institutional discontinuity and a resulting inadequate institutional infrastructure. In 1955 most of the institutional innovations of the Peronist government were dismantled, and few lasting new institutions were created for the formulation and implementation of economic policy. The Frondizi government was not especially concerned with institutional innovations, preferring to pursue its policies through its adhoc parallel policy network.[46]

As a result of institutional discontinuity and lack of interest in institution building, many institutions basic to state involvement in development were created in Argentina later than they were in Brazil. The National Budget Office was not established until 1964. The National Development Council (CONADE) was created in 1961, late in the Frondizi government, but did not begin to play an important role in economic policy making until the Illía government.[47]

In the absence of such auxiliary agencies, more burden fell on the office of the presidency and the appropriate ministries to formulate and implement development policy. Neither, however, had the necessary infrastructure or organization to carry out these tasks. A Pan American Union report on public administration in Argentina concluded that, as of 1965, the office of the president "does not have the adequate organization to carry out the vast and diverse powers of the presidency." Likewise, a lack of coordination complicated the work of the Ministry of Economics. "Without a profound reform of the ministerial institutions as an instrument of executive power—of juridical regulations, administrative formalities, work habits—it seems unlikely that the existing administration can transform itself into an administration for development."[48]

The institutional infrastructure for development in Brazil was a combination of such existing institutions as the Banco do Brasil and the Foreign Service, with new institutions set up during the second Vargas

46. One of Frondizi's close collaborators claimed that Frondizi saw formal institutional organization as an obstacle to his program, by increasing the power of lower-level officials and thus weakening the decisional power of the president. Nicholas Babini, *Frondizi: De la oposición al gobierno* (Buenos Aires: Editorial Celtia, 1984), p. 212.

47. An important interprovincial planning organization, the Federal Investment Council (CFI) was created in 1959. Although the CFI was an interprovincial organization, not a national one, it became the most permanent planning organism in the country, with a high degree of administrative continuity very unusual in Argentina. Antonio Federico Moreno, *El planeamiento y neustra Argentina* (Buenos Aires: Ediciones Corregidor, 1978), p. 111, and "La Historia del C.F.I.," *Todo es Historia* 106 (March 1976), 32.

48. Pan American Union, *Estudios sobre administracón pública en América Latina: Argentina,* pp. 94–95.

administration and during the Kubitschek administration, such as the Economic Development Council and its working groups and executive groups, SUDENE, and NOVACAP. At the center of the institutional network was the BNDE, which served as coordinator of Brazilian development strategy. Frequently, individuals moved from one institution to another, facilitated by a Brazilian civil service practice that permitted the "borrowing" of staff by institutions without them losing their seniority or position in their original institution.

In Argentina during the Frondizi administration no institutions played a training and coordinating role at the national level similar to the Brazilian institutions mentioned above. No state institution served as a training ground for economists, nor was the practice of lateral movement among institutions of the state common. The absence of a strong institutional infrastructure made it difficult for the state to have an adequate economic research base to plan its economic policy.[49]

Operating Procedures

Procedures for recruitment, promotion, dismissal, job classification, and salary can make an essential contribution to a coherent and effective public administration. They also help create conditions for increasing the intellectual talent available to the state apparatus and expanding institutional memory and institutional learning. Administrative capacity is enhanced by competitive entrance examinations for the civil service, in order to attract the most qualified people. For the civil service to keep qualified personnel over time it must have adequate possibilities for promotion based on merit, job security, and pay scales that are competitive with pay scales in the private sector.

In Brazil, prior to 1930, positions in the civil bureaucracy were generally acquired through political patronage. There were some exceptions to this rule; for example, the Ministry of Finance had required entrance exams for certain positions since the time of the empire. But in general there was a patronage system with no standard merit recruitment procedures.[50] It was not until a merit system was introduced during the first Vargas administration that public examinations began to be required for entry into the civil service. Even though the new system

49. Among the recommendations of a 1961 private consultants' report on industrial development in Argentina was the creation of an economic research staff to conduct the necessary research and to chart sound economic development policies for the government. "Some Aspects of Industrial Development in Argentina, Contract ICAC—1866," Report to the Government of Argentina and the International Cooperation Administration, prepared by Arthur D. Little, Inc., Cambridge, Mass., August 25, 1961, p. 2.

50. Wahrlich, *Administração de pessoal*, p. 23.

established the principle that public examinations would be required for all, in practice the great bulk of the public administration continued to be filled through political appointments.

One report shows that for a three-year period only 17.8 percent of new public servants gained admission to the public administration through public examinations. Although this figure appears low, many of the agencies responsible for formulating and implementing economic policy during the Kubitschek government had much higher levels of recruitment through merit exams. For example, the BNDE and Itamaraty both allowed admission only through public examination during this period.[51]

In 1957 Argentina first established more detailed recruitment procedures for the civil service, calling for competitive entrance examinations for certain positions. But entrance requirements were still vague: the applicant had to be Argentine, possess the moral and behavioral conditions and the physical aptitude for the job they hoped to get, and "prove their ability" to occupy the position.[52] Promotions were to be granted based on merit. Job security was guaranteed for civil servants, but only after three years of effective continuous service or five years of effective discontinuous service.[53] Given the extreme instability of Argentine politics, three years of continuous service or five years of discontinuous service can be rare in the public administration.

Intellectual Talent

It is difficult to separate the discussion of procedures from that of intellectual talent. Hiring and promotional practices potentially can increase state capacity by attracting and maintaining individuals with managerial and technical skills. The procedural orientation of the state influences the intellectual skills and talents it is able to recruit and maintain. Educational levels of bureaucrats are one indication of appropriate recruitment. The educational level of top Brazilian bureaucrats is high. A survey in 1968–1969 showed that 86 percent of public executives in Brazil had college degrees, compared to 81 percent in the United States, where college education is much more common.[54] No

---

51. Beatriz Wahrlich, "Normas para preservação e revigoramento do sistema do mérito," (Brazil: Ministro Extraordinario para a Reforma Administrativa, 1963), as cited in Graham, *Civil Service Reform in Brazil*, p. 129.

52. Ibid., p. 561.

53. Pan American Union, *Estudios sobre administracíon pública en América Latina: Argentina*, p. 81.

54. Robert Daland, *Exploring Brazilian Bureaucracy: Performance and Pathology* (Washington, D.C.: University Press of America, 1981), p. 310.

such complete information is available for Argentina, but a survey of forty-one top policy makers in 1960 revealed that 100 percent had graduated from the university or national military academy.[55] The most common professional background of Argentine bureaucrats is military training, followed by law and journalism. A study of top Argentine policy makers from 1943 to 1983 found that only 2.9 percent were trained as economists.[56]

Training of public employees in Brazil and Argentina. In addition to hiring and promotion procedures, the state may use training programs to improve the quality of intellectual talent involved in economic policy making. Training may not only expand technical expertise but also help reshape values toward a common rationality, contribute to the emergence of a shared esprit de corps, and increase the prestige of civil servants.

Training of public employees in Brazil on a wide scale was initiated by DASP in the late 1930s and early 1940s. After 1939 many public servants received scholarships from DASP to study abroad. In 1941 DASP began to offer administration courses for public officials and by 1943 they were attended by over four thousand students.[57] In 1958 a School of Public Service was set up as part of DASP to offer a broader range of training courses for public officials. By the time the Kubitschek administration came to power, training officials in public administration had been an institutionalized function of the bureaucracy for over fifteen years.

In addition to the training efforts within DASP, other training programs existed in the individual agencies and ministries. By far the most extensive training program outside of DASP was the Brazilian School of Public Administration, set up in 1952 as part of the Fundação Getúlio Vargas. The purpose of the new school was to offer university-level courses in public administration, a function not filled by DASP training courses. The United Nations agreed to provide technical and financial assistance to the school during the first four years, including sending international public administration specialists to help organize the school and its curriculum, providing scholarships for Brazilian professors to study abroad, and offering scholarships for Latin American students to attend the new school. Later, the school also received tech-

55. Silvert, "Liderazgo político y debilidad institucional en la Argentina," p. 172.
56. This was a survey of 136 bureaucrats who were at the secretary or subsecretary level in various executive offices from 1943 to 1983. Bonifacio, "Deseño organizacional de la presidencia en la Argentina," p. 173.
57. Fundação Getúlio Vargas, *Fundação Getúlio Vargas: 30 anos a serviço do Brasil* (Rio de Janeiro: Editora da Fundação Getúlio Vargas, 1974), p. 306.

nical assistance from U.S. universities contracted by the U.S. government as part of the Point Four Program.[58]

The experience of public administration training in Brazil is yet another example of the permeability of Brazilian institutions to international ideas and trends and the ability of Brazilian officials to solicit and receive international support for institution-building efforts. Much of the administrative reform during the 1930s and 1940s was based on the transplanting of U.S. theories of scientific management to the Brazilian context. The public administration training programs were often applied with excessive formalism inappropriate in the Brazilian setting. Nevertheless, the Brazilian public administration training programs soon became the strongest in the continent and contributed to the creation of a permanent trained body of public officials that could be tapped by the Brazilian state.

The idea and practice of training public employees took hold later in Argentina than it did in Brazil. No overall public administration training institution existed until 1957, when the Instituto Superior de la Administración Pública was created.[59] Other more specialized training institutes for public employees were also created in the late 1950s and early 1960s.[60] In 1968 a report on public administration commented that in-service training efforts had not yet led to "the transformation of the country's administration into an adequate instrument for the execution of the government's plans."[61] Whereas Kubitschek inherited a bureaucracy in which previous training efforts had already begun to bear fruit, Frondizi was faced with a bureaucracy that had just initiated its efforts to improve the training of public officials.

The impact of training on the behavior of the public administration

58. Marina Brandão Machado, *O ensino de administração pública no Brasil* (Rio de Janeiro: Fundação Getúlio Vargas, 1966), pp. 19–23. Also under the Point Four Program, the Joint U.S.-Brazil Economic Development Commission provided fellowships for training Brazilians in the United States in public administration. Report of the Joint U.S.-Brazil Economic Development Commission (Washington, D.C.: Institute of Inter-American Affairs, Foreign Operations Administration, U.S. Government Printing Office, 1955), p. 82.

59. No special schools for public servants functioned regularly during the Peronist administration. The Peronist Superior School was a training program in Peronist politics, but with no public administration component. Garcia-Zamor, *Public Administration and Social Changes in Argentina*, p. 145.

60. These included the National Foreign Service Institute, set up in 1963, which had as a forerunner the Diplomacy Specialization Institute, established in 1960–1961; the National Customs School of the Economics Ministry, in 1961; and the Public Health School of the Ministry of Welfare and Public Health, in 1959.

61. Pan American Union, *Estudios sobre administración pública en América Latina: Argentina*, p. 73.

depends on the nature of the training itself and the degree of continuity of public officials which would allow them to incorporate their training into their jobs. For example, Daland examined the effect of in-service training on the development orientation of public officials in Brazil. He found that training in their own agency actually reduced the level of development orientation of public employees, whereas graduate or foreign training increased it.[62]

The connection between the potential impact of training and the issue of bureaucratic continuity is apparent in the results of a study comparing Argentines and Brazilians who participated in the CEPAL basic training course in Santiago. Although more Argentines than Brazilians were trained in the CEPAL course, the potential impact of training on the bureaucracy was lessened because CEPAL-trained Argentines tended to leave the public sector for the private sector and for work abroad. Of a sample of CEPAL-trained Argentines, 41 percent had left Argentina and 55 percent had defected from the public sector to the private sector, either in Argentina or abroad. In Brazil the results were dramatically different. The public sector had a 72 percent holding power for its CEPAL-trained técnicos, and the sample even revealed a movement of the trainees from the private sector into government service.[63]

Continuity of employment for top officials in the Argentine and Brazilian bureaucracy. The Brazilian bureaucracy has much greater continuity than the Argentine. A survey of 325 top executives of the Brazilian national bureaucracy conducted in 1968–1969 found that 85 percent had originally entered the public service by age thirty and spent virtually their entire productive career there. Although there was high continuity within the bureaucracy, there was also a great deal of mobility from one part of the bureaucracy to another, so that the median tenure in one position was three and a half years.

Many Brazilian public officials were particularly identified with one administration, during which they received key promotions. Contrary to what was frequently the case in Argentina, however, at the end of the administration term bureaucrats did not leave or lose their jobs, but instead tended to make lateral moves within the bureaucracy until they reached a point where they might be promoted again. This lateral mobility serves what Daland calls a "conserving and talent banking func-

---

62. Daland, *Exploring Brazilian Bureaucracy*, pp. 166–67.
63. David Bruce, "The U.N. Economic Commission for Latin America and National Development Policies: A Study of Noncoercive Influence" (Ph.D. diss., University of Michigan, 1977), pp. 148–49, 162.

tion" for bureaucrats who will eventually be needed in another key position. "These data reinforce the image of an experienced stable bureaucracy with a relatively low level of partisan politicization. . . . Brazil's bureaucracy certainly falls at the stable end of the continuum among third world countries, and probably among all countries."[64]

No comparable study exists on the Argentine bureaucracy. Limited available evidence suggests much shorter tenure for government bureaucrats, especially at top levels. While it was not uncommon in Brazil for even top political appointee positions to be filled by civil servants, in Argentina the category of political appointees appears to reach deeper down into the bureaucracy, and these positions are rarely filled by civil servants. This is not to say that political appointees had no previous government experience. A study of 131 top-level executive policy makers found that 57 percent had some previous experience working at a high- to mid-level position in government.[65] Although specific information for the Frondizi period is not available, the level of previous government experience appears to have been much lower. Not one of the key economic policy makers during the Frondizi administration whom I interviewed was a government civil servant, and most had no previous administrative experience in government. In Brazil over half of the key policy makers from the Kubitschek administration interviewed held permanent positions in the bureaucracy. One survey of Argentine bureaucrats found that the greater tenuousness of Argentine civil service jobs led Argentine bureaucrats to be more security oriented; they failed to take new initiatives and opted for "a safe strategy of abstaining from the role of interest broker."[66]

The image of Brazilian government stability is reinforced by a study of bureaucratic turnover during the period 1946–1964. Ministerial and bureaucratic turnover rates vary from one administration to another, but high levels of instability existed only during the Goulart administration. The average length of a ministerial term during the Dutra administration was twenty-five months; during the second Vargas administration, 17.8 months; 22.7 during Kubitschek; and 6.7 during Vargas. The average term of the minister of finance was similar: 20 months during the Dutra administration, 21 during Vargas, 20 during Kubitschek, and 6.2 during Goulart.[67] These figures give us some idea of the continuity of the political appointees of various administrations, but

64. Daland, *Exploring Brazilian Bureaucracy*, pp. 306, 310.
65. Bonifacio, "Diseno organizacional de la presidencia en la Argentina," p. 174.
66. Ascher, "Planners, Politics and Technocracy in Argentina and Chile," p. 153.
67. Wanderley Gilherme dos Santos, "The Calculus of Conflict: Impasse in Brazilian Politics and the Crisis of 1964" (Ph.D. diss., Stanford University, 1979), pp. 201, 210.

they do not necessarily convey the actual degree of continuity between and within governments, which is also high in the case of Brazil during the period discussed. For example, of the thirty ministers that held one of the eleven ministerial positions during the five years of the Kubitschek administration, seven had held previous ministerial positions in one of the administrations since 1951.

Stability indexes for governmental agencies during the four presidential periods in Brazil are higher than the indexes for ministerial stability. Under Dutra six out of twelve top bureaucratic posts were administered by a single appointee throughout the period, whereas under Kubitschek eight out of fifteen agencies (more than 50 percent) were administered by the same person during his five-year term. Brazil's presidents attempted to protect parts of the state apparatus from the normal political game of influence and compromise.[68]

Argentina shows an even more dramatic pattern of declining ministerial continuity. During the Peronist government the average term of the minister of economics was fifty-six months; during the Aramburu government, ten months; nine months during the Frondizi government; and four and a half months during the caretaker Guido government that followed the overthrow of Frondizi. A similar though less drastic pattern existed for two other top economic policy posts in Argentina: the presidents of the Central Bank and the Banco Industrial. The average term of the president of the Central Bank was twenty-eight months during the Peronist government, ten months during Aramburu, fifteen months during Frondizi, and nine months during Guido; the average term of the president of the Banco Industrial was also ten months during the Aramburu government and fifteen months during Frondizi.[69] A survey of top-level political appointees (secretaries and subsecretaries) in the executive office during the period 1943–1983 found that the mean tenure was 18.3 months for the whole period. Over 40 percent of the bureaucrats served for under one year. If one factors out the Peronist period, which had relatively high job stability for bureaucrats, the lack of continuity would be even greater.[70]

---

68. Ibid., pp. 216–17. A second study of bureaucratic turnover rates in decentralized state agencies in Brazil during a twenty-year period (1945–1964) found that the Kubitschek government was the most stable period for bureaucrats in strategic positions in decentralized government agencies, except for heads of agencies, which had somewhat greater stability of tenure during the Medici government. Guilherme dos Santos, "Relatoria de pesquisa, centralização burocrática e renovação de elites," pp. 62, 67–68.

69. Figures calculated from data presented in Juan Carlos de Pablo, *La economia que yo hice* (Buenos Aires: Ediciones El Cronista Comercial, 1980), pp. 31–41; and the *Memoria y balance* of the Banco Industrial de la República Argentina.

70. Bonifacio, "Diseno organizacional de la presidencia en la Argentina," pp. 176–78.

DEVELOPMENT INSTITUTIONS COMPARED

I have argued that a stronger institutional framework in Brazil than in Argentina facilitated the acceptance and implementation of developmentalist ideas. Often, similar institutions existed in the two countries, but different procedures in Brazil gave greater autonomy to those institutions than they had in Argentina. Even in a situation in which similar procedures existed—for example, staff tenure—actual practice often differed from one country to the other. A brief comparison of two key state banking institutions, the BNDE in Brazil and the Banco Industrial in Argentina, will highlight the different institutional dynamics in Brazil and Argentina. Although these banks had somewhat similar mandates, their actual function in the development process was quite different. In Brazil the BNDE was the primary institution responsible for the formulation and implementation of the Targets Plan, whereas in Argentina the Banco Industrial was fairly marginal to the economic policies of the developmentalist period.

Banco Industrial de la República Argentina

In Argentina in the 1950s no single state institution, aside from the Ministry of Economics, played a central role in directing or promoting development. The Banco Industrial was an obvious candidate to play that role. Its failure to do so is an interesting puzzle that sheds light on the nature of the Argentine state.[71]

The Banco Industrial was created in 1944, during the government of Edelmiro Farrell.[72] The original goal of the bank was to grant medium- and long-term industrial credit, especially to industries that utilized national raw materials, giving preference to small and medium industry and to those that contributed to national defense and to the development of specific regions.[73] The bank was initially planned to be a development bank and not to duplicate the activities of existing official and

71. The Banco Industrial was almost never mentioned in my interviews with important economic policy makers. It is not referred to in major texts on Argentine economic development.

72. Banco de Credito Industrial Argentina, *Memoria y balance, 1944* (Buenos Aires, 1945), p. 27.

73. "If, then, a country does not try to enlarge its internal market and to progress along the path of being the first transformer of its own raw materials, it will remain dangerously exposed to the shocks of these unpredictable variations and in a position of permanent instability." Ibid., p. 16.

private banks. It emphasized intermediate industries such as textiles, food processing, and leather goods, a reflection of national populist economic policy of the Peronist government, which focused on horizontal industrialization for the internal market.

The bank was controlled by a president and by a board of ten directors, all appointed by the president of the nation. The directors were to represent specific ministries and institutions, and candidates were proposed to the president by the groups they were to represent, including two from the Ministry of Agriculture and three from the Argentine Industrial Union. This arrangement gave the institution less autonomy than it would have had if the directors were named independently.[74]

No special mechanism was created to generate an ongoing source of funds for the bank, thus further limiting its potential autonomy. It operated with funds granted by the Central Bank. Shortly after it was established, it began to act more like a commercial bank than a development bank by accepting deposits and granting both short- and long-term industrial credit. The bank played an important role in the expansion of industrial credit; by 1952 it accounted for 50 percent of the total amount of credit the banking system extended to the industrial area.[75] Throughout the Peronist government, the bulk of loans continued to be made to food processing, textile, machinery, and tool industries.

As one part of the Prebisch Plan, Raúl Prebisch recommended that the Banco Industrial be converted into an autonomous institution called the Economic Development Bank. The new bank would transfer its old short-term industrial credit business and would undertake only medium- and long-term investment financing operations. To finance these operations, it would issue bonds and carry out internal and international credit operations.[76] Prebisch also hoped that the Economic Development Bank would also serve to funnel Export-Import Bank funds

74. Later the number of directors was reduced, but the directors were still seen as representing those sectors of the economy served by the bank. Banco Industrial Argentina, "Carta Organica," *Memoria y balance, 1954* (Buenos Aires, 1955), p. 94. A 1961 consultants' report recommended that directors of the bank be appointed for three-year terms to give continuity and lessen political influence, and be removable only for malfeasance in office. "Some Aspects of Industrial Development in Argentina," p. 3.

75. Eduardo Jacobs, Nestor Huici, and Jorge Schvarzer, "National Dvelopment Bank and Technological Development: The Case of Argentine Industry," Centro de Investigaciones Sociales Sobre el Estado y la Administración, draft report, no date, p. 8.

76. *Review of the River Plate*, January 20, 1956, p. 38. A number of these recommendations were repeated in 1961 by a private consultants' report on industrial development in Argentina. "Some Aspects of Industrial Development in Argentina," p. 3.

to Argentine industrialists and to actively promote the formation of new industries rather than simply make loans to existing industries.[77]

The Prebisch recommendations for the conversion of the Industrial Banco generated controversy, however, especially among some industrialists and nationalists. Industrialists feared the loss of the short-term credit they had come to depend on.[78] Nationalists worried about the increase of international intervention as a result of international credit operations. An article in *Qué* magazine, under the editorship of Rogelio Frigerio, reflected this point of view: "By this proposal, the Banco Industrial would be transformed into an omnipotent investment organ, which could compromise the nation with international loans and sell bonds on the stock market. . . . In reality, this is exactly the type of financial organization the great international consortia want to create in colonial countries in order to transfer to these countries all the possible risks of their future investments."[79]

The bank was eventually reorganized in October 1957, incorporating a few of Prebisch's suggestions. In 1958, however, under the new Frondizi administration, short-term industrial loans were once again being granted by the Banco Industrial.[80] As part of the dramatic overhaul of the banking system in 1957, the Banco Industrial ceased to receive funds from the Central Bank. Banco Industrial lending fell to only 15.9 percent of total industrial lending in 1959. The bank was forced to look for additional funding sources and turned to foreign financing for the first time.[81] In 1959 a $10 million line of credit was secured from the U.S. Export-Import Bank to finance the import of capital goods produced in the United States.[82]

Although little is available on the technical capabilities of the staff of the Banco Industrial, a consultant's report in 1961 recommended that training programs be established to give senior and middle-junior staff members of the bank practical training in industrial finance institutions outside the country. The report stressed that among government officials, employees of the bank should receive priority for training abroad, and that the bank's capacity for evaluating projects would be increased by training bank staff.[83] Throughout the period 1944–1962 a large and

77. Raúl Prebisch, "Desarrollo económico y política social," Mesa redonda en la Universidad de Cordoba (Buenos Aires: Secretaria de Prensa de la Presidencia de la Nación, 1956), pp. 61-62.

78. Unión Industrial Argentina, *Memoria y balance, 1957*, p. 25.

79. *Qué sucedió en siete dias* 144 (August 1957), 14.

80. Banco Industrial Argentina, *Memoria y balance, 1958*, p. 11.

81. Jacobs, Huici, and Schvarzer, "National Development Bank," pp. 9, 13.

82. Banco Industrial Argentina, *Memoria y balance, 1959*, pp. 8–9.

83. "Some Aspects of Industrial Development in Argentina," pp. 3–4.

fairly consistent portion of the funds (40–59 percent) went to simple industrial activities involving local processing of domestic agricultural raw materials. This was consistent with the original mandate of the bank, which was to focus on the needs of small and medium-sized industry, with particular emphasis on those industries processing agricultural products. It is not consistent, however, with a developmentalist policy. Developmentalism called for more extensive state support of infrastructure, especially transport and energy, and of basic industries in which domestic entrepreneurs would encounter difficulties because high capital and technological requirements serve as barriers to entry.

The developmentalists failed to convert the Banco Industrial into a vehicle for the promotion of their economic goals. As figure 3 reveals, there was no major shift in lending policy as a reflection of the developmentalists' economic policy priorities. The percentage of loans directed to basic industry was virtually the same during the predevelopmentalist period (1953–1956) as during the developmentalist period (1958–1960). Second, during the two periods only a fraction of bank loans were devoted to infrastructural projects. In both cases, the bulk of loans continued to be made to the kind of light industrial activities that were not developmentalist priorities and easily could have found funding from commercial banks. Recurrent inflation in Argentina led to a situation in which official interest rates were usually much lower than inflation. As a result, official bank credit included a substantial subsidy to the borrower.[84] Since the developmentalists were unable to impose their development priorities on the bank, it continued to subsidize horizontal industrialization indiscriminately and failed to carve out a role for itself as a vehicle for long-term development finance.

One explanation for this failure is the rapid turnover of top management at the Banco Industrial. In the period 1954–1961 only one president served longer than a year at the post, and he only served a two-year term. Only one of the directors during this seven-year period served a full four-year term. Some of this turnover can be attributed to changes of governments, but a fair degree of turnover took place even during the term of a single president, corresponding to changes in the Ministry of Economics. The average term for a minister of economics in Argentina in the postwar period was less than one year, which would explain the high level of turnover of top management of the bank.[85]

84. Jacobs, Huici, and Schvarzer, "National Development Bank," p. 9.
85. Juan Carlos de Pablo, *La economia que yo hice* (Buenos Aires: Ediciones El Cronista Comerical, 1980). The average term of a minister of economics in Argentina during the period 1946–1976 was 347 days; that of a president of the Central Bank was 363 days (p. 31).

1953–1956

Light industry 52.4%

Infrastructure 6.0%

Other 7.8%

Basic industry 33.8%

1958–1960

Light industry 45.4%

Infrastructure 11.4%

Other 7.8%

Basic industry 35.4%

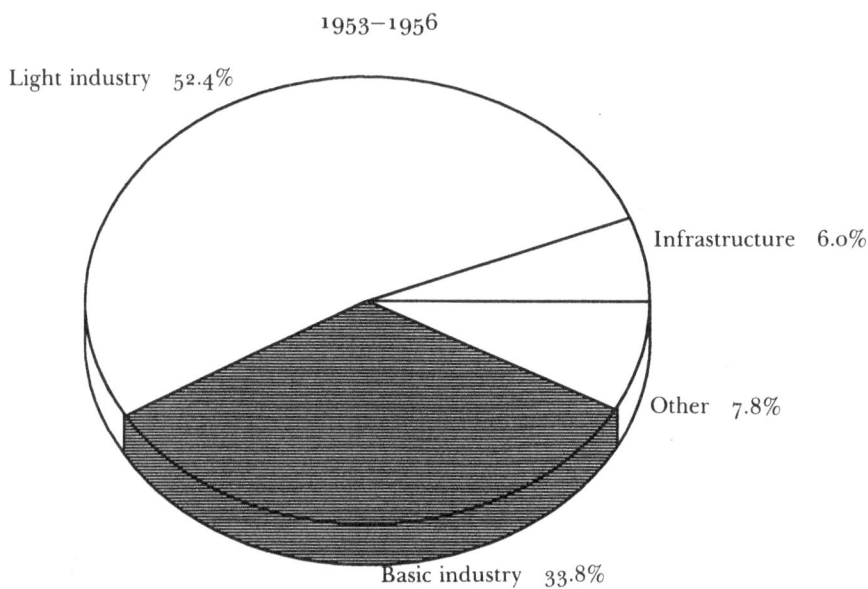

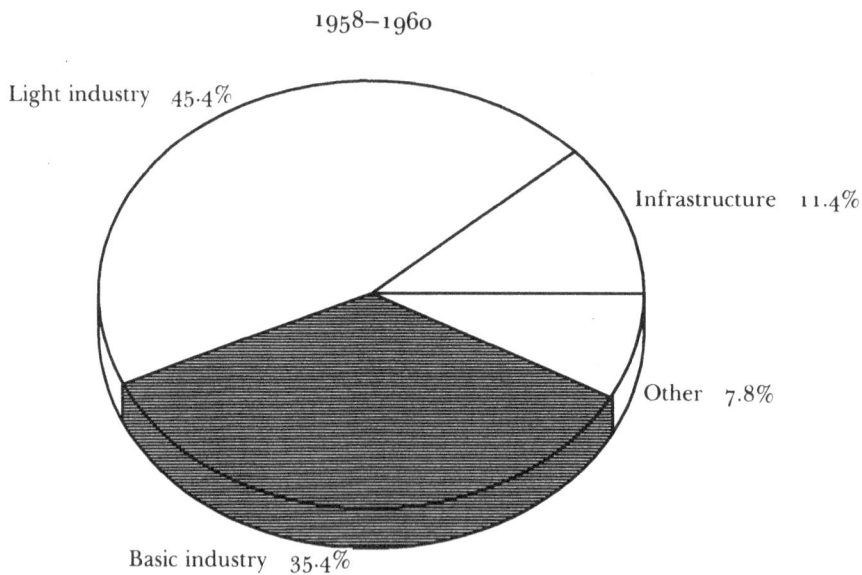

Figure 3. Argentine Industrial Bank loans by sector

Source: Banco Industrial de la República Argentina, *Memoria y balance.*

The developmentalist president of the bank held the position for only a year before being replaced by a new president named by Alsogaray.

In spite of the high turnover of top leadership during this period, the bank showed significant consistency in lending policy. The requirement that the directors represent those sectors of the economy served by the bank created a voting block of interests that tended to support short-term lending to existing industrial interests. Thus, the lack of institutional autonomy and the short tenure of top leadership of the bank hampered it from playing a more active role as a development bank. This could be an example of what O'Donnell means by a state "extensively colonized by civil society."[86]

The Banco Nacional de Desenvolvimento Econômico

The Brazilian National Economic Development Bank (BNDE) was set up later than the Argentine Industrial Bank. In 1950 representatives from the United States, the World Bank, and Brazil discussed the possibility of extensive World Bank and Export-Import Bank financing of Brazilian development efforts. One barrier to such funding, however, was the absence of an integrated Brazilian development plan and matching national funds to cover in-country expenses of funded projects. Thus, in 1952, at the recommendation of the Joint Brazil–United States Economic Development Commission, the Brazilian government set up a Rehabilitation Fund, based on a 15 percent compulsory tax/loan by individuals and firms that paid above a certain level of income taxes. It was to provide national funds to cover local costs of development projects. To administer the fund, the Brazilian government created the BNDE, a step not required by the World Bank or the Joint Brazil–United States Commission.[87] The Rehabilitation Fund provided the BNDE with an independent, noninflationary source of funding. The compulsory loan was temporary, however, and had to be renewed by Congress in 1956. After a period of nonrenewal, the tax was renewed for ten years, with the solid support of the Kubitschek government.[88]

The BNDE also served to channel foreign financing to domestic development projects, since it was empowered to give guarantees for the

86. Guillermo O'Donnell, "Estado y alianzas en la Argentina, 1955–1976," document CEDES/G.E. CLACSO/no. 5 (Buenos Aires, October 1976), p. 37.

87. Eliza Willis, "The State as Banker: The Expansion of the Public Sector in Brazil," (Ph.D. diss., University of Texas at Austin, 1986), p. 176.

88. BNDE finances were still sometimes precarious because the treasury had control over the Rehabilitation Fund money, which was not always released to the bank in its entirety. Ibid., p. 65.

Brazilian government for foreign loans obtained from public and private sources. Although the anticipated financing from the World Bank was never available, the bank did receive funds from the Export-Import Bank, the Inter-American Development Bank, and European banks. The bulk of its foreign resources came through the Wheat Agreement signed with the United States, which formed part of the P.L. 480 program.

In spite of certain limits on its autonomy, the BNDE was clearly a more independent institution than the Banco Industrial of Argentina. First, it was specifically mandated as a development bank, forbidden to take deposits, and obliged to focus primarily on long-term lending to "those initiatives that exercise an important influence in favor of the economic expansion of the country."[89] This was interpreted to mean areas characterized as bottlenecks to economic growth, especially essential services and industrial infrastructure, and other noninfrastructure activities construed as "growing points," which would stimulate further growth of the economy. These concepts emerged as the guiding principles of the BNDE's lending policies through the work of Roberto Campos and the Joint Brazil–United States Commission. Since Campos and other commission members held prominent positions in the bank from its inception until the late 1950s, they were able to oversee the implementation of this theoretical approach.

As a result of this mandate, the BNDE's lending concentrated heavily in three areas: energy, especially electric energy; transport, especially railroads; and basic industries.[90] Although the bank focused its loans consistently on transport, energy, and basic industry, there was a significant shift in lending priorities during the developmentalist government of Kubitschek. Bank lending began to concentrate more heavily on basic industry, reflecting the priorities of the government development plan. (See figure 4.)

Within the logic of the bottlenecks and the growing points, emphasis shifted from bottlenecks (primarily infrastructure) during the 1952–1956 period to growing points (primarily basic industries) during the developmentalist period of 1957–1961. Thus the Kubitschek administration saw its development goals reflected in bank lending policy. This

89. BNDE, *IX exposição sobre o programa de reaparelhamento econômico, exercício de 1960* (Rio de Janeiro, 1960), p. 8.

90. The BNDE staff defined the term "basic industry" to include eleven priority areas: the copper industry, aluminum industry and its alloys, steel and its derivatives, sulfuric acids, synthetic ammonia, soda, fertilizers, heavy electrical machinery, railroad material, agricultural machines, and vehicles. The definition was not used rigidly, and other industrial activities were considered for funding if it was believed that they satisfied the criteria. Ibid., p. 27.

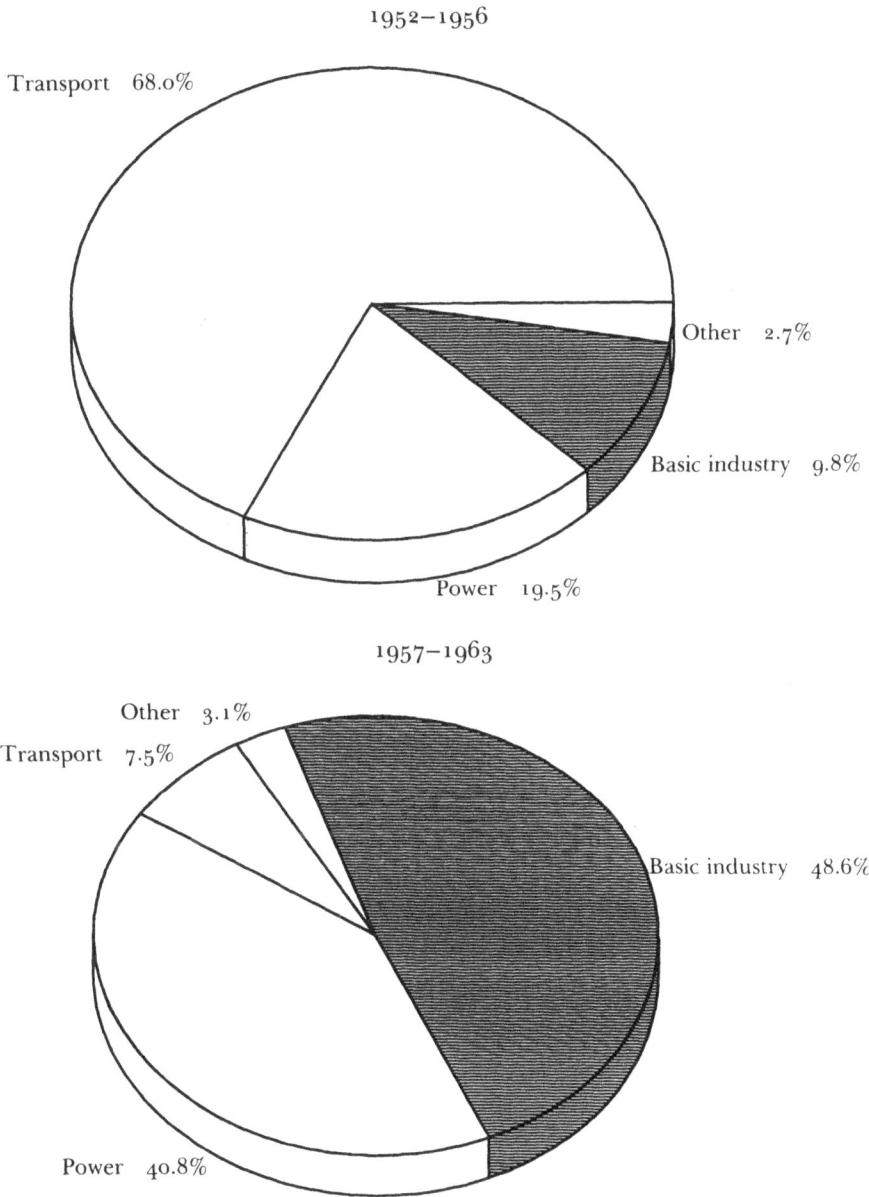

1952–1956

Transport 68.0%

Other 2.7%

Basic industry 9.8%

Power 19.5%

1957–1963

Other 3.1%

Transport 7.5%

Basic industry 48.6%

Power 40.8%

Figure 4. BNDE loans by sector

Source: Werner Baer and Annibal V. Villela, "The Changing Nature of Development Banking in Brazil," *Journal of Inter-American and World Affairs* 22 (November 1980), 429.

was the result of a convergence of goals and perspectives between Kubitschek and bank managers.

The bank was administered by a president, an administrative council, and a board of directors appointed by the president of the republic. Since there were no representational requirements, the president and other members of the bank's top management could be, and often were, professionals with training in economics. Obviously, the president's power of appointment gave the executive significant control over the bank, but the tenure of directors was respected more in Brazil than in Argentina. One story helps illustrate this point.

In 1954, only one month before Vargas's suicide, Cleantho de Paiva Leite was renominated by Vargas to a four-year term as director of the BNDE. When the government of Café Filho came into office, it adopted a more liberal economic policy under Minister of Economics Eugenio Gudin. Gudin sent a high-ranking official of the Banco do Brasil to ask Leite to resign from his position as a director of BNDE. Leite responded that he would not renounce the mandate that had been conferred upon him by President Vargas. Then he asked the official to tell Minister Gudin that Leite still expected to be in his position long after Gudin had left the ministry, a prophecy that was fulfilled only a few months later.[91]

The BNDE and the Banco Industrial Compared

The Brazilian BNDE was a much more coherent and central instrument of developmentalist policy than was the Argentine Banco Industrial. These differences were the result of different mandates, funding bases, and administrative structures and rules.

Whereas the BNDE was set up with a developmentalist mandate, the Banco Industrial's original mandate reflected the nondevelopmentalist pro-industrialization thought common in Argentina during the Peronist government. Second, by providing the BNDE with an independent source of financing, the Brazilian government gave it the capability to undertake the large long-term loans necessary to fulfill a developmentalist project. The Banco Industrial's lack of independent sources of financing made it dependent on deposits and rapid turnover of loans, causing it to behave more like a commercial bank than a development bank.

Third, the administrative structure of the Argentine Banco Indus-

91. Cleantho de Paiva Leite, *Cleantho de Paiva Leita (depoimento)* (Rio de Janeiro: Fundação Getúlio Vargas/CPDOC-História Oral, 1986), p. 177.

trial led to a management more responsive to external interests than to the overseeing of a national development project. The BNDE had an initial management that shared the common experience of having participated in the Joint Brazil–United States Economic Development Commission.[92] They brought with them a similar theoretical framework derived from that experience, which gave continuity to BNDE policy. Because bank managers did not represent any special sector, they were able to frame policy more clearly in terms of the bank's mission and their own theoretical framework, which was very similar. The Kubitschek years were the high point of BNDE activity, since a unique concurrence of goals and perspectives between the executive and the bank led to fruitful mutual support and collaboration.

The different nature of institutions in Brazil and Argentina did not influence the timing of the appearance of developmentalist ideas or the content of those ideas, but it did influence the implementation of developmentalist policies and their success and failure. The fact that Kubitschek's development priorities were clearly reflected in the lending policies of the BNDE supported the achievement of these priorities. The failure of the Argentine Banco Industrial to implement a developmentalist lending policy was just one indication of a broader breakdown of implementation of developmentalist policies in Argentina.

For a government that built a reputation as the most modern and technically oriented option in Argentine politics, the Frondizi administration did little to increase the capacity of the state to direct economic policy. But did this institutional fragility really matter for the implementation of developmentalist policies? The importance of the state for formulation and implementation involved not only the technical capacity to draw up and carry out development plans, but also the degree to which the state was able to generate support or acquiescence for economic policy through using a policy process that was perceived as legitimate. One of the most serious obstacles faced by the Frondizi administration was its perceived lack of legitimacy, partially a result of the way it won the 1958 election—by making a deal with Perón to have his supporters vote for Frondizi. But the illegitimacy of the Frondizi government and its policies also resulted from opposition to the "process" of making and implementing decisions. The policy formulation and implementation process was not perceived as legitimate. It was carried

92. Four of the first five presidents of BNDE—Ary Torres, Glycon de Paiva, Lucas Lopes, and Roberto Campos—and the first superintendent-director, Jose Soares Maciel Filho, had all collaborated in the Joint Brazil–United States Economic Development Commission.

out by illegitimate interlocutors in secret, without adequate channels for input from societal groups.

The institutional weakness of the Argentine state, its lack of autonomy and capacity, reinforced Frondizi's move to an ad hoc and secret policy formulation and implementation process. The greatest economic "successes" of the Frondizi administration were those that relied almost solely on private initiative. Thus the expansion of petroleum production and the establishment of the automobile industry were the result of private efforts, with the government's main role being to remove barriers, offer incentives, and give the green light. The areas of the developmentalist program that required more active state participation—such as planning in general, the expansion of steel production through joint public-private enterprises, the construction of roads and other infrastructural projects, the careful oversight of private investment efforts, and development assistance to domestic industry—were those in which the Frondizi government had much less success, in part because the state apparatus did not have the capability or continuity to take on these functions.

CHAPTER SIX

Implementing Developmentalism: The Mobilization of Financial, Technical, and Political Resources

Successful implementation of economic programs depends on the existence and mobilization of resources—financial, technical, and political. Hirschman has argued that "development depends not so much on finding optimal combinations for given resources and factors of production as on calling forth and enlisting for development purposes resources and abilities that are hidden, scattered or badly utilized."[1] By mobilization of resources we generally think of economic resources, but mobilization of political resources may often be just as important for development. Mobilization of political resources involves not only the process by which state officials design policies and put them into effect but also the broader process of gaining support or acquiescence of social groups for those policies. Successful formulation and implementation of development policy requires both technical skills in the state apparatus and persuasive ability and legitimacy of the government. The following discussion first examines the economic outcomes of the developmentalist programs and then focuses on the existence and mobilization of financial, technical, and political resources that contributed to the implementation of developmentalist programs in Brazil and Argentina.

---

1. Albert O. Hirschman, "A Dissenter's Confession," in *Rival Views of Market Society and Other Recent Essays* (New York: Viking, 1986), p. 13.

Table 4. Comparative economic growth: Brazil and Argentina, 1955–1962 (percentage annual change)

Year	Real gross domestic product		Per capita gross domestic product	
	Brazil	Argentina	Brazil	Argentina
1955	6.9	7.1	3.7	5.0
1956	3.2	2.8	0.2	0.9
1957	8.1	5.1	5.0	3.3
1958	7.7	6.1	4.6	4.3
1959	5.6	−6.4	2.5	−8.0
1960	9.7	7.8	6.5	6.2
1961	10.3	7.1	6.7	5.5
1962	5.3	−1.6	2.1	−3.0

Sources: Banco Central de la República Argentina; Fundação Getúlio Vargas, Centro de Contas Nacionais.

ECONOMIC OUTCOMES OF THE DEVELOPMENTALIST PROGRAMS

Brazil's overall and per capita economic growth was higher than Argentina's throughout the period under study. (See table 4 and figures 5 and 6). During the period 1955–1960 the Brazilian gross domestic product (GDP) grew 7.8 percent on average annually, and the Argentine GDP grew 3.0 percent annually. Thus in spite of much more rapid population growth in Brazil, Brazilian per capita GDP increased 2.7 percent annually during 1955–1960, as compared to 1.2 percent in Argentina. If we compare annual growth rates for the precise periods the developmentalist governments were in power, Brazil's growth is even more striking. The annual average increase in GDP during the Frondizi presidency (1957–1961) was 2.4 percent as compared to a rate of 8.9 percent during the Kubitschek administration (1955–1961), while the annual increase in per capita GDP in Brazil during the same period was 5 percent, compared to only 0.8 percent in Argentina.[2] Nevertheless, it is important to keep in mind that in terms of per capita GDP,

2. These numbers are based on calculations from Argentine figures from the Banco Central de la República Argentina, Sistema de cuentas del producto e ingreso de la Argentina: Cuadros estadísticos (Buenos Aires, 1975), pp. 180, 184, and Brazilian figures from Albert Fishlow, "Foreign Trade Regimes and Economic Development: Brazil," table A-I, based on Brazilian Central Bank figures (Author's summary of study being prepared for the Special Conference Series on Foreign Trade Regimes and Economic Development undertaken by the National Bureau of Economic Research, 1975).

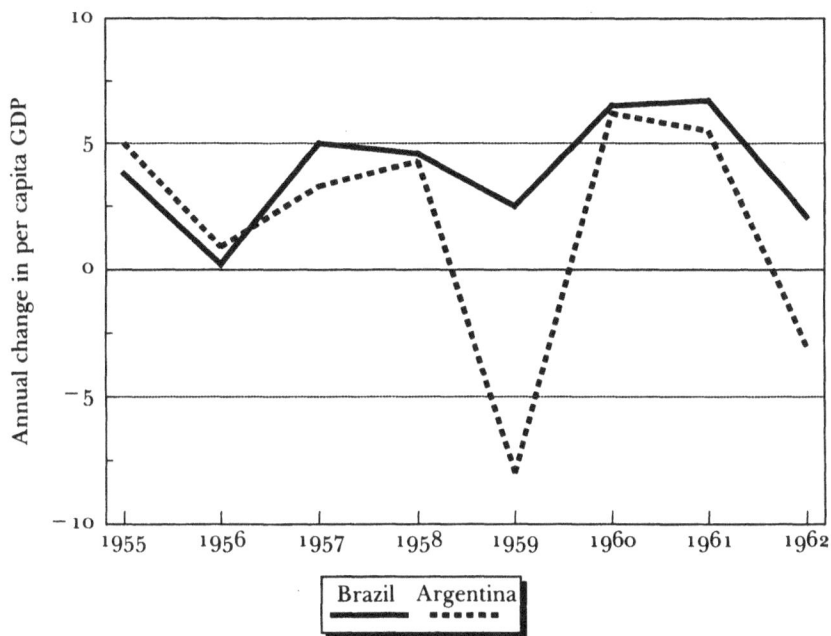

Figure 5. Percentage annual change of per capita economic growth (GDP per capita)

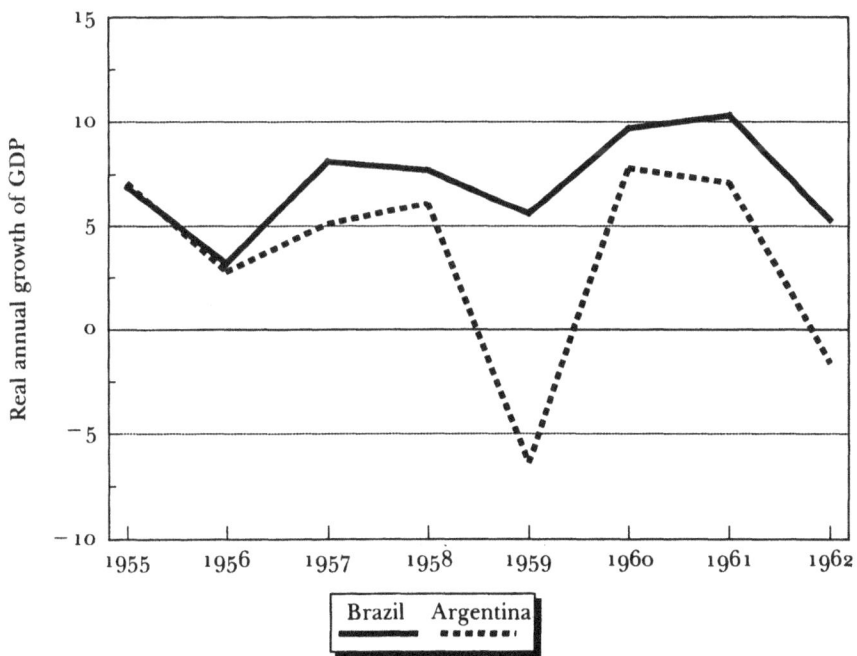

Figure 6. Percentage annual change of real GDP, Brazil and Argentina, 1955–1962

Source: Data for figures 5 and 6 are from table 4.

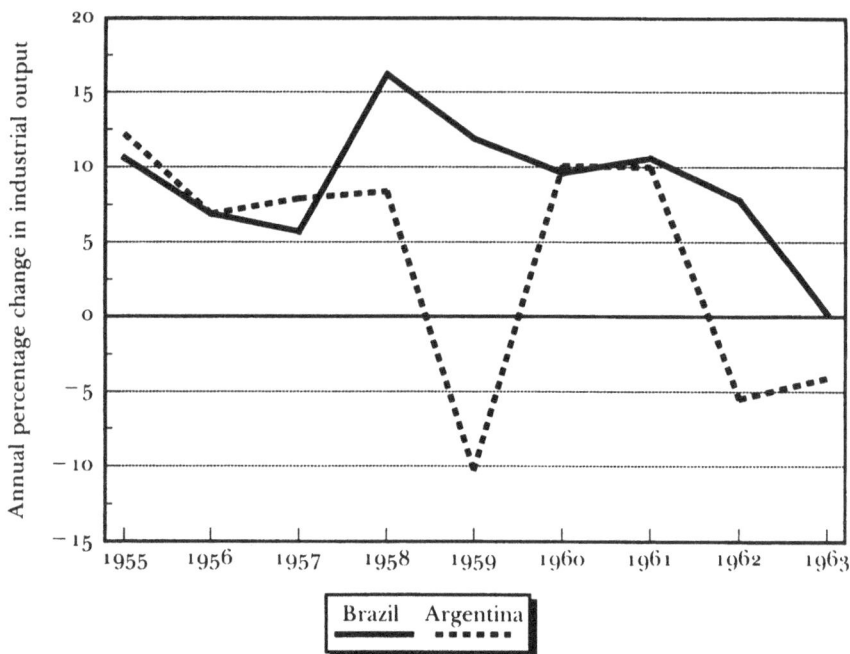

Figure 7. Real annual percentage change of industrial output

Brazil was starting from a much lower level than was Argentina: in 1955 Brazilian per capita GDP was half that of Argentina.[3]

Growth in manufacturing, the sector most emphasized by developmentalism, was also considerably higher in Brazil than it was in Argentina. (See figure 7.) During the period 1955–1960 the average annual growth rate of manufacturing in Brazil was 12.2, as compared to 4.6 in Argentina. Industrial output increased by an annual average of 13.3 percent during the Kubitschek government (1956–1961), whereas during the Frondizi government, industrial output increased annually by a much smaller amount, 2.2 percent on average.[4]

The Argentine stabilization plan succeeded in substantially reducing levels of inflation (see figure 8), and the economy bounced back with

3. Argentina per capita GNP was $1,380, Brazil's was U.S. $670 of 1970 purchasing power. Carlos F. Diaz Alejandro, "No Less Than One Hundred Years of Argentine Economic History, Plus Some Comparisons," Economic Growth Center, Yale University, Center Discussion Paper no. 392, p. 5.

4. Banco Central de al República Argentina, *Sistema de cuentas del producto e ingreso*; Fishlow, "Foreign Trade Regimes."

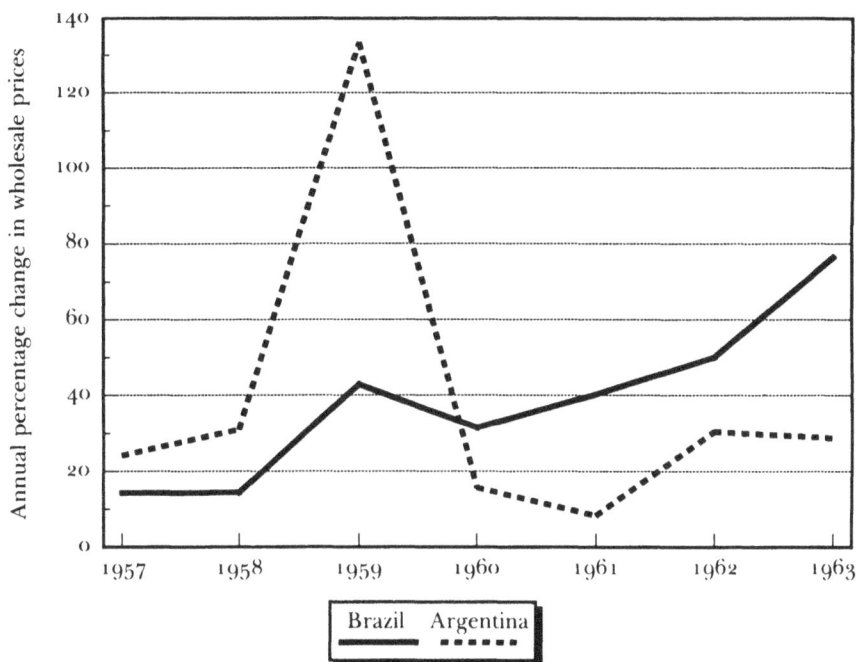

Figure 8. Annual rates of inflation, changes in wholesale prices, 1957–1963

high levels of overall and industrial growth in 1960 and 1961. Brazil, in contrast, maintained high growth levels without suffering any major recession, but inflation levels continued to rise dramatically throughout the period, as shown in figure 8.

To what degree can the greater success of the Kubitschek program in promoting overall and industrial growth be accounted for by differences in the formulation and implementation of the program itself? The next section looks at the existence and mobilization of financial resources for development programs in the two countries.

Financial Resources

Both Argentina and Brazil attracted similar amounts of direct foreign investment during this period, but Brazil received more bilateral and multilateral assistance from other sources. Both governments succeeded in attracting large amounts of direct private foreign investment. (See table 5.) Frondizi's success in this basic goal of his program was more dramatic, increasing annual flows of investment by over seven

Table 5. Direct foreign investment, 1955–1963 (in millions of U.S. dollars)

	Argentina	Brazil
1955	10.0	43.0
1956	22.3	90.0
1957	17.3	144.0
1958	20.5	110.0
1959	152.6	124.0
1960	151.6	98.0
1961	189.9	108.0
1962	54.2	69.0
1963	35.2	30.0
Total, 1955–1963	653.6	816.0
Total, 1956–1960		566.0
Total, 1958–1962	568.8	

Sources: Joel Bergsman, Brazil: Industrialization and Trade Policies (New York: Oxford University Press, 1970), p. 76; Peter Fischer, "El capital externo en el desarrollo economico de Argentina, 1880–1964" (Santiago, Chile: Instituto Latinoamericano de Investigaciones Sociales, Estudios y documentos 28, 1973).

times the levels of the mid-fifties. But if one compares the period of the Kubitschek administration (1956–1960) to the Frondizi administration (1958–1962), the absolute amount of direct foreign investment that entered the two countries during this period is almost identical, U.S. $566 million in Brazil and U.S. $568 million in Argentina.[5]

At first glance, the Frondizi government appears to have faced a more benevolent international situation than did Kubitschek, who took office two years earlier. The Frondizi administration overlapped more with the Kennedy administration in the United States, which expressed its interest in Latin America and development issues in the Alliance for Progress program. Adoption of the IMF stabilization program early in the Frondizi administration increased the confidence of investors and financial institutions. International investors responded well to the incentives provided, and international financial institutions offered ample support.

5. Argentine figures based on Peter Fischer, El capital externo en el desarrollo económico de Argentina, 1880–1964 (Santiago, Chile: Instituto Latinoamericano de Investigaciones Sociales, 1973), p. 140; Brazilian data from Joel Bergsman, Brazil: Industrialization and Trade Policies (New York: Oxford University Press, 1970), p. 76. These dollar figures underestimate the full amount of direct foreign investment in Brazil and Argentina during this period because of depreciation of the currency in both countries against the dollar. See U.S. Department of Commerce, Office of Business Economics, U.S. Business Investment in Foreign Countries (Washington, D.C.: Government Printing Office, 1960).

But in spite of the apparently more benevolent international climate that the Frondizi administration faced, the Kubitschek government still received substantially larger sums of foreign capital in the form of long- and medium-term loans from public sources. This is often obscured by Kubitschek officials' complaints that the United States and international financial institutions neglected their development program. The Brazilians were frustrated because they expected much higher levels of financial support, but Brazil received more international financial support than other countries in the region.

Brazil had ongoing positive relations with international financial institutions and with bilateral U.S. institutions, which provided a continuing flow of loans that generally exceeded levels given other countries in Latin America. In the case of bilateral aid, these positive relations dated back to the Second World War, when Brazil received substantial assistance to develop the steel industry and to exploit strategic minerals that the United States thought were important for the war effort. Once these bilateral lending relationships were established, they helped secure ongoing flows of capital, as lending institutions developed special interests in certain sectors and projects. For example, in Brazil, the Export-Import Bank of the United States had provided large loans for the establishment of the Volta Redonda steel complex. Later the Export-Import Bank had a "fierce proprietary interest in Brazil's steel industry," and in the late 1940s and early 1950s it even competed with the World Bank over who would finance certain Brazilian development projects. Since World Bank interest charges were higher than Export-Import rates at this time, borrowers often went first to the Export-Import.[6]

Through the Joint Brazil–United States Economic Development Commission, Brazil also established a positive bilateral lending relationship with the World Bank and with U.S. development assistance agencies. Although the actual amount of assistance forthcoming fell way below Brazilian expectations, total World Bank funding to Brazil still exceeded levels in all other Latin American countries. From the time of the founding of the World Bank until the end of 1961, Brazil received over five times more development assistance than Argentina.[7] Argentina did not join the World Bank until 1956, after the fall of Perón, and did not receive its first loan from the bank until June 1961. So during

6. Edward Mason and Robert Asher, *The World Bank since Bretton Woods* (Washington, D.C.: Brookings Institution, 1973), pp. 496–98, 532.

7. Argentina received a total of $48.5 million and Brazil a total of $267 million in World Bank loans and credits as of the end of 1961. IBRD, *The World Bank and the IDA in the Americas* (Washington, D.C.: IBRD/World Bank, 1962), p. 1.

Table 6. Inflow of World Bank capital to Brazil and Argentina, 1956–1962 (in millions of U.S. dollars)

Year	Brazil	Argentina
1956	13.0	0
1957	4.0	0
1958	2.0	0
1959	20.0	0
1960	15.0	0
1961	26.0	0
1962	18.0	18.8
Total, 1956–1962	98.0	18.8

Source: International Monetary Fund, *Balance of Payments Yearbook* (Washington, D.C.: International Monetary Fund), vol. 12 (1955–1959) and vol. 16 (1959–1963), sections on Argentina and Brazil.

the years of the developmentalist governments (1956–1962), World Bank assistance to Brazil equaled more than five times that of loans to Argentina. (See table 6.)

This was the relative situation despite Brazil's sense of being "ostracized" by the World Bank because of Vargas's 1954 decision to limit profit remittances to foreign companies. The bank approved no new loans for Brazil during the 1955–1957 period, but inflows from past loans continued, and in 1958 the bank approved a large new loan for electric power ($86.4 million).[8]

The bank was clearly impressed with Frondizi's development program and collaborated fully with his administration,[9] but because of the slow process of loan approval, World Bank financing did not make an important contribution to Argentina until after Frondizi was overthrown. By the end of 1961 negotiations had been completed on a $95 million loan to Argentina for electric power,[10] but this money arrived too late to aid Frondizi's program.

Indeed, just as Frondizi's domestic situation worsened, the relationship and prospects of his government with international financial insti-

8. Mason and Asher, *The World Bank since Bretton Woods*, p. 657.

9. In a 1961 publication, the bank praised Frondizi's economic program. "Argentina's rigorous program of financial stabilization, which was initiated at the end of 1958, has successfully laid the basis for resuming the long-interrupted expansion of the Argentine economy." The bank also collaborated with the Frondizi government to survey the present situation and long-range requirements of all forms of surface transportation in Argentina, and to assess Argentina's power situation and prospects. IBRD, *The World Bank and IDA in the Americas*, pp. 7, 9.

10. Ibid., p. 9.

tutions brightened. In 1962, shortly before Frondizi was deposed by the military, his representatives in Washington had discussions with the World Bank about the possibility of an international consortium, headed by the World Bank, to arrange financing for an integrated development plan up to a sum of $1–2 billion. These discussions specifically mentioned resources available through the Alliance for Progress and the International Development Association.[11] The international environment in the early sixties was more favorably disposed toward the developmentalist agenda than it had been in the mid-1950s, when Kubitschek first took office, but the Frondizi administration was unable to reap the benefits of this improved international environment.

Both Argentina and Brazil relied heavily on loans from the Export-Import Bank of the United States to support their development programs. Here also, Brazil received substantially more assistance than Argentina did during the developmentalist period. The Export-Import Bank was set up in 1934 to promote U.S. exports by providing export financing at favorable rates. All of the bank's loans had the approval of the U.S. State Department, which was accorded veto power.[12] Throughout the life of the Export-Import Bank, Brazil has always been a major recipient of credits. From 1934 to 1963 total Export-Import Bank commitments of credits to Brazil, $732,382,231, made Brazil the largest recipient in the region, while credits to Argentina for the same period equaled less than half as much—$334,386,392.[13]

Although the disparities in funding are not as great if one compares per capita assistance levels, Export-Import Bank support for the developmentalist program in Brazil was still significantly greater than its support of the Argentine program, as is clear from table 7.

The same pattern emerges from a comparison of U.S. bilateral economic and technical assistance grants to the two countries during this period. The U.S. assistance program was the only important bilateral economic assistance program in the 1950s, and the amounts of the grants were meager compared to the larger volume that would be available later, during the Alliance for Progress. Nevertheless, Brazil received seventeen times the bilateral economic and technical assistance grants from the United States that Argentina received during this period. (See table 8.)

11. Letter and memorandum from Emilio Donato del Carril, Argentine ambassador in Washington, D.C., to President Frondizi, dated March 10, 1962.

12. Rita M. Rodriguez, ed., *The Export-Import Bank at Fifty: The International Environment and the Institution's Role* (Lexington, Mass.: D. C. Heath and Company, 1987), pp. 6–7.

13. Export-Import Bank of Washington, "Cumulative Record of Activities by Country," in the *Semi-Annual Report of the Export-Import Bank to Congress*, July 1–December 31, 1963 (Washington, D.C.: Government Printing Office, 1964), pp. 37, 45.

Table 7. World Bank capital to Brazil and Argentina, 1956–1962 (in millions of U.S. dollars)

Year	Brazil		Argentina
1956	31.0		0
1957	46.0		7.9
1958	189.0		61.9
1959	63.0		44.7
1960	52.0		48.9
1961	60.0		41.7
1962	11.0		55.9
Total, 1956–1962	452.0		260.1
Total, 1956–1960	381.0	Total, 1958–1962	252.2

Source: International Monetary Fund, Balance of Payments Yearbook (Washington, D.C.), vol. 12 (1955–1959) and vol. 16 (1959–1963).
*Includes loans to private business but excludes loans to the Central Bank categorized under monetary sectors in Balance of Payments Yearbook.

But neither the multilateral nor the bilateral sources of assistance and loans were adequate to finance the substantial requirements of the developmentalist economic programs. In order to complete their programs and especially to satisfy large demands for capital goods imports, both Brazil and Argentina relied heavily on suppliers' credits from industrialized countries. Many were medium-term credits with higher interest rates than other forms of multilateral and bilateral assistance. Table 9 gives an idea of developmentalist programs' dependence on suppliers' credits as a form of development finance. In Brazil "other" credits, which were for the most part suppliers' credits to the private

Table 8. U.S. government grants for economic and technical assistance (in millions of U.S. dollars)

Year	Brazil	Argentina
1956	4	0
1957	5	0
1958	6	.1
1959	8	.5
1960	11	.6
1961	7	1.2
1962	29	1.7
Total	70	4.1

Source: International Monetary Fund, Balance of Payments Yearbook (Washington, D.C.), vol. 12 (1955–1959) and vol. 16 (1959–1963).

Table 9. Suppliers' credits as a percentage of total external credits (million of U.S. dollars)

	Brazil			Argentina		
Year	Suppliers' credits*	Total external credits†	%	Suppliers' credits*	Total external credits†	%
1956	105	240	44	69	132	52
1957	182	304	60	52	129	40
1958	214	518	41	90	271	33
1959	282	357	79	15	61	25
1960	198	375	53	180	255	71
1961	260	811	32	238	460	52
1962	149	512	29	316	427	74
Totals						
1956–62	1390	3117	45	960	1735	55
1956–60	981	1794	55			
1958–62				839	1474	57

Source: author's calculations based on information from the International Monetary Fund, *Balance of Payments Yearbook*, vols. 12 and 16.

*In the Argentine case, these figures are reported specifically as suppliers' and trade credits (and exclude Export-Import Bank loans); in the Brazilian figures, these come from an unspecified "other" category of private capital flows which apparently correspond to suppliers credits (and also exclude Export-Import Bank loans).

†This column for both Brazil and Argentina is a total of inflows of foreign capital excluding direct foreign investment and credits received by the Central Bank and listed under the monetary sector in the *Balance of Payments Yearbook*. This includes U.S. government economic and technical assistance grants, loans from the IBRD and the Export-Import Bank, suppliers' and trade credits, commercial bank loans, and sales of government securities.

sector, totaled 32–63 percent of total credits from abroad (not counting direct foreign investment) during the Kubitschek administration; in Argentina suppliers' credits provided 25–74 percent of total external financing during the Frondizi government.

What stands out is the extraordinary dependence of both countries on suppliers' credits as a form of development finance. Argentina appears to have relied more heavily on suppliers' credits, although this could be the result of the somewhat different manner in which the credits were reported in the balance of payments summaries. A World Bank survey of suppliers' credits to developing countries, which covered only publicly guaranteed suppliers' credits, found that among all the countries surveyed, Brazil and Argentina had among the highest ratios of both suppliers' credits to total indebtedness and service payments on suppliers' credits to total service payments.[14] In addition, the

14. In Argentina suppliers' credits totaled 30.5 percent of total indebtness, and in Brazil, 29.8 percent; in Argentina service payments on suppliers' credits accounted for 59 percent of total service payments, and in Brazil, 63.1 percent. IBRD, *Suppliers' Credits from Industrialized to Developing Countries*, A Study by the Staff of the World Bank re-

study noted that the service burden of suppliers' credits to exports was particularly noteworthy in the cases of Brazil and Argentina.[15]

Because of the shorter maturity and higher interest rates of suppliers' credits as compared to other forms of finance, heavy reliance on these credits led to rapid debt-servicing problems. In both Argentina and Brazil use of suppliers' credits contributed to the need for debt rescheduling operations during this period.[16]

These figures shed new light on the developmentalist model. The Argentine and Brazilian developmentalist experiments were clearly early cases of "indebted industrialization."[17] The levels of foreign investment were roughly similar in the two countries, but Brazil received much more of the kind of assistance with the best terms—U.S. government grants, Export-Import Bank loans, and IBRD loans. Argentina, on the other hand, received more credits from the IMF during this period, apparently because it was receiving less assistance from other sources than was Brazil.

Much of the assistance received by the Kubitschek government was the result of the continuation of a long-standing aid relationship between Brazil and the United States and the World Bank, rather than specific benefits negotiated by Kubitschek. Both the U.S. government and international financial institutions were impressed with the Frondizi program, but as explained earlier, much of the financial help they eventually provided came too late to be of much help to the Frondizi development program. Once again, the continuity of policy making and of bilateral and multilateral relationships with the Brazilian state is one of the most important factors explaining the differences between the Brazilian and the Argentine cases.

But some of the similarities are more important than the differences. For both countries, the actual levels of economic aid from grants was

---

quested by the United Nations Conference of Trade and Development, rev. ed., April 3, 1967, p. 6.

15. In 1965, the ratio of service payments on suppliers' credits as a percentage of commodity exports was far higher in Brazil (20 percent) and Argentina (12.4 percent) than in any of the other countries surveyed. IBRD, *Suppliers' Credits from Industrialized to Developing Countries*, annex 5, table 4.

16. Argentina's reschedulings took place in 1957, 1961, 1962, and 1965, and the 1965 agreement contained specific limits on the use of suppliers' credits. Although Brazil's reschedulings took place in 1961 and 1964, after the end of the developmentalist government, they reflected the debt burden acquired during the Kubitschek administration. Ibid., p. 22.

17. Jeffrey Frieden, "Third World Indebted Industrialization: International Finance and State Capitalism in Mexico, Brazil, Algeria and South Korea," *International Organization* 35 (1981).

only a tiny portion of total external financing. The great bulk of external finance came in two forms: direct foreign investment and trade and suppliers' credits. Both of these forms had the virtue of being fast— they responded quickly to new incentives offered by the developmentalist governments and allowed them to get their programs off the ground rapidly. But they had costs as well. They were expensive: suppliers' credits usually had higher interest rates and shorter terms than other development finance, and the profits from direct foreign investment were usually remitted to foreign owners. Both governments chose this riskier strategy because they saw few alternative means to finance their development programs.

Technical Resources

The Kubitschek government more successfully mobilized the technical resources available to it for implementing the developmentalist program. It drew on a wide range of domestic technical expertise and took advantage of past planning experiences and international technical assistance. Kubitschek's economic program was more clearly presented in a simple plan than was Frondizi's economic program. Although the Targets Program was not a sophisticated planning effort, it nevertheless allowed for a far greater degree of coordination and planning than did Frondizi's less clearly articulated program. The Kubitschek administration incorporated economic measures of previous administrations, such as SUMOC Instructions 113 and 70, as integral parts of its program and relied on earlier planning efforts, such as the report of the Joint Brazil-United States Economic Development Commission and the studies of the BNDE-CEPAL joint study group.

The Frondizi administration was much less successful in mobilizing technical resources to implement the developmentalist program. In Argentina the desarrollistas adopted most of their economic program from scratch, relying on neither the policies, the personnel, nor the plans of the preceding administrations. Because the Argentine desarrollistas decided to not rely on previous efforts at development planning, such as the Prebisch Plan or the massive CEPAL study of the Argentine economy, the task they faced in formulating their economic program was much more daunting than Brazil's. They did not attempt even a modest planning exercise along the lines of the Targets Program. Frondizi also failed to mobilize the technical resources present within his own party, because the best-trained economists in his party did not hold policy positions in the federal government. These differences in the two countries are related to differences in the nature of the state and in the continuity of policy and personnel in state institutions, as discussed in Chapter 5.

Political Resources

Implementation of developmentalist policy depended not only on financial and technical resources to put the program into effect but also on the ability to generate support for the policies. There is a tendency to think of the government's resources only in material terms, but one of the most important differences between the implementation of the Kubitschek and the Frondizi programs was that Kubitschek mobilized political resources more effectively than did Frondizi. The legitimacy of Kubitschek's government was one of the most important political resources in implementing policy. The majority of the Brazilian public saw Kubitschek as a legitimate political leader, whereas after the first year of Frondizi's administration much of the Argentine public did not see their president as highly legitimate.[18] In part, Kubitschek's legitimacy was electorally derived. Although he received only a plurality of the vote, he won in open elections in which all the major political parties, except the Communists, participated. Frondizi, on the other hand, won in elections that excluded a majority political party, the Peronists.

But political resources were not only the result of the different origins of the developmentalist governments. Political resources, like financial and technical resources, also depended on careful efforts to accumulate, conserve, and spend wisely. The desarrollistas were acutely aware of the need to accumulate financial capital for the development effort, but they were curiously oblivious of the need to accumulate symbolic capital.[19] Much of their early efforts went toward the creation of a secure climate for international investors, but much less attention was directed to the need to mobilize the energies and capture the imagination of the Argentine people for the development effort.

The next sections examine various means by which the developmentalist governments accumulated, conserved, and spent political resources. In particular, it focuses on the acquisition of symbolic capital,

18. I use Juan Linz's definition of legitimacy: "At the very least, legitimacy is the belief that in spite of shortcomings and failures, the existing political institutions are better than any others that might be established, and they therefore can demand obedience." *The Breakdown of Democratic Regimes: Crisis, Breakdown, and Reequilibration* (Baltimore: Johns Hopkins University Press, 1978), p. 16.
19. The concept of symbolic capital is from Pierre Bourdieu, *Outline of a Theory of Practice* (New York: Cambridge University Press, 1977), pp. 171–83.

the role of political leadership in securing a balance between reform and accumulation, and the importance of political style and discourse.

SYMBOLIC CAPITAL

Pierre Bourdieu developed the concept of symbolic capital in relation to a small village where the severity of climate and limited technical resources led to a demand for collective labor. Accumulated symbolic capital in the form of the prestige and renown attached to a family and a name, was convertible back into economic capital, in the form of labor power. We must modify the concept in order to apply it to politics at a national level, yet the translation is useful, since it offers a unique way of understanding the value of symbolic action in relation to other resources. Bourdieu also discusses the role of symbolic investments, which require both material wealth and the investment of time. In Bourdieu's society, symbolic capital can only be accumulated at the expense of the accumulation of economic capital, but symbolic capital can later be reconverted back into economic capital.[20] In politics, the direct fungibility between symbolic capital and economic capital no longer exists. It remains true that symbolic capital is sometimes accumulated at the expense of economic capital, but in politics symbolic capital is rarely directly convertible back into economic capital. Rather, the accumulation of symbolic capital through symbolic action, which often requires expending economic resources, contributes to political legitimacy. Political legitimacy, in turn, is the coin for maintaining political power and for implementing a political and economic program.

By using the terminology "symbolic capital," we stress that legitimacy is not a constant or an either/or situation; rather, it is a flow that can be accumulated, stored, spent, or squandered. Second, we raise the notion that symbolic capital may be accumulated at the expense of economic capital, and we emphasize that legitimacy is often bolstered through symbolic action. Third, by discussing symbolic capital as a component of legitimacy, we have a better chance of communicating with the desarrollistas themselves, who do not understand symbols but do understand accumulation.

In terms of the substance of the implementation of the economic programs in Brazil and Argentina, the differences were most pronounced in the handling of two issues, petroleum and stabilization policy, which were central to the divisions within the developmentalist gov-

20. Ibid., pp. 171–83.

ernments of both countries. The two governments faced these issues in very different ways. Kubitschek's eventual decision to break with the IMF and to end the stabilization effort led to the resignation of some of his top economic policy makers and the loss of support from international financial institutions. It permitted him, however, to hold together his domestic political coalition for the remaining two years of his government. Kubitschek's action can be interpreted as a symbolic gesture to reaffirm his defense of the nation against external interests. It helped Kubitschek accumulate the symbolic capital needed to reenergize his coalition and hold it together for the rest of his term. But it was not without costs. In a very real sense, Kubitschek sacrificed economic capital—the IMF funds as well as the private funds that would have followed—in order to accumulate symbolic capital.

In both Brazil and Argentina during the developmentalist governments, stabilization plans were adopted not as a desertion of or an alternative to development and investment programs, but as part of them. The architects of the stabilization plans believed that stabilization was necessary to protect fundamental aspects of the development efforts, in particular to assure continued access to foreign investment and loans upon which their programs depended. But this understanding was not shared by all or even by a majority of the members of the developmentalist political coalition. For many, the adoption of the stabilization plans in consultation with the IMF signaled a surrender to foreign pressures and interests, as well as a desertion of the more populist aspects of the development programs—higher wages, easy credit to domestic entrepreneurs, and subsidies for basic goods and inputs. In this sense, stabilization, like the petroleum issue, centered on nationalism, which has traditionally permeated much of political symbolism and mythology of Latin America across the political spectrum from Right to Left. Nationalism, although not central to the economic program of developmentalism, and perhaps in contradiction to its internationalizing aspects, was one of the important political "glues" that held the developmentalist coalition together. By appealing to nationalism when he broke with the IMF, Kubitschek was able to galvanize his coalition, secure added support from nationalist sectors in the military, and insure the completion of his term. The long-term economic cost of such a strategy was the exacerbation of inflation. But as Lourdes Sola has argued, within the political constraints of the existing system of class collaboration in Brazil, the alternatives were limited.[21]

21. Lourdes Sola, "The Political and Ideological Constraints to Economic Management in Brazil, 1945–1963" (Ph.D. diss., Oxford University, 1982), p. 191.

Frondizi's choice of a different path shows that the alternative policy of implementing harsh stabilization measures was politically costly. Argentina faced a more dramatic economic situation in 1959 than Brazil did: inflation levels were much higher and the balance-of-payments crisis was greater, leading to a more serious depletion of foreign exchange reserves. At the same time, Frondizi sensed the need to send a more dramatic signal to the international investment community, which was wary of Argentina after Peronist nationalist policies. Stabilization measures succeeded in bringing inflation levels down dramatically and correcting the foreign exchange disequilibrium, while enhancing the international reputation of Frondizi's economic policy, securing access to international sources of finance, and attracting foreign investors. But it also undermined the desarrollista coalition early in the Frondizi administration.

With his stabilization plan, Frondizi chose to promote economic accumulation rather than engage in symbolic action that would appeal to Argentine nationalism. But in some ways, he also chose between two types of symbolic action: the IMF stabilization plan was a symbol to the international community and domestic entrepreneurs of the seriousness of his program. Frondizi engaged in one form of symbolic action, his defense of a positive investment climate, at the expense of another, his role as defender of nationalism. Alternatively, using the terminology of political survival discussed in Chapter 1, these positions might be explained in terms of two different types of survival strategies. Frondizi believed that by pursuing the first, he insured his survival by generating positive economic outcomes. But by choosing that survival strategy, he lost support from key nationalist groups, thus undermining other survival strategies. The choice of a survival strategy is not obvious or straightforward. It is driven by the ideas of politicians.

Even with implementation of the stabilization plan, however, the Frondizi administration was not able to gain the broad support it had hoped for from domestic industrial groups and rural producers. Stronger symbols interfered: domestic entrepreneurial groups could not overcome their distrust of Frondizi's connections with Peronism and with leftists and thus could not wholeheartedly embrace the government and its policies. A multilayered game of symbolic action was going on in which different actions had different repercussions for different audiences. As far as the entrepreneurial groups in Argentine society were concerned, Frondizi was sending mixed symbols. The pact with Perón, and the conciliatory gestures made to the organizations of the Peronist era, the CGT and the CGE, came through as stronger symbolic action than his efforts to promote a positive investment climate.

Petroleum policy can be interpreted in much the same way. The petroleum contracts with foreign firms functioned as a symbolic gesture to the international community. But for the domestic audience, the contracts were seen as the very negation of nationalism. Frondizi lost the symbolic capital he had accumulated over the years as a defender of nationalism and YPF, while he gained the economic capital and technological know-how of the foreign petroleum companies. The immediate result was a dramatic increase in petroleum production, but the indirect effect was Frondizi's loss of legitimacy and support from many of his coalition partners. In the imperfect and imprecise exchange between economic and symbolic capital, it is difficult to assess whether more was won than lost. The total effect of Frondizi's actions in the first year of his government, however, was an overemphasis of economic accumulation at the expense of symbolic capital. Once such reserves of symbolic capital were lost, the government found it difficult to build them up again, which left it isolated and vulnerable.

Perhaps the purest example of the accumulation of symbolic capital as intended by Bourdieu was *the* symbolic capital—Brasília. Kubitschek invested considerable expense and time in the construction of a new capital when many of his advisers warned him that it was draining resources from more essential projects. The construction of Brasília and the organized pageantry of its inauguration were Kubitschek's ways of capturing visions of hope, wealth, and the future in order to accumulate prestige and renown for himself and his administration.[22]

LEGITIMACY AND MEDIATIONS

O'Donnell has outlined three essential mediations through which the state derives its legitimation: (1) the mediation of the nation; (2) the mediation of citizenship; and (3) the mediation of *lo popular*, a "we" that is the carrier of the demands for substantive justice for the poor. The successful operation of these three mediations are what allow the state institutions to appear as agents of a general interest of a community. The state derives its legitimacy from its role as the organizational focus of consensus in society, and consensus is created through the operations of the three mediations.[23] To these three mediations a fourth

22. Alex Shoumatoff, *The Capital of Hope: Brasília and Its People* (Albuquerque: University of New Mexico Press, 1980), pp. 19, 55.

23. Guillermo O'Donnell, "Tensions in the Bureaucratic-Authoritarian State and the Question of Democracy," in *The New Authoritarianism in Latin America*, ed. David Collier (Princeton: Princeton University Press, 1979), p. 289.

should be added: the mediation of effectiveness, or the capacity to implement policies with the desired results.[24] O'Donnell does not clarify all the possible means through which these different mediations function. I suggest that symbolic action is one of the means through which all four mediations operate, and that symbolic action is particularly important as regards the mediation of the nation. "The nation is expressed through a dense symbolism epitomized by the flag and national anthem, as well as by an official history that mythologizes a shared, cohesive past and extols a collective 'we' which should prevail over the cleavages (not only those between social classes) of civil society."[25]

In both Argentina and Brazil, the campaigns for national control of petroleum resources was one of the issues around which the national identity was formed. Thus both Petrobras and YPF were more than producers of a scarce resource. They were part of the "dense symbolism" of nationalist mythology. Condensation symbols "evoke the emotions associated with the situation. They condense into one symbolic event, sign, or act of patriotic pride, anxieties, remembrances of past glories or humiliations, promises of future greatness."[26] In both Argentina and Brazil YPF and Petrobras essentially became condensation symbols for national independence. Their names and existences evoked the emotions associated with the struggle to establish the oil monopoly, a struggle central to public awareness of nationalism. This puts Frondizi's oil policy in a different light. Inviting foreign participation in the exploration and exploitation of Argentine petroleum was not simply a rational choice to expand production capacity. It was a symbolic action of the highest order in violation of the mediation of "nation." The reaction of outrage it provoked in Argentine civil society can only be understood in these terms.

Although no other single area was as clearly symbolic as the petroleum issue, foreign investment in general was also an issue that impinged on the concept of the nation. This presented a dilemma for the developmentalist governments: their economic programs depended on extensive foreign investment, but their legitimacy depended on presenting themselves as the defenders of the general interest of the nation. They addressed this dilemma in different ways. In particular they tried to redefine the very concepts of nation. These concepts were not easily transformed. Much of the ideological activity of the developmen-

24. According to Juan Linz, ineffectiveness "weakens the authority of the state, and as a result, weakens its legitimacy." *The Breakdown of Democratic Regimes*, p. 22.

25. Ibid., p. 288.

26. Murray Edelman, *The Symbolic Uses of Politics* (Chicago: University of Illinois Press, 1985), p. 6.

talist government, however, can be interpreted as attempts to alter the old symbols of the nation and replace them with an alternative national ideology. One example was the distinction made by developmentalists between "nationalism of ends" and "nationalism of means," when they argued that as long as policies pursued nationalist ends (rapid growth to reach a national destiny of greatness), it was not important that they used nonnationalist means (such as foreign investment).

The second mediation of citizenship consists of that notion of abstract equality embodied in universal suffrage and rule of law, which is the foundation of the claim that the power exercised by the state is based on the consent of the citizens.[27] Although both the Kubitschek and the Frondizi period were formally democratic, the limitations of the semidemocracy in Argentina were more apparent than those in Brazil. The proscription of the Peronist party during the Frondizi government fundamentally undermined the possibilities of legitimation based on the mediation of citizenship. During the Kubitschek period, on the other hand, respect for political freedoms, full freedom of the press, and tolerance for political activity contributed greatly to the legitimacy of the government and bolstered claims that the state represented the general interests of society. The exclusion of illiterates from voting in Brazil, although it affected a substantial portion of the population, was not perceived as a limitation of citizenship in the same way as the exclusion of a political party was in Argentina.

Through the third mediation, *lo popular*, the government responds to demands for substantive justice of the *pueblo*, a notion of "we" that forms the basis for the state's obligations toward the less favored segments of the population.[28] The Peronist party in Argentina has traditionally identified itself as the party of the *pueblo*, and the legitimacy of the Peronist government was derived in part from its actions in favor of the poorest parts of the population. In many ways, Peronism as a movement became identified with *lo popular*. The exclusion of the Peronist party in Argentina thus had a double effect: it undermined the operation of both the mediation of citizenship and of *lo popular*.

These categories help us understand some fundamental differences in the development of consensus around the developmentalist model in Argentina and Brazil. Consensus was more likely to emerge where these three mediations were reinforced by the practices and symbolic action of the developmentalist governments. So whereas in Brazil dur-

27. O'Donnell, "Tensions in the Bureaucratic Authoritarian State," p. 288.
28. Ibid., p. 289.

ing the Kubitschek period all three mediations were functioning to a greater or lesser degree, in Argentina they were truncated.

The fourth mediation, that of effectiveness, is the ability to implement policies with the desired effect—to deliver the goods, especially the economic goods. Both the Frondizi and Kubitschek governments were highly aware of the need to legitimate themselves through effectively implementing policies designed to promote rapid growth. Frondizi was perhaps excessively concerned with effectiveness, to the detriment of other mediations. As the economic data at the beginning of this chapter indicate, Brazil experienced higher growth rates during this period. Frondizi's record, in retrospect, was also good. But effectiveness in and of itself is not sufficient to legitimate a democratic government in the absence of the successful operation of the other mediations. In those areas where the Frondizi program was most effective— the expansion of petroleum production and the reduction of inflation levels—it was least able to use this effectiveness to legitimate itself, since the petroleum and stabilization program had breached other mediations.

What are the qualities that permit leaders successfully to use symbolic politics to their advantage? Leaders need to be sensitive to the symbolic dimension of politics. They must be aware of how certain issues are perceived symbolically by the wider public, and of the powerful symbolic impact of many of their actions. But also the context itself determines the definitions and limits of what is possible. The presence of João Goulart as Kubitschek's vice-president served as a symbolic guarantee that at some level workers were incorporated within the government coalition.[29] In Argentina if Frondizi had wanted a Peronist in a similar position to provide the same kind of symbolic integration, it was simply not possible; in 1958 it was unimaginable for a Peronist to serve in a top government position. At times it seemed that Frondizi and his advisers lacked sensitivity to the symbolic dimension of politics. The secret meeting between Ché Guevara and Frondizi in 1961 is an example of a gratuitous symbolic gesture that exacerbated already tense relations between the executive and the military without providing Frondizi any clear benefit.

---

29. Goulart's position was more than symbolic, in that he helped settle labor disputes, determined who got jobs in the Labor Ministry bureaucracy and the social security institutes, and participated in policy making at the national level.

THE BALANCE OF REFORM AND ACCUMULATION

Earlier we discussed the entrepreneurial or accumulation function and the distributive or reform function, identified by Hirschman.[30] Developmentalism was basically an ideology of accumulation, since its primary aim was to accelerate industrialization of key sectors. But different developmentalists advocated striking a different balance between the accumulation and reform functions.

The reform function is similar to the mediation of *lo popular*. The need to balance the reform and the accumulation function is another way of talking about the need to assure the operation of the mediation of both *lo popular* and effectiveness, necessary for governments to achieve legitimacy. How were the developmentalist governments able or unable to achieve this balance between accumulation and reform?[31] The tactical alliance between cosmopolitans and nationalists which took place within the developmentalist administrations was the main way in which the reform and accumulation functions were integrated in developmentalist policy making. The nationalists argued for reform policies, whereas cosmopolitans focused more on accumulation. The coexistence in administrative positions of individuals advocating reform and accumulation policies was one way that these two functions were balanced in practice. Kubitschek was successful in temporarily achieving a balance between the demands for the accumulation and reform functions, but Frondizi was perceived as overemphasizing the accumulation at the expense of the reform function.

A "correct balance" between the demands for reform and accumulation does not exist in the abstract; it is socially determined and emerges from the nature of state-society relations. The more mobilized Argentine civil society demanded more attention to the reform function than did civil society in Brazil. Likewise the correct conditions for accumulation are not predetermined. Domestic and international entrepreneurs in Argentina may have been more wary because of past policies and thus demanded higher levels of profits and security than their counterparts in Brazil. Frondizi was aware that in order to reestablish the confidence of both international and domestic entrepreneurs in Argentina,

30. Albert O. Hirschman, "The Turn to Authoritarianism in Latin America and the Search for Its Economic Determinants," in *The New Authoritarianism in Latin America*, ed. Collier, p. 88.

31. Cavarozzi discusses this tension between accumulation, reform, and legitimation in developmentalist governments, although he does not use this terminology. "El 'desarrollismo' y las relaciones entre democracia y capitalismo dependiente en, 'dependencia y desarrollo en América Latina,'" 17 (1982), pp. 157–59.

he would have to provide extensive evidence and guarantees of the good "accumulation" intentions of his government. Thus, Frondizi faced a more difficult situation: he confronted greater demands for reform at the same time that he was obliged to offer more extensive guarantees to insure accumulation.

The degree to which a balance can be struck between the demands for reform and accumulation depends on how these processes have been historically articulated in a given setting. Hirschman gives two examples of a successful balance: in the Colombian case a united private political elite assured some minimal performance of both functions; in Venezuela the state and its bureaucracy, rather than a "private" ruling group, were responsible for carrying out both functions.[32]

We can argue that Brazil combined elements of the Colombian and the Venezuelan cases; both the private elite *and* the state and its bureaucracy were split between two groups, the cosmopolitans and the nationalists, which advocated in turn the accumulation and the reform functions. But historically these two functions were connected to a single political personality and tradition, that of Getúlio Vargas. The two political parties founded by Vargas can be seen as embodiments of the two functions: the PTB advocated reform and the PSD emphasized accumulation. Kubitschek was political heir to the Vargas tradition, and thus heir to the historical association of the two functions. Both Vargas and Kubitschek, who stressed the centrality of the PTB-PSD coalition, understood implicitly the importance to their government of the coexistence of the accumulation and reform functions.

In Argentina the main division around which society was organized —Peronist versus non-Peronist—corresponded to and reinforced the division between the demands for reform and the demands for accumulation. The Peronist party was identified with nationalism and with reform and *lo popular*, whereas the private groups of entrepreneurs and rural elites were identified with the accumulation function. Thus the historical tradition was one of division rather than balance of the two functions. The state was viewed not as an arena where these two tendencies might interact but as a prize to be captured by one group or another and to be used for its ends.

Frondizi attempted to integrate reform and accumulation in his government, but the historical divisions of Argentine society were so profound that his attempt to balance or merge the accumulation and reform functions earned his government the mistrust of both sides. Frondizi's move to reintegrate Peronists into Argentine political life can

32. Hirschman, "The Turn to Authoritarianism," p. 95.

be seen as an effort to address issues of reform and distribution, since the Peronist party was the bearer of these concerns. At the same time the bulk of his government's efforts addressed the accumulation function: his stabilization plan and the efforts to open the economy to foreign investment, to provide incentives for domestic industrialization, and to establish an infrastructure.

The Peronists and the nationalists identified the Frondizi government with the accumulation function. At the same time, Frondizi's attempt to forge an alliance with the Peronists also made him suspect in the eyes of entrepreneurial elites upon which the success of his economic program depended. Many different groups shared some of the economic ideas of the Frondizi government, but the political divisions of the period, and in particular the division over incorporating the Peronists into the political and economic life of the country, made them bitter opponents representing different parts of the political, if not the economic, spectrum. Since the Peronist party was the primary symbolic carrier of the reform function in Argentina, the debate over incorporating the Peronists into political life was essentially a debate about incorporation of the reform function. These bitter divisions meant that the accumulation and reform functions were never reconciled within the Frondizi administration, as indeed they have rarely been reconciled within any single Argentine government.

In this situation the president, as arbiter and the balancer of these two currents, is an essential figure. Kubitschek played this role masterfully, never fully identifying with either one or the other group. Frondizi, on the other hand, failed to perceive the importance of his role as arbiter. His exclusion of reformist elements from his administration and his excessive identification with the accumulators was responsible in part for the failure to legitimate his policies.

The essential aspect of the Kubitschek political leadership style was his ability to hold together the tactical alliance of cosmopolitans and nationalists within his government. Likewise, the stability of the PSD-PTB coalition was due in part to Kubitschek's compliance with campaign agreements between the parties.[33] He cultivated a co-optive and inclusive policy-making style, with particular emphasis on involvement of industry and military figures in the executive groups of the Targets

33. Kubitschek's political style is frequently listed as an explanation for the stability of his government and for his ability to implement his economic program. Benevides has stressed the importance of the balance he maintained between the PSD and the PTB within his government. Benevides, *O governo Kubitschek: Desenvolvimento econômico e estabilidade política* (Rio de Janeiro: Paz e Terra, 1979), pp. 59–76.

Program. Frondizi displayed a more exclusionary and closed style, in which, for example, policies designed to benefit industrialists were made without input from the industrialists themselves.

Although both the Frondizi and the Kubitschek governments started out precariously, without clear electoral mandates, and with considerable unrest in the military, the cumulative effect of events in the two countries soon began to look and feel very different. In Argentina one senses a layering of conflict, deception, and divisions, accompanied by increased disillusionment even among some of the government's allies. In Brazil, for the initial three years of the government, a surprising degree of convergence and optimism emerged around the administration's economic program. The developmentalist governments confronted the issues faced by any government of a capitalist state: balancing accumulation and reform, and assuring legitimacy. Their task was greater because developmentalism reserves a special role for international investment; the government had to convince international investors of the benefits and security of their investments, while at the same time retaining support and guaranteeing adequate benefits for domestic groups. The developmentalists were playing to two audiences simultaneously, one international and one domestic. Symbols were used to communicate with both audiences, but sometimes the symbols used to appeal to one audience alienated the other.[34]

The differences in the nature of the state in the two countries influenced the manner in which the ideological struggles over developmentalist policies played out. In Brazil the tactical alliance between cosmopolitans and nationalists was manifested by incorporating and co-opting key elites into the state, and thus much of the debate over developmentalism took place within the state. In addition, this elite debate extended to a handful of other privileged groups, in particular groups of industrialists and military. It is interesting to note that the members of the different groups of técnicos themselves understood and accepted the need for balance within the state. Cosmopolitan Roberto Campos recalled that he had recommended that Kubitschek nominate Celso Furtado as one of the directors of the BNDE, "to satisfy the avid nationalists who thought that Lucas Lopes and I had more of a globalist mentality. So Celso would be a nationalist element who would bring in

34. For example, one consulting firm offering advice to the Frondizi team on industrial policy advised it to abandon preaching economic nationalism, because this would alienate foreign capital necessary for industrialization. Concord Sociedad Anónima Industrial Comercial, "Sugestiones para una política de industrialización del pais," Buenos Aires, January 15, 1958, p. 2.

a coefficient of xenophobia to counterbalance our more cosmopolitan vision of the Brazilian reality."[35]

In Argentina divisions over incorporating the Peronists into political life made it more difficult to strike a balance between the accumulation and reform functions. As opposed to the Brazilian case, where almost all the developmentalist técnicos were incorporated into federal economic policy making in one form or another, the Frondizi government called only on cosmopolitan developmentalists. Later Frondizi called on policy makers of an economically liberal perspective to reassure industrialists and military figures about the economic policy of his government. Thus instead of a struggle within the state, as in Brazil, the conflict between nationalists and cosmopolitans took the form of a conflict of parts of society against the state.

POLITICAL STYLE

In spite of the similarities between the ideas of developmentalists in Brazil and Argentina, the two groups differed dramatically in their political style, discourse, and understanding and manipulation of the symbolic and mythical elements of the political debate. The two developmentalist governments operated in democratic or semidemocratic situations, and their success depended on their ability to forge a developmentalist coalition, holding together disparate elements and effectively negotiating the necessary compromise between external and internal demands.

In this task a higher level of economic growth afforded the state greater flexibility since it was negotiating the division of an expanding pie rather than a static one. Still, actually forging the coalition depended on the political ability of the leaders, which rested on such issues as political style and discourse.

Hirschman, among others, has pointed to the importance of "political style" in the failure of the Frondizi program:

> It could be argued that Frondizi's industrialization drive faced less favorable structural conditions than the similar drive that Kubitschek had launched two years earlier. But the more important difference may lie elsewhere: Kubitschek was able to create, during most of his mandate, a political and popular coalition that was held together by some minimal ideological fervor and backed his policies. Frondizi, on the other hand,

35. BNDE, Oral History Project, "Participação do BNDE na economic brasileira ao longo de sua historia," interview with Roberto de Oliveira Campos, March 27, 1982, p. 8.

became involved, from the very beginning of his term, in a series of policy reversals (e.g., with regard to petroleum) and ambiguities (the Frigerio-Alsogaray coexistence within his Cabinet) through which he forfeited the trust of large sectors of opinion which should have been his allies but soon turned against him. He even managed to give, in Argentina, the term "desarrollismo" a bad name from which it has still to recover. It was an unfortunate style of policy making rather than the strategy of unbalanced growth that caused his ruin.[36]

Marcelo Cavarozzi has also argued that a clearer analysis of political style, what he calls "ways of doing politics," is important for a better understanding of Argentine politics, and that "it would be erroneous to suppose that these ways of doing politics can be explained simply on the basis of an understanding of the interests of social groups and their interrelations."[37]

Central to understanding the Frondizi period in Argentina is the notion of *engaño* or deception. There was a strong perception, fueled by opposition political parties, that Frondizi had willfully deceived the Argentine people on a number of different occasions. The disillusionment created by the perceived deception blocked the potential energizing and mobilizing capacities of the developmentalist administration in Argentina.

Hirschman has suggested in a recent article that new ideas in economics and social science can be devices that serve as occasional and temporary boosters of public spirit. Thus, he argues that "Keynesianism's most important political effect in the U.S. may well have been to have raised public spiritedness in a crucial period of its recent history."[38] Developmentalism as a new idea had the potential to create this new public-spiritedness through the recruitment of a cadre of idealistic individuals who believed that they now held in their hands the tools to propel their countries from underdevelopment to development.

But developmentalism in Argentina was able to tap into this well of political energy for only a short period of its existence. Frondizi had the potential for broad appeal. Throughout his political career as a leading opposition figure, party leader, and intellectual, he had accumulated important symbolic capital that he could now call upon in his

36. Albert O. Hirschman, "Argentina's Economic Development and Policies during the Frondizi Period (1958–1962): Comments on the Paper by Alberto Petrecolla," unpublished manuscript to be published in a volume edited by Guido DiTella.

37. Marcelo Cavarozzi, "La política argentina contemporanea 1955–1985: Propósito del curso," course syllabus, 1985, p. 2.

38. Albert O. Hirschman, "How the Keynesian Revolution Was Exported from America, and Other Comments," in *The Political Power of Economic Ideas*, ed. Peter A. Hall (Princeton: Princeton University Press, 1989), p. 357.

bid for the presidency. Through a series of political moves during the candidacy and in the early months of his presidency, Frondizi essentially squandered this accumulated symbolic capital and undermined his potential for mobilizing and energizing a new political generation. Three key decisions created the climate of deception: the secret electoral pact with Perón, the reversal of petroleum policy, and the decision to let religious universities grant degrees. Each of these policies was adopted by Frondizi with the advice of Rogelio Frigerio. As a journalist and polemicist, Frigerio was brilliant, as witnessed by the success of *Qué* magazine under his editorship. As a political strategist, he was dismally unaware of the symbolic dimension of politics. Capable of arousing intense admiration and loyalty from a small coterie of disciples, he generated mistrust and dislike among a broad range of individuals otherwise sympathetic to Frondizi's ideas.

The concern with Frondizi's perceived deception took on such proportions because it was fueled by political groups and individuals of many persuasions. The Right and the military had their own version of Frondizi's deception. It focused on Frigerio and his followers as covert Communists infiltrating the state. In gentle versions, Frondizi was a dupe of his Communist advisers; in more venal versions, Frondizi was himself a Communist. At the same time military and anti-Peronist groups focused on the pact with Perón as further evidence of Frondizi's deception and untrustworthiness. From the Left, the criticism focused on the reversal of petroleum policy and the lay education debate. Defense of the national oil monopoly and anticlericalism had long been banners of the Left in Argentina.

Both Frondizi's party members and his opponents found it hard to accept that the president had honestly changed his mind about certain policies and that he had found an intellectual blood brother in Frigerio. The change was too rapid and unexpected. They could only conclude that he had been misled and used in his association with Frigerio. Frigerio's penchant for secrecy and intrigue only intensified the belief that he was involved in underhanded activity.

This perceived deception had far-reaching effects on the Frondizi administration and the future of developmentalism in Argentina. Conflicts between the desarrollistas and other groups centered around particular issues that took on profound symbolic meaning beyond their apparent importance. The watershed issues were essential in defining whether or not a particular group would support Frondizi's policies. Peronism, communism, foreign capital, and petroleum each became a watershed issue that took priority over other shared concerns and goals. Frondizi and Frigerio hoped to make Development (with a capital *D*) the new watershed issue, overriding all previous divisions to meld together a powerful coalition capable of producing industrialization and growth. They never succeeded in imposing their new agenda, and instead were defeated by the multiple fractures of the coalition around the other watershed issues.

The vehemence of the response to Frondizi's policies reveals that what was at stake were intensely held national myths and tacit agreements. Catalina Smulovitz has elucidated one of the tacit agreements that Frondizi's policies violated. Examined rationally, the extreme vehemence of the political response to Frondizi's pact with Perón is surprising. Politicians are expected to maximize votes. Because the Peronist party was not permitted to participate in the elections, Peronist voters would have to vote for another party's candidate or turn in a blank ballot. Given this situation, why should Frondizi's agreement with Perón provoke such opposition? Smulovitz argues that by dealing with Perón, Frondizi broke a tacit pact between all the non-Peronist political groups to weaken Peronism as an independent political actor. Frondizi's decision to negotiate directly with Perón served to relegitimize Perón as a political actor.[39]

THE DISCOURSE OF DEVELOPMENTALISM IN ARGENTINA

Desarrollistas in Argentina attempted to restructure political and economic discourse by taking existing words and concepts and giving them new meaning. They used the existing concepts of nationalism, foreign investment, economic independence, and agro-import structure in ways that varied from commonly accepted speech practices in Argentina. Frondizi argued that developmentalist policies were aimed at leading Argentina to greater economic independence and breaking down the traditional agro-import structure.[40] He identified the sources of economic dependence not with foreign ownership but rather with lack of industry and low productivity. Rapid industrialization and economic growth with the help of foreign investment would thus increase Argentine economic independence. In Argentina, however, the concept of economic independence was generally associated with national ownership of industry, infrastructure, and natural resources.

The writings and speeches of the desarrollistas were peppered with

39. Catalina Smulovitz, "Relaciones entre la oposición partidaria y el gobierno durante el periodo de Frondizi," Informe Final, Beca de Perfeccionamiento, CONICET, March 1987, p. 66.

40. Felix Luna, *Dialogos con Frondizi* (Buenos Aires: Editorial Desarrollo, 1963), p. 72.

references to large landholders, the oligarchy, and the traditional agro-import structure of the economy.[41] To many Argentines, such a vocabulary implied a political concern with the need for land reform. But the desarrollistas argued that "the question of ownership has nothing to do with the solution to the Argentine agrarian problem," and that the "claim for land ownership is one of the most reactionary issues that has been taken up by the Left in our countries."[42]

The developmentalists frequently attacked "foreign interests,"[43] by which they did not mean all foreign involvement in Argentina but rather only "bad foreign investment" as opposed to "good foreign investment." According to the desarrollistas, bad foreign investment, associated with Great Britain, did not contribute to the rapid development of basic industries. Good foreign investment, associated with the United States, was concentrated in basic industrial areas prioritized by the desarrollistas.[44] Just as there was good and bad foreign investment, there was also false and true nationalism. According to the desarrollistas, true nationalism was the nationalism of ends, not of means. As long as the ends were truly national, it did not matter if nonnational means were used to achieve these ends.[45]

The desarrollistas hoped to define these words and concepts on their own terms, but they did not take into account that the political language they were using was an inherited language, built up over time through use. Certain meanings had become institutionalized in the language, and thus it was not sufficient for developmentalists simply to intend to use them in a certain way. They also had to consider how the words they were using would be interpreted in a context they could not control. As a result, they were accused of trying to deceive the public by using words commonly perceived in one way in a totally different fashion.

> Two incidents in *Alice Through the Looking Glass* would seem to be making this point. Humpty Dumpty, as is well known, avers that "when I use a word, it means what I want it to mean, neither more not less. . . . The

41. See, for example, ibid., pp. 72–73.

42. Fanor Diaz, *Conversaciones con Rogelio Frigerio* (Buenos Aires: Hachette, 1977), p. 29.

43. Rogelio Frigerio, *Las condiciones de la victoria* (Montevideo: A. Monteverde, 1962), p. 167.

44. "In synthesis, this thesis argues that capital—national or foreign—is colonialist when it is dedicated to items that strengthen dependency—and, on the other hand, is liberating when it is invested in basic sectors of the economy." Arturo Sábato, "Prologo," in Arturo Frondizi, *Petroleo y nación* (Buenos Aires: Transicion, 1963), p. 15.

45. Diaz, *Conversaciones con Rogelio Frigerio*, p. 54.

question is who is to be master, that's all." This poor being is in the linguistic equivalent of a Hobbesian state of nature; it has not occurred to him that words subject to one person's totally arbitrary control may become unintelligible to those hearing them, and so of very little use for purposes even of mastery. . . . At a later stage in the story, the Red Queen remarks: "When you've said a thing, that fixes it and you must take the consequences." Without going too deeply into her use of the word "fixes," we can interpret her as meaning that to use language at all, you must make commitments. You have not merely performed upon yourself; you are inescapably perceived as having performed in ways defined by others' acceptances of the words you have used. You have performed upon them, but the means by which you have performed are in some degree not at your power but at theirs.[46]

The desarrollistas exhibited a disdain for Argentine discursive traditions. "See the harm to the country caused by the repetition time and time again of slogans that don't have anything to do with reality," argued Frigerio, referring to such slogans as the call for an immediate and profound agrarian reform, which was part of the platform of the Radical party.[47] One of their explicit political goals was the destruction of certain "mental categories," as represented by certain kinds of language that they found detrimental to Argentine development. In its place they hoped to substitute the new mental categories of developmentalism, based on a scientific analysis of the economy and society. But since they believed that their categories were scientific, as opposed to the "slogans" or the "ideological stupidity" of the opposition,[48] they were unwilling to recognize the intersubjectivity of language. If, as they argued, their ideas were based on science, on economic laws, there was no room for debate. "Can we oppose an objective law of political economy? Can we oppose the process of concentration and centralization of capital? It would be like opposing the law of gravity or that the earth rotates around the sun," Frigerio argues.[49]

A second cause of the exclusionary discourse was the desarrollistas' view of themselves as revolutionaries fighting for the cause of development. "The character of language as a two-way communication system is hard to reconcile with revolution as a one-way act of power. Therefore, the verbal strategy characteristic of the revolutionary is the reduc-

---

46. J. G. A. Pocock, "Verbalizing a Political Act: Toward a Politics of Speech," in *Language and Politics*, ed. Michael Shapiro (New York: New York University Press, 1984), pp. 31–32.

47. Diaz, *Conversaciones con Rogelio Frigerio*, p. 29.

48. Ibid., p. 54.

49. Ibid., p. 113.

tion of You to a choice between We and Them."[50] This dichotomy between "you" and "them" is evident in the discourse of the desarrollistas. Thus, Frondizi states, "For me, in this country and in the world, the reactionaries are those who don't want to help the economic development of underdeveloped countries, those of us who want this development are the revolutionaries."[51] Frigerio makes frequent references to the "enemy," never clearly defined, except as those who supported foreign interests and the maintenance of the agro-import structure.

Although it is not surprising that the desarrollistas used this rhetoric—it was shared by many of their political allies and opponents—it may have contributed to the continuation of a typical discursive pattern that could be used against them effectively. In many ways, the desarrollistas recognized that the success of their program depended on breaking down these traditional antinomies of Argentine thought: nationalism or "selling out," Peronist or anti-Peronist. They decided to break down the old antinomies by trying to substitute a new and equally rigid one—desarrollista or enemy—rather than urging a more nuanced interpretation of politics. Their rhetoric gave fuel to many opponents, who used it to justify their belief that Frigerio and Frondizi were Communists or Peronists in disguise; it also confused and angered potential political allies, who felt betrayed by what they read as unkept promises and Machiavellian twists.

The interests of each sector of Argentine society were filtered through an ideological interpretation that included a certain sense of discursive congruence; certain things made sense and fit together, and others did not. The statements and justifications of the Frondizi government contradicted this historically formed pattern of discursive congruence. The developmentalists claimed to be democratic, yet they benefited from an exclusionary electoral system; they claimed to be nationalist, yet they made a series of significant concessions to international capital; they claimed to be legalists, and yet Frondizi gave in to the golpistas in the military; they claimed to be anti-Communist, and yet they voted against Cuban exclusion from the OAS; they returned the CGT to the labor unions, and yet they severely suppressed strike activity. The sense of discursive congruence of each sector of Argentine society was violated by a series of activities and justifications that made sense within the bounds of the intricate reasoning of the desarrollistas' thought but shocked anyone not immersed in this thought. This attack

50. Pocock, "Verbalizing a Political Act," p. 42.
51. Luna, *Diálogos con Frondizi*, p. 102.

on discursive tradition could only be explained as the result of Machiavellianism, infiltration, payoffs, and corruption.

Meanwhile, the desarrollistas themselves, faced with an unprecedented wave of opposition to a wide variety of their policies, retreated into their own simplifications. They believed, given that their actions were congruent with their ideology and given their view of politics, that the opposition could only be the result of the maneuvers of the enemy and of psychological warfare. They justified, indeed took pride in, the opposition as an indication that they were the group most threatening to established interests. "Frigerio's methodology consists in discovering tendencies based on an analysis of the dynamic conditions of reality. Since this has absolutely no precedent in Argentine political thought, it explains why he was rapidly identified as the most dangerous of enemies by reactionary interests in Argentina and abroad."[52]

Intentional misinformation and blatant distortions, including those originating from the intelligence agencies of the armed forces, were being circulated and published about the desarrollista government, and this fueled the paranoia and the lack of self-criticism of the desarrollistas. Categorizing much of the political opposition as the insidious maneuvering of traditional colonial interests led to the desarrollistas' failure to take them seriously.[53]

As has been discussed above, the mobilization of financial, technical, and symbolic resources was an essential ingredient for the successful implementation of developmentalist policies. In each of these three areas, the nature of political leadership and of the state in the two countries conditioned the outcomes. Both countries mobilized large amounts of foreign investment and suppliers' credits to support their development programs. Brazil, however, received more bilateral and multilateral public assistance than did Argentina, primarily as a result of the positive continuous aid relationship between Brazil and the U.S. government and the World Bank. Such an ongoing institutional relationship did not exist in Argentina.

Symbolic action, political leadership style, and political discourse were the basic tools for mobilizing the public to support developmen-

52. Oscar Camilion, "Prologo a la segunda edición," in Rogelio Frigerio, *Crecimiento económico y democracia* (Buenos Aires: Paidos, 1983), p. 3.

53. "The enemies of the nation work without rest to undermine the public confidence in the institutions and in the men of the government and to block, with insidious campaigns, the plans for recuperation and economic progress. Traditional colonialist interests are at work behind the most innocent appearances of social and democratic fervor." Frigerio, *Las condiciones de la victoria*, p. 180.

talist projects. Kubitschek mobilized political resources through powerful symbolic action and a convincing political style that concentrated on balancing the reform and accumulation function, and making tradeoffs between the accumulation of symbolic and economic capital. But this mobilization of political resources essentially depended on Kubitschek's leadership and the maintenance of the PTB-PSD coalition that he represented, and thus was not easily sustainable once Kubitschek left office. It also depended on the elasticity of the economy, which was beginning to give out. Kubitschek accumulated symbolic capital at the price of inflation, and that exchange could not continue indefinitely.

CHAPTER SEVEN

Conclusion

Theorists explaining differences in development patterns in the Third World, either between countries within regions or between regions, have pointed to the choice of development model as a crucial factor in determining economic outcomes. In Chapter 1 I discussed four alternative explanations for the adoption and implementation of economic models in Latin America: theories of economic interest groups, relative state autonomy, power and discourse, and rational choice and political survival. Each of these explanations provides some insights into actions taken during the period under study, but none of them alone, nor any combination of them, can answer the central question of this research: why was developmentalism adopted in Latin America?

Nor can any of these models convincingly account for the differences between the experience of Brazil and Argentina during this period. Explanations that focus on changing internal class configurations, state autonomy, political survival, or the power of discourse cannot explain the depth of the opposition to the Frondizi government and its policies, even from groups that benefited from those policies; nor can they explain the breadth of support for the Kubitschek program. In particular, these explanations cannot grasp how and why developmentalism took on different meanings in Brazil and Argentina. These explanations fall short because they are not concerned with how people's beliefs motivate their actions.

In Latin America new ideas about development that surfaced in the postwar period had a profound influence on the economic policies adopted by Latin American governments. Perhaps the central shift in economic policy in Latin America in the last fifty years was a perceptual one in favor of import-substituting industrialization. The move away from liberal free trade models in Latin America and toward some form of import-substituting model was the result of a broad-based ideological shift, reflecting widespread public support for national industrialization and broader state involvement in the supervision of the economy. A number of different economic models were equally viable in Latin America in the postwar period. But import-substituting industrialization was the most captivating model to a continent traumatized by memories of its vulnerability during the Depression and the Second World War.

Moving from a national populist model to a developmentalist model involved a narrower ideological shift, taken among a smaller group of intellectuals and policy makers, in light of the limitations of national populism and the new external constraints and opportunities. Once again, it was not the only model they could have chosen, but it was a compromise model that allowed them to try to respond to their belief and the public's belief in and commitment to industrialization, and at the same time operate within the domestic and international economic constraints.

But disembodied ideas did not waft through the air and have an abstract influence on political debates. Nor did I find clear evidence of particular classes serving uniformly as the carriers of particular ideas, as I had originally expected. Ideas were carried by specific individuals and institutions and served as a basis for guiding policy—policy that is not fully intelligible without understanding beliefs.

RECENT THEORIZING ON THE INFLUENCE OF IDEAS

A number of interesting new works on the influence of ideas have recently emerged in the study of comparative politics, political economy, foreign policy, and history. Each of these studies is concerned with related but somewhat different questions in different countries and time periods.[1] But all focus on policies and outcomes that cannot

1. See, for example, Peter Hall, ed., *The Political Power of Economic Ideas: Keynesianism across Nations* (Princeton: Princeton University Press, 1989); Hall, *Governing the Economy* (Oxford: Oxford University Press, 1986); Judith Goldstein, "The Impact of Ideas on Trade Policy: The Origins of the U.S. Agricultural and Manufacturing Policies," *International Organization* 43 (Winter 1989); Goldstein, "Ideas, Institutions, and Trade Policy," *International Organization* 42 (Winter 1989); Ernst B. Haas, *When Knowledge Is Power: Three Models of Change in International Organizations* (Berkeley: University of California Press, 1990); John Odell, *U.S. International Monetary Policy: Markets, Power, and Ideas as Sources of Change* (Princeton: Princeton University Press, 1982); Michael Shafer, *Deadly Paradigms:*

be explained solely by changes in objective conditions or material interests, and all attempt to provide alternative explanations that incorporate a concern with the role of ideas.

Yet there is still a strong lack of systematic theoretical attention to the role of ideas. What exists are mainly isolated studies, not yet borrowing insights from one another or building a common framework. Little cumulative knowledge about the role of ideas in a broad comparative sense has emerged. Efforts to theorize about the impact of ideas and the interaction of ideas and institutions can be enhanced by comparing findings from related studies. In this spirit, the purpose of this chapter is to relate some of the theoretical arguments arising from this book to other studies on the role of ideas, highlighting common themes and possible areas for future research.

Some of the current work on ideas and politics presents ideas as a kind of intervening variable that mediates between interests and outcomes.[2] My work specifically rejects this conceptualization of the relationship between ideas and interests. Ideas are the lens, without which no understanding of interests is possible. Ideas transform perceptions of interests.[3] Ideas about economics and about politics are present from the beginning in the very process of formulating interests, shaping not only actors' perceptions of possibilities but also their understanding of their own interests. Anti-Peronism among many businesspeople in Argentina did not interfere with their pursuit of their economic interests. It is the lens through which they interpreted their interests. Anti-Peronism was not an irrational consideration; the incorporation of a powerful and independent labor movement is a fundamental concern of business interests. But one cannot speculate on how Argentine business groups will act without knowing the ideas that motivate them.

Others argue that ideas influence policy by interfering with decisions based on economic rationality. This sometimes is discussed in terms of

---

The Failure of U.S. Counterinsurgency Policy (Princeton: Princeton University Press, 1988); Emanuel Adler, *The Power of Ideology: The Quest for Technological Antonomy in Argentina and Brazil* (Berkeley: University of California Press, 1987); Eric Foner, *Politics and Ideology in the Age of the Civil War* (Oxford: Oxford University Press, 1980).

2. One example of a work that essentially views ideas as intervening variables is Aaron L. Friedberg, *The Weary Titan: Britain and the Experience of Relative Decline, 1895–1905* (Princeton: Princeton University Press, 1988). Friedberg portrays ideas as intervening between "objective changes in the structure of the international system" and the policy actions taken to respond to these changes.

3. Ernst Haas makes a similar argument when he discusses the relation between interests and values. "Contrary to lay usage, interests are not the opposite of ideals or values. . . . Interests cannot be articulated without values. Far from (ideal) values being pitted against (material) interests, interests are unintelligible without a sense of values-to-be realized." *When Knowledge Is Power*, p. 2.

the "ideological and political constraints" on economic policy making. My concern is to emphasize the absolute centrality of political and ideological factors in not only determining the outcomes of economic policy but influencing the very meaning and interpretation of economic ideas and recommendations. In this sense, the debate is not between politics and economic rationality but over what was economically rational, which is a political and ideological debate. The debate between liberals and developmentalists was not over economic rationality and politics but over two totally different visions of economic rationality. While it may be possible to try to evaluate from the perspective of the 1990s which vision of rationality yielded the best results, it is problematic to read that evaluation back into history and assume that some actors were advocating economic rationality and others were putting politics first. Rather, the discussion here centers on why one set of economic ideas won out over another in this period of Latin American history.

IDEAS AND INDIVIDUALS

The adoption of new economic models is the result of the changing ideas of top policy makers, who respond to what they perceive as the constraints and opportunities of the international and domestic economic scene. This study signals an important role for individual policy makers, such as Frondizi and Kubitschek, their top advisers, and intellectuals like Raúl Prebisch. This emphasis on the importance of ideas held by individuals, especially top policy makers, is shared by many recent theorists on the influence of ideas.[4] The connection between ideas and individuals has been conceived of alternatively as the connection between ideas and political entrepreneurs, who seek to put together political coalitions in which ideas serve as the glue.[5] Both Frondizi and Kubitschek are prime examples of political entrepreneurs who attempted to use ideas as the basis of pulling together disparate political coalitions. Frondizi failed to maintain the ephemeral developmentalist coalition. Kubitschek succeeded brilliantly for most of his presidency, but the coalition began to unravel near the end of his term and then fell apart during the Goulart presidency. Ideas are often symbol-

4. Adler, Hall, Haas, Goldstein, Odell, and Friedberg are primarily concerned with the ideas held by individuals, especially by policy makers and intellectuals who have influence on policy, although some also discuss broader societal ideas and discourse.

5. This point has been made by Judith Goldstein and Robert Keohane, in their "Conference Report" for the Conference on Ideas and Politics, March 5, 1990, p. 11.

ized by an individual or group of individuals who are the most important representatives of the ideas. Kubitschek, Frondizi, and Prebisch are all key examples of individuals who symbolized developmentalism and whose personal histories became entwined with the history of the ideas they championed.

Others argue that ideas are often held by "epistemic communities."[6] One author defines epistemic communities as "professionals . . . who share a common causal model and a common set of political values."[7] Although epistemic communities may take the form of an "invisible college" network, they are usually found within institutions and organizations. The community of people who worked at CEPAL, were trained there, or shared their ideas could certainly be thought of as an epistemic community that held common ideas about development. One difficulty with this approach, however, is that it is often possible for external observers to impose a coherence upon a community not shared by the so-called members of the community. The types of developmentalist thought that I initially had lumped together in the same category were not always internally perceived as being the same. I had believed, for example, that desarrollistas in Argentina, and those who believed in the ideas of CEPAL and Prebisch (CEPALinos), would be one and the same. I discovered that in Argentina in the 1950s desarrollistas and CEPALinos were often opponents. These groups had the potential of belonging to the same epistemic community because the ideas they held were very similar, but this potential community was never realized.

One difficult question is why individuals come to hold new ideas. Some authors have suggested that ideas often emerge in response to dramatic policy failures or disillusionment.[8] Ideational arguments have

6. John Ruggie, the first to use the term "epistemic communities" in the political science literature, borrowed the term from Michel Foucault and used it to refer to "a dominant way of looking at social reality, a set of shared symbols and references, mutual expectations and a mutual predictability of intention." John Gerard Ruggie, "International Response to Technology: Concepts and Trends," *International Organization* 29 (Summer 1975), 570.

7. Haas, *When Knowledge Is Power*, p. 41. Peter Haas has developed the concept of epistemic communities in *Saving the Mediterranean* (New York: Columbia University Press, 1990).

8. John Odell argues that a "major failure of past policy, or rather, extreme or accumulated evidence that can be readily interpreted as a consequence of past policy," is an important impetus to cognitive change. *U.S. International Monetary Policy*, p. 371. Albert Hirschman makes a related argument when he discusses disappointment as one of the main factors motivating social action. *Shifting Involvements* (Princeton: Princeton University Press, 1982).

also been used to explain why policies remain unchanged despite repeated failure, as in the case of U.S. counterinsurgency policy in the Third World.[9] In the case of Latin America, the original adoption of national populist import-substituting industrialization was clearly a response to the perceived failure of the liberal model during the Depression and the Second World War. But the same experience of failure was simultaneously perceived as an opportunity. Prebisch recognized this in the first paragraph of the so-called CEPAL manifesto: "Two World Wars in a single generation and a great economic crisis between them have shown the Latin American countries their opportunities, clearly pointing the way to industrial activities."[10] The Depression and the war led to a dual set of perceptions on the part of many Latin Americans. The first was that the international economy was unpredictable and undependable, and was likely to remain so in the future. The second was that the efforts to "go it alone" through import-substituting industrialization had been surprisingly successful and were the most promising route for future economic policy. The combination of perceived failure and initial success contributed to the adoption of national populist policies.[11] Although these perceptions were not irrational, given the past performance of the international economic system and the domestic economies in the 1930s and 1940s, they turned out to be poor predictors of future economic developments.

I hesitate to suggest, however, that this pattern of dramatic failure of past policies combined with initial success of the new is always the best explanation for why policy makers come to hold new ideas. The change from national populism to developmentalism did not correspond to this pattern. By the 1950s the national populist model was beginning to have problems, but these problems (often referred to by the catchy but somewhat misleading phrase "exhaustion of the easy stage of ISI") did not amount to a dramatic failure along the lines suggested by Odell. Nor did some initial successes generate broad support. To a certain extent both "success" and "failure" are in the eye of the beholder. From one point of view, the most successful policy implemented by the Frondizi administration—attaining self-sufficiency in petroleum produc-

9. Shafer, *Deadly Paradigms*.

10. Raúl Prebisch, "The Economic Development of Latin America and Its Principal Problems" (New York: United Nations Economic Commission for Latin America, 1950), p. 1.

11. This relates to Goldstein's argument that "nothing establishes the legitimacy of a policy like success. Policies become institutionalized because they work." "The Impact of Ideas," p. 71.

tion—also generated the most public opposition. Whether the policy was a success or a failure depends on what kinds of yardsticks were used to measure success: national ownership or overall production goals.[12]

Perhaps more useful than either failure or success as a way of thinking about what causes people to adopt new ideas is Peter Hall's notion of persuasiveness. What makes an idea persuasive is the way the idea relates to the economic and political problems of the day.[13] Success and failure are interpreted in terms of what are perceived as the most pressing problems facing a country at a particular time. What was it that made developmentalist ideas persuasive? They addressed directly and forcefully the issue that was seen by many as the central economic problem of that time in Latin America: the need for rapid industrialization. But developmentalism was appealing to policy makers because it offered a compromise program between the demands of the international economy and the demands of domestic groups. For new models to be adopted, they need only be persuasive to a fairly small group of policy makers and intellectuals; for a model to be consolidated, however, it must be persuasive to a broad range of societal groups. Leaders can use material incentives and symbolic appeals to try to make new models more persuasive to the public. If the new model fits well with existing ideologies, it will be less difficult to persuade society to accept it. If the new model is in stark contrast to existing ideologies, the people may be persuaded only if they perceive that old models have suffered dramatic failure, or if the new offers stunning success.

Developmentalism gained appeal in the mid-1950s because changing economic and political circumstances made it appear to be the best response to a situation of foreign exchange crisis and new availability of international finance. In general one could suggest that external events impinge more strongly in the case of Third World countries, so that the notion of persuasion is more externally coercive than in the case of Western Europe or the United States. Policy makers may adopt economic policies based on ideas that are not internally persuasive, as is often the case with the economic policies advocated by the International Monetary Fund.

12. Even the most ingrained orthodoxy will eventually respond to long-term economic failure. But it is not clear how long certain models must sustain failure before new models are sought. One interesting question is why certain policies have been able to be maintained for so long in spite of abundant evidence of failure.

13. Hall, *The Political Power of Economic Ideas*, p. 369.

IDEAS IN INSTITUTIONS

Powerful individuals are important for the adoption of ideas, but if these ideas do not find institutional homes, they will not be able to sustain themselves over the long term. Institutions take on more importance at the stage of policy implementation and consolidation than at the stage of the adoption of new policies. Frondizi was able to adopt the developmentalist model in Argentina in spite of fragile institutional support for such a model. Institutional weakness, however, complicated implementation and consolidation of the model.

Peter Hall and Emanuel Adler also stress the importance of institutions for carrying and disseminating ideas.[14] In his study of science and technology policy in Brazil and Argentina over the last twenty years, Adler presents a convincing argument that technocrats in institutions who hold collective understandings can "catalytically affect" events, leading to outcomes that would not otherwise occur. Adler argues that embodying optimistic, forward-looking ideologies in insulated institutions led to the successful adoption and implementation of technology policies. But Adler fails to provide a more systematic framework to specify when ideas make a difference, how ideas become connected to institutions, and why some ideas and institutions make a difference and others do not.

The institutional structure and the formal and informal rules that govern the state have a decisive impact on the potential stability of state institutions and the possibility of ideas becoming embodied in these institutions. In Argentina, for example, the lack of any significant civil service reform leads to personnel discontinuity and difficultly recruiting and retaining qualified personnel. The successful example that Adler gives, the case of the National Atomic Energy Commission and the nuclear power issue in Argentina, is in some ways an exception that proves the rule, since it was one of the few insulated institutions in the Argentine state that had personnel continuity and was not subject to constant changes in leadership.[15]

Yet we still lack a satisfactory understanding of how and why ideas

14. Hall, *Governing the Economy*, pp. 276–80; Adler, *The Power of Ideology*, pp. 11, 327–29.

15. Adler argues that Argentina's success in developing a near autonomous nuclear development capacity can be credited mainly to one institution, the National Atomic Energy Commission, which enjoyed extraordinary continuity of leadership and political autonomy, consensus and insulation, at the same time that "other institutions were being shattered by ideological conflict and political and economic instability." He recognizes that CNEA was the exception to Argentine "fracasomania." Adler, *The Power of Ideology*, p. 329.

become embedded in institutions and what happens to them once they are. To answer these questions, I place importance on: (1) the institutional structures and procedures that facilitate emergence and maintenance of strong institutional ideas and purpose; (2) the congruence between particular institutions and certain ideas; and (3) the role of pivotal institution builders and their ideas.

First, the institutional structure of the state influences the degree to which ideas can become embodied in institutions. A minimum level of merit civil service procedures, continuity of personnel, and insulation is necessary to develop an institutional orientation. The nature of state institutions in Brazil, especially the existence of an "insulated bureaucracy" governed by merit criteria and with significant personnel continuity, made it easier for ideas to become embedded in state institutions. In Argentina the general weakness of state institutions and constant shifts in personnel made it difficult for ideas to become embedded in state institutions. Institutions with little autonomy or continuity are much less likely to become carriers of influential ideas.

In Argentina and Brazil the structure of the civil service had important implications for the successful implementation of new ideas. The almost complete absence of a civil service in Argentina led to a failure to develop and maintain economic expertise in the state, and the high personnel turnover meant that ideas did not have the opportunity to take hold within the state structure. Peter Hall suggests that Keynesian ideas made the strongest inroads in those countries where the civil service was more permeable to outside influence, but that once accepted in Britain, the strong civil service rendered them an entrenched component of the policy process.[16] The Latin American cases suggest that excessive permeability and turnover make it difficult for any idea to become embodied in an institution. Nevertheless, once ideas have become embedded in an institution, this institution is less permeable to the influence of other ideas. This supports the notion discussed above that the factors necessary for adoption of a new model are different from those needed for the implementation and consolidation of the model.

Second, certain ideas have affinities with particular state structures.[17] Developmentalist policies were more likely to find an institutional home within planning ministries and development banks. In Argentina

16. Hall, *The Political Power of Economic Ideas*, pp. 378–79.

17. This is supported by a point made by Peter Hall, who suggests that the role of the Central Bank was especially important in the case of Keynesianism. Where the Central Bank played a powerful role in the process of economic policy making, it was likely to inhibit the pursuit of Keynesian policies. Ibid., p. 379.

the absence of a planning ministry and a development bank meant that there was no institutional structure predisposed to embody developmentalist ideas. Brazil had no all-powerful Central Bank at this time, which allowed the Development Council and the National Development Bank (BNDE) more power to supervise policy. At the same time, new ideas can lead to the formation of new institutions. The wave of developmentalist ideas in the 1950s led to the formation of new planning agencies and development banks throughout the region.

Third, pivotal institution builders often leave an ideological legacy within their institutions. Thus Perón left a national populist legacy in the Argentine Banco Industrial that continued throughout the developmentalist government. The ideological legacy can be incorporated into the specific rules governing institutions. For example, the requirement that the board of directors of the Banco Industrial be made up of representatives of industry and agriculture assured that the loan policy of the bank would respond to the short-term credit concerns of existing industrial sectors. On the other hand, Vargas and the individuals responsible for founding the BNDE instilled in it a clear set of developmentalist orientations. At other times the legacy is incorporated in the ethos or the training programs of the institutions. Itamaraty's ethos of professionalism and cosmopolitanism was transmitted to young Foreign Service officials through the official training program. But institutions are able to transform and take on new ideas. In the early 1950s, for example, Itamaraty became increasingly concerned with the need for economic development and diplomacy, concerns that had not previously been an important part of its institutional orientation. In this sense, members of the Itamaraty group helped the institution respond to changes in the international economic diplomatic environment. Institution builders can help instill their ideas in institutions, but once ideas have become embedded within institutions, they no longer require the presence of the founding individual to maintain their vigor.

Institutions were not only important for the implementation of policy, in the narrow sense of the word, but they also helped secure broader support for developmentalist policies from domestic groups. In Brazil industrialists were incorporated into economic policy making through a series of institutional arrangements that facilitated their involvement in economic decision making. Likewise, labor was incorporated as a subordinated partner in the developmentalist coalition. Labor incorporation was the result of specific corporatist institutional mechanisms such as the consolidated labor law and the social security institutes. As for the Brazilian military, one of the important ways Kubitschek secured military support was through a co-optation process that included an unprecedented number of appointments of military figures to key policy posts.

But no amount of insulation, continuity, and civil service regulations will lead to innovative and successful policy in and of themselves. It would be a mistake to attribute the successful formulation and implementation of developmentalist policies solely to institutional factors. Issues of political leadership and legitimacy were also crucial for mobilizing political resources and support for developmentalist policies. Kubitschek was a talented political leader and a masterful manipulator of symbolic politics. Frondizi failed to achieve similar levels of legitimacy, haunted by the legacy of the pact with Perón and unable to understand that the symbolic nature of politics implied that many of his moves led to the simultaneous gain of economic capital and loss of symbolic capital. It was the dynamic interaction between a skillful leader who mobilized public support and a group of policy makers in an insulated sector of the state which permitted effective implementation of policy during the Kubitschek administration.

IDEAS AND INTERPRETATION: CONSENSUS AND CONSOLIDATION

Ideas alone do not account for the different outcomes in Brazil and Argentina. Rather, the degree of ideological consensus on economic policies in the two countries is one of the primary variables explaining consolidation of an economic model. One reason for the different levels of acceptance of developmentalist ideas in Brazil and Argentina is that although the economic policies adopted by Frondizi and Kubitschek were very similar on paper, developmentalism did not "mean" the same thing in both countries. Explanations based on the "meanings" that I attributed to ideas, or to the "objective interests" that I attributed to actors, did not adequately explain the success or failure of developmentalist ideas in Brazil and Argentina. Instead it was necessary to discover the meanings that developmentalism had for the actors of the period and the process of interpretation that led to the emergence of those particular meanings. Second, I had to understand the ways in which these meanings served as a basis on which different actors decided their political positions and actions and how the relevant political actors perceived their interests.

There are some interesting points of connection between the impact of developmentalism in Latin America and Peter Hall's conclusions on the influence of Keynesian ideas in Western Europe, one of the most systematic attempts to address this issue. Hall argues that "many complex sets of ideas are ambiguous and far from immediately comprehensible. In these cases, interpretation is a necessary prerequisite to understand; and to make such interpretations, individuals tend to refer to the existing stock of knowledge that is generally conditioned by prior historical experience. Hence, the same set of ideas can be interpreted quite differently in settings where the relevant historical experiences diverge."[18] Although Hall is novel in his application of the concept of interpretation to understand the political power of economic ideas, there is a body of literature that provides insights into how interpretation occurs.[19]

How and why do ideas acquire meaning in a political setting, and how are meanings transformed? This study suggests that the meaning and acceptance of new ideas derive not only from the content but also from: (1) powerful symbolic issues; (2) the nature of the political and ideological context into which new ideas they are introduced; (3) the nature of who interprets or carries the ideas.[20] Economic ideas in Latin America are open to multiple interpretations. They have one set of meanings for the author, which we can try to uncover by reading memoirs and interviewing individuals, but they may have a different meaning for members of the public. The public does not construct meaning through the "text"—in this case a series of economic plans. The text itself is often ambiguous, with apparently inconsistent or contradictory parts. Most of the people in Argentina and Brazil never read the Prebisch Plan or the Targets Program, or the CEPAL documents, but they nevertheless developed strongly held opinions on these programs. The meanings of ideas are interpreted within the context into which they are inserted, in this case the political and economic context of the country in question at a particular historical moment.

First, meanings emerged from these debates about specific policy issues with strong symbolic significance. In Argentina, desarrollismo became associated with *entreguismo*—with "selling out to foreign interests." In Brazil the nationalist developmentalists appeared to maintain the balance of policy making in their favor against the wishes of the cosmopolitan developmentalists, especially after Kubitschek broke off

18. Ibid., p. 370.

19. See, for example, Michael Gibbons, "Introduction: The Politics of Interpretation," in *Interpreting Politics*, ed. Michael T. Gibbons (New York: New York University Press, 1987); Brian Fay, "An Alternative View: Interpretive Social Science," in his *Social Theory and Political Practice* (London: Allen and Unwin, 1975).

20. Kathryn Sikkink, "The Influence of Raúl Prebisch on Economic Policy Making in Argentina, 1950–1962," *Latin American Research Review* 23 (1988), pp. 108–9.

negotiations with the International Monetary Fund in 1959. Although most of the economic policies of the developmentalist governments in Brazil and Argentina were very similar, they differed on two central issues with profound symbolic implications: foreign investment in the petroleum industry and IMF stabilization policies.

But meanings were also created by the way new ideas were inserted into the political context, and how they articulated with existing political and economic ideas. In Argentina, for example, after Prebisch wrote an economic program for the Aramburu government, the ideas of Prebisch and CEPAL became identified with anti-Peronism. In Brazil neither developmentalism nor the ideas of CEPAL in the 1950s were seen as opposed to the legacy of Vargas.

CEPAL's ideas were less influential in Argentina than in a number of other countries in Latin America: they achieved the most influence in Chile and Brazil, met with enthusiasm in Central America and the Caribbean, but enjoyed less influence in Argentina, Mexico, Peru, and Colombia. It is difficult to attribute the varying degree of influence and penetration of CEPAL's ideas in the region solely to the correctness of CEPAL's economic diagnosis in relation to the various economies. The notion of persuasiveness itself is interpreted. One must also look at the political and ideological conditions in the various countries that influenced the acceptance and nonacceptance of CEPAL's ideas.

Third, the individuals and institutions responsible for introducing new ideas shape the way these ideas are received and play a crucial intermediary role in interpreting them. If the persuasiveness of new ideas depends in part on interpretive exercises, "who" interprets and what are the key factors that can lead us to expect one type of interpretation over another?[21] In the Latin American context, the greater institutional weakness of parties and the nature of the presidential political systems create much more autonomy for interpretation and adoption by individual leaders. Political leaders in Latin America have had more success playing the role of intellectual entrepreneurs, adopt-

21. Hall argues that in the European cases, the orientation of the governing political party is particularly important for suggesting whether Keynesian ideas are adopted or not. Thus, in the European case, we could say that parties are the key mediating institutions responsible for interpretation. This has been less clearly the case throughout the developing countries; for example, the orientation of the governing party was less important in the case of the adoption of developmentalism in Brazil and Argentina, or with the adoption of national populist ISI policies in both countries. In some cases, however, parties have played an important role in the creation of meaning for new ideas. The Peronist party was very active in discrediting Prebisch's ideas in Argentina, by associating Prebisch with the traditional anti-Peronist working class, but Prebisch's history and actions contributed to this interpretation.

ing new ideas and policy once they held political power.[22] In Brazil Kubitschek emerged as a powerful and persuasive interpreter of developmentalist ideas. Kubitschek interpreted developmentalism broadly, attempting to include more and more groups under the developmentalist umbrella. But interpretation is also carried out through dramatic symbolic gestures—especially those of the government and the president. Kubitschek interpreted developmentalism for the ordinary Brazilian partly through the focus on Brasília. He presented developmentalism as something modern, new, and dramatic. For Kubitschek, Brasília was part of the developmentalist program. The construction of the new capital symbolized Brazil's integration of its national territory and its movement into the future. The construction of Brasília and the organized pageantry of its inauguration could also be seen as Kubitschek's effort to interpret developmentalism in substance and form.

There is a difference between the message, the attempt at interpretation, and the reception—the meanings ascribed to actions by the public. One of the central questions for the developmentalists was how to have their actions interpreted as nationalist, in spite of the bias in favor of foreign capital and investment. But the Argentine desarrollistas were unable to gain broad support for this interpretation. The understanding of foreign investment as antinationalist was too ingrained in the Argentine consciousness to permit any reinterpretation of that point.

If we are to take the role of ideas in development seriously, we must come to terms with the processes through which meanings are created in social settings. The conclusions of this study stress a number of points, some of which may be applicable more broadly to Third World or newly industrial countries in general. The same ideas do not take on the same meanings in all settings. Meanings emerge through a process of interpretation, in which certain actors play a more privileged role as interpreters. In the Latin American setting individual leaders and intellectuals played a significant role in the process of interpretation and adoption of ideas. Attention to the role of ideas in developing countries, where political institutions and parties are weaker, may focus more directly on the role of key individuals as "carriers" and "inter-

22. This is the case of Jorge Sabato in Argentina's nuclear policy, Jose Pelusio in Brazil's science and technology policy (as Emanuel Adler discusses in his book), Celso Furtado in SUDENE (as discussed in Hirschman's study of reform mongering), and Lucio Meira in the Brazilian automobile industry (discussed in my study of developmentalism). There are also stories of individuals at critical moments who are not able to play the reform-mongering role: Prebisch with the Prebisch Plan of 1955–1956; Aldo Ferrer at the Junta de Planificacion in the Province of Buenos Aires.

preters" of new ideas. As such, the individuals take on a symbolic role; they come to stand for the ideas themselves, and thus the interpretation of the idea is intertwined with the success and interpretation of the individuals and their political life.

The strength, continuity, and success of new ideas once implemented depend on the degree to which they become embodied within institutions, especially state institutions. The ideas that have been successfully implemented and consolidated are those that have been instilled within an institutional home, where a team of like-minded people transform their individual ideas into institutional purpose. Many of these institutions were state institutions, part of the economic apparatus of the state, but others outside the state also played important roles in the transmission of ideas. How individuals and institutions were connected to the state and how much continuity they had within the state were particularly important in determining the translation of ideas into coherent economic policies. Certain types of ideas have affinities with particular institutions and are more likely to survive when these institutions are strong. Rules governing state practices that permit personnel and institutional continuity facilitate the process of embodying new ideas within institutions.

The consolidation or persistence of a new idea depends on the degree of consensus that forms around the idea. Actors respond to new policies on the basis of their perceptions: perceptions of their interests and of reality. These perceptions are structured by existing ideas and historically formed ideologies in different settings. Consensus is more likely if new ideas interact or "fit" well with the ideological currents and institutional structures, and with the political and economic concerns of the time.

Interviews

Argentina

Roberto Aleman (minister of economics, 1961–1962), Buenos Aires, July 29, 1985.

Oscar Alende (governor of the province of Buenos Aires), Bamfield, November 27, 1985.

Nicolas Babini (technical advisor to President Frondizi), Buenos Aires, July 7, 1985.

Carlos Borzone, Buenos Aires, November 1 and November 5, 1985.

Alfredo Eric Calcagno, Buenos Aires, July 11, 1985.

Oscar Camilion, Buenos Aires, June 3, June 12, and August 5, 1985.

Nestor Grancelli Chá, Buenos Aires, July 17, 1985.

Hector Dieguez, Buenos Aires, June 28, 1985.

Adolfo Dorfman, Buenos Aires, June 6, 1985.

Isaias J. Garcia Enciso, Buenos Aires, November 7, 1985.

Aldo Ferrer (minister of economics, province of Buenos Aires, 1985–1960), Buenos Aires, November 27, 1985.

Rogelio Frigerio, written responses to interview questions, received July 15 and October 5, 1985.

Arturo Frondizi, written responses to interview questions, November 22, 1985.

Eduardo de la Fuente, Buenos Aires, July 27, 1985.

Juan Martin Oneto Gaona, Buenos Aires, November 25, 1985.

Roberto Huerta, Buenos Aires, November 21, 1985.

Mariano Lorenzes, Buenos Aires, November 20, 1985.

Arnaldo Musich, Buenos Aires, October 29, 1985.

INTERVIEWS

Alberto Petrecolla, Buenos Aires, July 2, 1985.

Raúl Prebisch, Buenos Aires, October 23, 1985.

Roberto Jose Rebousin, Buenos Aires, November 27, 1985.

Manuel Rodriguez, Buenos Aires, November 1 and November 5, 1985.

Arturo Sábato, Buenos Aires, July 23, 1985.

Alberto Virgilio Tedin, Buenos Aires, August 10, 1985.

Daniel Vilas, Buenos Aires, July 3, 1985.

Brazil

Roberto Campos, Rio de Janeiro, June 20, 1986.

Roland Corbisier, Rio de Janeiro, June 25, 1986.

Jose Pelusio Fereira, Rio de Janeiro, May 12, 1986.

Alberto Venancio Filho, Rio de Janeiro, April 24, 1986.

Juvenal Osorio Gomes, Rio de Janeiro, April 30, 1986.

Helio Jaguaribe, Rio de Janeiro, June 20, 1986.

Sidney Latini, Rio de Janeiro, May 20, 1986.

Cleantho de Paiva Leite, Rio de Janeiro, May 21, 1986.

Lucas Lopes, Rio de Janeiro, May 19, 1986.

Lucio Meira, Rio de Janeiro, May 24, 1986.

João Batista Pinheiro, Rio de Janeiro, June 19, 1986.

Ignacio Rangel, Rio de Janeiro, May 12, 1986.

Affonso Heliodoro dos Santos, Brasilia, June 5, 1986.

Ezio Tavora dos Santos, Rio de Janeiro, June 20, 1986.

General Macedo Soares e Silva, Rio de Janeiro, May 14, 1986.

General

Manuel Balboa, Santiago, Chile, September 13, 1985.

Ricardo Cibotti, Santiago, Chile, September 5 and September 9, 1985.

Norberto Gonzáles, Santiago, Chile, September 13, 1985.

Anibal Pinto, Santiago, Chile, September 6, 1985.

Anibal Quijano, New York City, May 5, 1983.

Octavio Rodriqugez, Montevideo, Uruguay, May 23 and May 24, 1985.

Osvaldo Sunkel, Santiago, Chile, September 10, 1985.

Index

Cornell Studies in Political Economy

EDITED BY PETER J. KATZENSTEIN

Library of Congress Cataloging-in-Publication Data

Sikkink, Kathryn, 1955–
Ideas and institutions: developmentalism in Brazil and Argentina
/ Kathryn Sikkink.
    p.   cm.—(Cornell studies in political economy)
    Includes index.
    ISBN 0–8014–2488–7 (alk. paper).
    1. Brazil—Economic policy.   2. Argentina—Economic policy.
3. Brazil—Politics and government—1954–1964.   4. Argentina—
Politics and government—1955–1983,   I. Title.   II. Series.
HC187.S445   1991
338.981—dc20   90–55713

www.ingramcontent.com/pod-product-compliance
Lightning Source LLC
Chambersburg PA
CBHW022304280326
41932CB00010B/973